Three Screenplays

LUCHINO VISCONTI

THREE SCREENPLAYS

White Nights
Rocco and His Brothers
The Job

Translated from the Italian by Judith Green

The Orion Press   New York   1970

Copyright © 1970 by Grossman Publishers, Inc.
Published by Grossman Publishers, Inc.
125a East 19th Street, New York, N.Y. 10003.
Published simultaneously in Canada by Fitzhenry and Whiteside.
All rights reserved, including the right of reproduction
in whole or in part in any form.
Library of Congress Catalogue Card Number: 73-86126.
First Printing.
Manufactured in Belgium.

CONTENTS

White Nights (1957)

Credits

Producer:	Franco Cristaldi
Production Manager:	Pietro Notarianni
Director:	Luchino Visconti
Screenplay:	Suso Cecchi d'Amico, Luchino Visconti, from a short story by Dostoyevsky
Director of Photography:	Giuseppe Rotunno
Camera Operator:	Silvano Ippoliti
Editor:	Mario Serandrei
Art Directors:	Mario Chiari, assisted by Mario Garbuglia
Music:	Nino Rota
Costumes:	Piero Tosi
Choreography:	Dick Sanders
Sound:	Vittorio Trentino

Cast:

Natalia:	Maria Schell
Mario:	Marcello Mastroianni
The Lodger:	Jean Marais
The Prostitute:	Clara Calamai

Outside. Night.

The neighborhood streets are almost deserted, although it is not very late. We are in one of those urban landscapes in transition between the old and the new.

In entire sections of the area the remains of wrecked buildings survive alongside new ones. From one of these new streets we can see the lights and the neon signs and hear the voices of a more lively existence. The muffled sound of cars and buses filters through almost continuously from the nearby central square. Now we hear the strident screech of the brakes of a bus stopping at the end of the line and the voices of the few people who are getting off. The bus starts up again with another screech and turns around to start back on its route in the opposite direction. A small group of passengers remains in the middle of the street after getting off the bus. The group is composed of a man of about forty-five, a woman no longer young, two children, and a young man of about twenty-five (Mario).

The older man turns to the younger.

OLDER MAN: You're already home. The canal's at the first bridge and you'll be home in a few minutes.

MARIO: Right.

WOMAN *(complaining, to her husband)*: Should we take the trolley? The kids are sleeping on their feet. *(Points to children).*

OLDER MAN: If they haven't stopped running for the night. We'll take a look. *(To the young man)* See you tomorrow.

The older man takes one of the children by the hand and walks off toward the lighted street, followed by the others.

The young man walks along with the others for a few yards; they are heading in a direction opposite to his own.

YOUNG MAN: Thanks again.

OLDER MAN: What for? We enjoyed your company. *(To the woman)* Right, Maria?

WOMAN: Huh?

OLDER MAN: We enjoyed his company! The next time we go—if there's another day as nice as today—I'll let you know.

WOMAN: Wait till he gets settled here and then you'll see, he'll find some better way of spending his weekends.

A trolley is heard approaching. The older man turns slightly to urge his family to hurry.

OLDER MAN: Hurry up, hurry up, there's the trolley!

The man begins to run, pulling one child along by the hand. The woman begins to run too.

The young man has been trying to say a last goodbye but finds himself suddenly alone.

VOICE OF WOMAN SHOUTING: Stop! Wait a minute! Wait, stop!

The young man listens as if trying to hear whether his acquaintances have made the bus. The trolley is heard pulling off, and its sound is lost in the stillness of the night.

The young man shrugs his shoulders, sighs, and looks uncertainly toward the well-lit street for a moment. Evidently he is uncertain whether to prolong his evening out or to return home. He walks a little way in the street, where the neon lights are still on. A small crowd is exiting from a movie theater not far off.

With another shrug of his shoulders the young man makes up his mind. He turns around and starts back toward his home at a good pace. Now he enters a broad deserted piazza.

Beyond the piazza is the old section of town, crisscrossed with long shallow canals leading directly to the port. There is very little light and the tall squalid buildings seem uninhabited. In the great empty piazza there stands only a neon-lit café where coffee and drinks are sold.

The young man slows his pace. His reluctance to consider his day at an end becomes ever more obvious. When he notices the light of the café, Mario turns toward it after a moment's hesitation.

Inside of café. Night.

Inside the café, which is about to close, the only customer is a treasury agent. He stands at the bar, intent on corking a bottle, while the barman is busy closing the shutters. When the young man enters, the agent has raised the bottle against the light to check its contents.

AGENT: Did you put sugar in?

BARMAN: Three packages!

The agent nods and again sets about corking the bottle, which he then turns upside down to be sure that it does not leak.

The barman points to the tiny bottle of cognac displayed in the window; it has a screwed-on cap that serves as a little cup.

BARMAN: You ought to take one of those...

AGENT: Too expensive.

Mario has leaned up against the bar and clearly would like to join the conversation. Now he points to the corked bottle in the agent's hand.

MARIO: That's still the best system going. *(Pointing to the bottle on display)* But even there if you don't put in the cork. ...

Mario shakes his head and grimaces, as if to illustrate the disastrous consequence of those systems too.

BARMAN: You're wrong there.

The young man points to the espresso machine.

MARIO: Cup of coffee, please.

The barman has begun to pull down the sliding doors.

BARMAN: Don't you see I'm closing? I can't start the machine up again just for one coffee.

MARIO: All right, forget it if it's too much trouble. Give me a beer, it's all the same to me. *(Turning to the agent)* You won't notice, will you? *(Trying to start a conversation)* What is the closing time for cafés in this town? I still haven't figured it out.

AGENT: Well, it depends on the kind of license.

BARMAN: I'm licensed to stay open all night long if I want to.

Mario takes out a pack of cigarettes and offers one to the agent, who accepts it. Mario offers one to the barman, who does not accept. Then he lights his own and the agent's.

MARIO: That's what I thought. Just a few days ago, when was it? The night I first came. I passed by here and... it was late, but you were still open.

BARMAN: Probably. When there's business...

The young man grins as if to say, "And now there's no business? Here I am." The barman now opens a bottle of beer.

BARMAN: Here you are.

The foam immediately runs over the glass. The barman makes a gesture of impatience, then sets the half-full bottle down next to the glass full of foam.

BARMAN *(irritated)* : When you're in a hurry...

The young man does not notice, or pretends not to notice, the barman's irritation. He takes the glass and turns to the agent.

MARIO: I really needed something to drink. When you've been out in the open all day long, the way I've been... Beautiful place, though. I'd never been there before... *(Takes another two sips)* ...You get thirsty...and you're not at all sleepy.

The barman has finished closing up. He buttons his jacket and stands at the door, making it clear to the young man that he's waiting for him to leave.

MARIO *(with simplicity, to the agent, pointing to the barman)*: He wants to kick us out. *(To the barman)* Right?

AGENT *(walking to the door)*: I have to go anyway. I'm on duty.

Mario is about to pour the rest of the beer into his glass, but the barman's attitude discourages him. He puts the bottle down and walks toward the door. Without waiting for him to reach it, the barman turns out the light.

The young man is forced to count out his money by the light of the street lamp.

MARIO: A night like this...and no one's out.

BARMAN: Just goes to show that people sleep better when the weather's good.

MARIO *(laughing)*: Here they sleep in all weather. What a town! And to think what they told me...

The agent has taken his bicycle and pedals slowly along with one foot, dragging the other along the pavement as a brake, while he waits for the barman to catch up.

AGENT *(insinuating)*: They told you right. Some people sleep... but the others can have a good time, and how.

MARIO *(still hoping to start a conversation)*: Really? Where?

The barman has caught up to the agent on his motorbike. Mario finds himself alone. The other two men ride out of the piazza side by side.

BARMAN *(to the agent)*: If you hadn't been there he'd have kept me there an hour listening to his private life. ... An awful lot

of that kind come in... people who haven't any other way
to waste their time.

AGENT: I get that way sometimes too, when I'm off duty. I think
about a lot of things... and I end up doing nothing... Maybe
I never do anything because I want to do too many things.

*The men's conversation fades out in the distance along with the sound of
the barman's motor.*

*The area is now plunged into almost total silence except for the distant sounds
from the center of town, though even these are muffled and intermittent.*

Street along the canal. Night.

*The young man walks slowly along the street bordering the canal. His
head is lowered and he seems resigned to considering his evening at an end.
He whistles. He kicks some stones in his path.*

*A dog crosses the piazza hesitantly, his nose to the ground as he sniffs along.
He stops to search through a pile of garbage.*

*The young man turns to the dog, speaking softly as if ashamed to be talking
all by himself but unable to resist the desire to speak.*

MARIO: Get out of there. *(He stamps his foot to catch the dog's attention; frightened, the dog lifts his head and gazes at the young man.)*
Leave that garbage alone. Are you hungry? *(After a moment's hesitation the dog turns and edges a few steps off.)* What an
ugly thing you are, poor fellow. What a mess. Come here.
*(The dog has stopped and looks at the young man, who is amused
and smiling.)* Come here.

*He whistles. The young man experiments with several types of whistles
to find the one usually used to call dogs. He crouches down, snaps his
fingers, smiles....*

*The whistling finally arouses the dog's suspicions, and he begins to trot
away.*

The young man picks up a stone, possibly to throw it at the dog. But he continues to hold onto it and juggles it in his palm. He walks off, singing softly now. He crosses a bridge over the motionless dark canal.

Halfway over the bridge the young man notices that the dog has stopped as if waiting for him. The young man stops too and smiles. He does not move, waiting to see whether the dog will take courage and come to him. They watch each other. The dog takes a few cautious steps forward.

MARIO: But I haven't anything to give you, old boy. You look. Something always turns up.

The dog trots on ahead. The young man follows him with his eyes, curious to see whether the dog (who returns in the direction they have come from) has really understood. But the dog stops again. He takes a few steps in one direction, then in another. Finally he starts to bark and races off to chase a cat. The young man is standing still. He looks up toward the cloudy sky, then turns to look at the water and the lights reflected in it. For a little while he remains lost in thought, then he throws the stone he has been holding into the water. The tarry black water barely ripples.

At this point a bell rings in a nearby church tower. Eleven slow clangs sound in the deserted air. Mario raises his head to listen attentively to the bell.

He rests with his hands against the guard rail. He looks up into the cloudy sky. A window that had still been lighted suddenly darkens; the crash of shutters swinging in the wind is heard.

Suddenly something catches his attention. Some little distance away, on another bridge about fifty yards from where he stands, is the motionless black figure of a woman leaning on the rail over the canal. The figure is dim but she is definitely leaning over and gazing at the water.

The young man is startled; he leaves the bridge and walks along the canal between the high façades of the buildings and the black water. After a few steps he stops, leans against the rail again, and continues to watch the motionless figure.

The woman is rather small, with hair so blond it appears luminescent in the feeble light issuing from the doorway of the Sport Café, which is still open on the far side of the canal. The sound of a radio filters from the café. The young mans draws a few steps nearer. The woman does not seem to notice him and continues to gaze at the water.

Uncertain, the young man halts; he is trying to decide whether to pick the girl up or not.

The girl is still motionless at the rail. Evidently, he thinks to himself, she is only waiting to be approached. He walks up onto the bridge and slows his pace as he walks behind the girl. He opens his mouth to say something. But the only thing that comes out is a sound as if he is clearing his throat.

MARIO: Hmmm...

The young man goes on a few steps and then suddenly stops. He has heard a sob behind him. He turns. He takes a step toward the girl but dares not go any closer, since she is crying and is shaken by desperate sobs. The young man is evidently perplexed about what to say or do. As if sensing rather than hearing the man's presence, the girl looks rapidly about, pulls herself together, and sees the young man. Immediately she lowers her eyes in fright, slips past him, and runs off.

The young man does not move. The girl, nevertheless, seems to fear his following her. After a moment's hesitation she crosses the bridge resolutely in the direction of the houses along the canal. The young man also moves now toward the houses, as if to follow her, and he keeps his eyes on her.

Preceded by an ear-shattering noise, a motorcycle with two boys riding on it now sweeps into the scene from a nearby street. The motorcycle arrives from the far side and is about to cross to the right side of the street when the driver notices the girl. With the obvious intention of giving her a scare, he accelerates and heads toward the sidewalk where the girl is walking.

The girl jumps and cries out in fright, crosses the street, and begins to walk rapidly along the opposite wall.

ONE OF THE BOYS: Scared you! Hop on! There's room for you in the middle. Come on, miss.

The girl continues to hurry along. The driver starts up the bike again and departs apparently deciding not to bother her any more. But the motorcycle speeds around the block and reappears rapidly and suddenly before the girl just as she reaches the corner of the building and is about to cross the street. The bike cuts her off so suddenly that she is obliged to step back. She gives another little cry of fright.

The young man hurries toward her and arrives just as the two boys, still on their bike, again laughingly invite her to get on.

BOYS: Come on, blondie. There's room for you too. All three of us... snuggled tight.

MARIO *(violently)*: Will you leave this lady alone?

BOY: What d'you want? Where'd this character come from?

MARIO: I'll show you what I want! The lady is with me, understand? Get out of here.

The boy is about to answer back but the driver starts off again, partly because he is worried by the sound of an approaching vehicle. As they go off, the boy on the back turns to shout.

DRIVER: Leave that ass, blondie, and come with us.

BOY BEHIND *(shouting)*: What'll you show us? Stupid! Some nerve!

The boy's shout resounds loudly in the silence of the night, which is now interrupted by the sound of an approaching truck.

The truck driver looks out curiously at the young man, who is shouting after the departing motorcycle.

MARIO: You scum! Come on back! You're cutting out, eh? Some courage!

Noticing that the truck driver is slowing down to look at him, the young man suddenly stops shouting and turns to make sure that the girl is still behind him. He takes a few steps toward her.

The girl is still there. She raises her head to shoot a rapid glance at the young man. Then she blushes and lowers her eyes again. Her face, which we see now for the first time, is extremely pretty. When she raised her eyes they were still shining from her tears, and her cheeks are wet.

MARIO *(indignantly)*: Did you see how they ran away? They enjoy bothering people. Stupid kids!

The girl lowers her eyes. Mario observes her more attentively. There is a long silence between the two. Then the young man chances.

MARIO: If you hadn't rushed away, then...

Now the stray dog Mario had been playing with a short while before

reappears suddenly and rubs against the young man's trousers. Mario jerks away.

MARIO *(to the dog)*: Get away! What d'you want?

Amused, the girl smiles. The young man believes he has found a subject with which to start up a conversation. He turns to the dog.

MARIO *(to the dog)*: You're a real pest, you know.

Smiling, the young man turns back to the girl. But his expression is immediately transformed: the girl has disappeared.

Mario instantly looks toward the alley and then toward the canal guard rail, which the girl is now approaching. Annoyed, the young man steps quickly to her side.

NATALIA: But I don't know you...please, leave me alone.

MARIO: I don't know you either. But do allow me to walk you home. Those two fellows were bothering you and maybe... It's my duty, I think.

Natalia looks at him shrewdly.

NATALIA: Don't trouble yourself. I live right nearby.

MARIO: Can't I walk you home?

NATALIA: Thanks... but no. You'd better not.

MARIO *(trying to protest)*: You don't think that I... would want to bother you too...

Natalia stops and looks at him.

NATALIA: Yes, I do think so... A little while ago, on the bridge, you...

Mario tries to protest, but the girl's look disarms him.

MARIO *(stammering)*: Well... Perhaps... You may have thought... but really ...I...

The girl smiles more openly.

MARIO *(as if concluding an address)*: Anyway I came right over when you... *(More kindly)* were crying. It broke my heart. *(Sincerely)* And I thought... excuse me if I say it.

Natalia shrugs her shoulders slightly. She stares at the water in the canal. Then, hearing footsteps in the distance, she suddenly turns.

Not far from the two young people, a local prostitute is walking by. She is no longer young and anything but pretty. She looks at the two without interest, yawns, and continues on her way, walking a little awkwardly on heels too high for her. She is heading toward a part of the street where men's voices are heard as they leave a restaurant.

Mario is watching Natalia, who is again staring at the waters of the canal. He observes her more closely now, and from his expression it is clear that he is beginning to notice her beauty.

MARIO *(kindly)*: Now will you let me walk you home? You can trust me....

Natalia does not even turn toward him. Mario is annoyed and starts to walk away, but immediately stops and returns to her side.

MARIO *(annoyed)*: No. I won't leave you here alone. Come on. *(The girl looks at him in surprise.)* So many times you hear that some misfortune makes people...

Mario completes his thought by indicating the water of the canal. He sits down on the wall.

MARIO: That's not what you had in mind, I hope. A pretty young girl like you...

A group of men passes by on the far side of the canal. One of them, drunk, gesticulates emphatically.

MARIO *(to Natalia)*: Well? *(After a pause)* What'll we do? *(Natalia shrugs her shoulders slightly.)* Well—will you tell me what you're doing here? *(Pause)* And why you were crying?

The girl looks at Mario with a lost and very sweet expression. Then softly, childishly, she answers.

NATALIA: I live near here. There...

MARIO: That's what you were crying about? I live near here too. *(Points across the bridge)* There. But I'm not crying.

Natalia smiles as if to excuse herself, then immediately averts her glance. The distant church bells sound the hour. Mario hops down from the wall. He seems annoyed.

MARIO: Midnight already. This day sure went fast. *(He is uncertain what to do; he looks at the girl, then looks around him.)* Today I was out of town all day, with a man from my office and his family. Nice people. Dull, but nice. It was the first time since I was transferred here that I've been out with anyone. I enjoyed myself. But... *(He laughs.)* I was quiet as a mouse with them.... Then when I was by myself again.... I felt like talking...like being with people.... I was feeling good. I wanted to end the day well. Then I saw you....

The young man shrugs his shoulders and smiles as if to comment ironically on his poor luck.

Off-camera noise of a distant car. The girl becomes upset once again. She looks about, then sighs. She looks at the young man.

GIRL *(with a melancholy smile)*: If you still want to, you may walk me home.

Mario, who was not looking at Natalia, turns to her in surprise. Natalia is still smiling. Clearly Mario is again thinking how pretty she is. He immediately becomes gallant.

MARIO: Shall we go have a bite somewhere? There's a place still open in Piazza Grande.

The girl shakes her head slightly and abruptly walks off.

NATALIA *(walking quickly)*: It's too late.

The two walk a little distance in silence, Natalia a step ahead and Mario following, observing her with growing curiosity. As if perceiving his stare, Natalia turns and smiles at him.

NATALIA: I'm sorry if I spoiled your evening.

MARIO *(embarrassed)*: Not at all. I enjoyed it. I didn't have anything to do anyway, I told you. *(Laughing a little awkwardly)* I wanted some company... and... I was lucky.

His embarrassed tone contrasts so obviously with his words that the girl cannot help smiling. Mario is ever more embarrassed. He stops.

MARIO: Forgive me. I'm ...terribly timid. I mean with girls. I'm not used to them. I don't even know how to talk to them. The women I know...

NATALIA *(smiling)*: Women usually like timid men. Me too...

Mario looks into the girl's eyes and is increasingly attracted to her, so much so that he is forced to lower his eyes.

MARIO *(laughing in embarrassment)*: Is that so? But you shouldn't say so or you'll make me forget I'm timid... and that would be the end of my secret weapon....

NATALIA *(already distracted)*: What weapon?

Mario is a little startled by her sudden change of tone.

MARIO: You said women like timid men and that you do too.

Natalia begins to walk rapidly again and turns into a narrow alley.

NATALIA: Here's where I live.

Natalia stops and points to a little house a few yards away. She obviously intends to dismiss the young man now.

MARIO *(disappointed)*: Sure.

The girl nods only slightly. She is again distracted and agitated, but the young man seems not to notice.

MARIO: I'm sorry. Do I really have to go?

Now Mario notices the girl's impatience.

Noise of a window opening and closing again. Mario looks toward the window and then at the girl. Evidently he thinks the girl does not want to linger right outside her house.

MARIO *(hurriedly)*: Listen. Tomorrow night I'll come back to where I saw you tonight....

NATALIA *(immediately)*: Perhaps we'll meet.

Mario did not expect this prompt acceptance. He smiles happily.

NATALIA *(almost to herself)*: If nothing happens in the meantime...

MARIO: I'll wait for you.

But the girl has placed her hand on his arm as a brief sign of farewell, and immediately runs toward her house.

Mario is about to say something, but the girl has already opened the door; she disappears immediately and closes the door behind her. For a moment Mario remains watching the door through which the girl has disappeared. Then he slowly turns and starts to walk away. But his curiosity returns and he starts back, as if wishing to check the street number of the house. This time he walks right up to the door and looks at the house. But he hears a sound which makes him lower his eyes.

The door has been opened again and Natalia reappears in the doorway. The girl is surprised and almost terrified to find Mario there, but she immediately recovers her poise and tries to smile.

NATALIA: I wanted to tell you... I'll be there at ten tomorrow....

MARIO: At ten...

Before he can say another word, the girl has disappeared again and closed the door behind her. This time Mario smiles with satisfaction and immediately walks off at a good pace.

Interior, entrance hall and stairwell, girl's house. Night.

The girl has remained just inside the doorway, leaning motionless against the closed door. The narrow entrance hall is almost entirely dark; it gives the impression of poverty. The stairs are all badly worn and the frame of a little window giving out from the stairs is squeaking.

The girl waits without moving. Then she turns slowly, opens the door a crack, and tries to hear, rather than see, whether the young man is still outside. Reassured that he has gone, she opens the door again and slips out into the street. She runs along the wall back toward the canal.

Interior, Mario's bedroom. Day.

The room Mario occupies in a rooming house is tiny and badly furnished with objects of various but equally depressing styles. Mario has tossed his clothes over a chair and he is still sleeping soundly.

Sound of knocking at the door.

LANDLADY'S VOICE: Aren't you going to work today? You know what time it is? It's after eight.

Mario moves in his sleep without awaking. More knocks on the door.

Mario pulls himself up and begins to open his eyes. The landlady has opened the door and appears in the doorway.

LANDLADY: Hey! Aren't you going to work today?

MARIO: Oh hell! What time is it?

LANDLADY: I just told you! It's after eight.

Mario starts to get up. Then he falls back again.

LANDLADY: Big deals at night, but in the morning it's another story, eh? I heard you come in last night, you know.

The young man does not look at his landlady; he stares straight ahead as if savoring a pleasant memory. Only when the landlady has gone out does Mario seem to start awake; he jumps out of bed and calls her.

MARIO: Ma'am, ma'am…

LANDLADY'S VOICE: What?

Mario has jerked open the door of the decrepit wardrobe, which rocks with the shock.

MARIO: Ma'am! *(The young man opens the drawers of the wardrobe, then turns to look toward the door, where the landlady has re-appeared.)* My white shirt, my good one…

LANDLADY: How should I know where it is?

MARIO: I gave it to you to wash last Thursday. I need it.

LANDLADY: If it's not there it means it's not ready.

The young man looks at the only suit hanging in the wardrobe.

MARIO: I told you when I first came that this was to be cleaned and pressed.

LANDLADY: We'll do it. I told you, didn't I, that these services are extra?

MARIO *(impatient)*: All right, all right.

Mario pulls the suit from the wardrobe and throws it to the landlady.

MARIO: Do it right away.

LANDLADY: Right away, right now?

MARIO: Right now. I have to go to the office.

LANDLADY: But I can't do it now. It takes time.

The young man is looking at a shirt he has pulled out of the open drawer.

LANDLADY'S VOICE: You ought to think of these things ahead of time, dear boy.

MARIO: I've been telling you since I got here.

LANDLADY *(immediately argumentative)*: Did you tell me you needed it today? *(Conciliating)* It'll be ready tomorrow morning. The shirt too.

MARIO: But I need them tonight.

LANDLADY *(magnanimously)*: All right, tonight. But not now.

MARIO *(annoyed)*: If I leave the office late... I'll have to come all the way back here and... *(Changing his tone)* All right... I'll come back and change. But don't forget the white shirt, will you?

The young man is cheerful once again. He goes to the mirror and examines himself, passing his hand over his cheeks. He whistles.

MARIO: Yes... I'll shave tonight too.

LANDLADY'S VOICE: Good boy. Women's skin is so delicate.

The Sport Café. Interior. Evening.

The waiter brings a cup of coffee to Mario (who is wearing his dark suit). Other customers come up to the espresso machine with their cashier's receipts.

To make room for the new customers, Mario edges down along the bar toward the door. He begins to sip his coffee, turning to look outside. Suddenly his expression becomes more attentive. Instinctively he lowers his cup to rush outside, but he checks himself with a pleased smile and finishes the coffee, then walks out of the café at a moderate pace.

Outside. Night.

The young man leaves the café and walks toward the bridge over the canal.

At the corner stands the local prostitute, who passed Mario and Natalia the evening before. Mario does not even notice her. Hurrying his steps a little, he nears the canal.

Although it is fairly late, the street is much more animated than it was the night before. Some stevedores are still unloading coal from the boats and transferring it to the warehouses lining the canal with their lit door-ways. There are still some people in the streets.

Natalia, whom Mario had evidently seen a moment before from the café, is walking along the wall about ten yards ahead of him. Instead of follow-ing her, Mario turns along the quay with an amused smile, intending to circle around and meet her head on at the meeting place.

A man is sitting on the quay fishing. Two passers-by are watching him.

PASSER-BY *(ironically)*: What're you fishing for? Dead fish?

Now Mario sees that instead of walking toward the bridge, the girl has disappeared inside a doorway. Mario hurries his step and goes beyond the bridge. He looks inside the doorway, certain that the girl is waiting there just behind the sill. The girl is not there.

Mario is sorely disappointed. He crosses the street slowly, goes over to the guard rail along the canal and leans on it, preparing to wait and watching the doorway of the building opposite.

Entranceway of the building on the canal. Interior. Night.

We see Mario from where the girl is hiding in the darkest corner of the entranceway. He looks at his watch, walks up and down, then resolutely crosses the street again and approaches the doorway.

Natalia immediately shrinks back in order not to be seen. From her hiding place we see Mario stopping in front of the doorway. He looks toward the courtyard inside the building. It is enormous and cluttered with wheel-

barrows and bicycle trucks. Then he turns away and walks, hands in pockets, to wait at the edge of the sidewalk.

Careful not to make a sound, the girl slips away into the courtyard. This courtyard is even larger than it appeared from the entranceway. It is lit only by the windows opening onto it, which transmit voices and noises like those of all the courtyards of poor apartment buildings. Here too, as in all similar courtyards, there are endless lines of washing hung between the windows. The girl must keep to the wall to avoid the water dripping from the laundry hanging from the second-floor windows.

On the far side of the courtyard a disheveled woman is walking in slippers. When she sees the girl she slows her steps.

CONCIERGE: Are you looking for someone?

The girl is somewhat embarrassed. She does not want to speak loudly and she doesn't want to cross the courtyard either, for fear of being seen from the outside. She remains in her corner, smiling as if to excuse herself.

The concierge draws nearer.

CONCIERCE: Who're you looking for?

NATALIA: No one, thank you. I... I have an appointment here. And...

The concierge frowns.

CONCIERGE: You waiting for somebody who lives here?

Having made up her mind to lie, Natalia nods affirmatively. But she does not know how to lie, and immediately corrects herself.

NATALIA: No, no. Not in this building.

The concierge is annoyed and out of patience.

CONCIERGE: Well? You can't stay here. I have to close the door. It's already late. I can't...

The concierge walks toward the entrance, certain that she has said enough to make the girl leave. But after a few steps she must stop, and she turns to look at Natalia, who has not followed her.

Natalia has remained in her corner; she motions the concierge to come to her and immediately draws farther back into the shadows. When the concierge, by now more astonished than annoyed, walks back toward her, Natalia begins to speak softly.

NATALIA *(begging the concierge, very charming)* : Could I stay here a moment, please? I'll close the door afterward. You can trust me. Perhaps you've seen me around the neighborhood.

CONCIERGE : I think I have, but...

NATALIA *(louder)* : I'll only be here a minute. There's a person outside I don't want to see me. He'll go away soon....

The girl suddenly stops. Beyond the concierge she has seen Mario enter the courtyard. His expression makes it clear that he has heard her last words. He immediately turns around and walks out. Natalia runs after him in dismay, leaving the concierge, who has not seen the young man, bewildered.

Outside. Night.

Natalia catches up with Mario just outside the door, panting a bit with the effort of trying to keep up with him.

NATALIA: Please don't be offended. You mustn't be offended. There's no reason why you should be, I assure you.

MARIO *(rather violently)* : I may be very bothersome… informal… but if you didn't intend to see me you had only to say so. It would have been…so simple…wouldn't it?

The young man is actually stammering in his embarrassment, humiliation, and irritation. Natalia cannot help but smile. She says nothing but raises her eyebrow. Then her expression becomes serious again, almost sad.

NATALIA *(softly, her eyes lowered)* : Don't be offended. I… last night I made a mistake… and… *(She looks at Mario with resolution.)* …I behaved like a child. I thought about it all day today. What kind of girl must he think I am, making a date with someone I don't even know? That's what you thought, isn't it?

MARIO *(in consternation)* : I… I didn't think anything.

NATALIA: Of course you thought so. And you were right to think so. And since it's not true, the easiest way to prove it to you was not to meet you.

MARIO *(puzzled)* : So you came here.

NATALIA *(impatient)* : But I had to come here.

MARIO *(again irritated and ironical)* : Sure! But not to be with me. So you're terribly sorry and that's that.

NATALIA *(with extreme simplicity)*: It would be all right if you kept me company. I mean if we were friends... acquaintances.

About to walk off, Mario turns to look at Natalia.

MARIO *(astonished)*: What did you say?

NATALIA *(timidly)*: I mean... if we'd known each other for a long time and we were friends...

MARIO *(exploding)*: You're a pretty funny kind of girl, you know? Can I help it if we met by accident and there's no one around to introduce me, to guarantee I'm not a thief or a cad?

NATALIA *(serious)*: I realize that. But... if I make an appointment with you, you'll certainly think...

MARIO *(still puzzled and irritated)*: That you made an appointment with me. All right. I don't think so.

NATALIA *(timidly)*: Are you cross with me?

MARIO *(who is)*: Who, me? No, no. What an idea.

NATALIA *(as above)*: And you really don't think so?

There's a brief pause. Mario does not answer, but he sighs as if his patience is being sorely tried.

NATALIA *(laughing gaily)*: Then it's all right. We can take care of the introductions by ourselves. *(She extends her hand to the young man.)* My name is Natalia. Now quick, tell me everything about yourself, who you are, what you do. And it'll be as if we've been friends forever.

The young man is ever more puzzled. But on the other hand, it is clear that the contact with Natalia's hand and her luminous smile are attracting him despite himself. Little by little his expression relaxes. Now he begins to laugh too.

MARIO *(laughing)*: What's my story? But... I don't have a story.

NATALIA *(gaily)* : How did you ever live so long without a story?

MARIO *(shrugging)* : I just lived.

NATALIA *(gaily vivacious)* : But you must have someone, a family, even if it's very small, like mine. I have only an old grandmother, old and blind. All the others ran off. First my father. So long ago I can't remember him. Then my mother... with someone who wasn't my father. *(With a little laugh)* So then my grandmother, for fear that I'll get into some kind of trouble... and since she's blind and can't keep after me, sometimes she doesn't want to worry about me so she takes a pin and pins my dress to hers. Really...

MARIO : What? What? What do you mean?

NATALIA : It's the truth. Don't you believe me? She really does. *(Changing her tone and becoming more serious)* But don't laugh at my grandmother. She can't help being the way she is. I love her all the same. But... we weren't talking about me. You were supposed to tell me who you are, what you do, how you live, who you live with...

Mario takes the girl's arm and walks along with her.

MARIO : There's plenty of time for that. First let's decide where we want to go. It's too late for the movies, and anyway we wouldn't be able to talk. Why don't we go...

Natalia halts abruptly, obliging the young man to stop too.

NATALIA *(disappointed)* : But... I thought you understood. I have to stay here. *(With her eyes lowered and her voice trembling slightly)* I'm waiting for someone.

Dismayed, Mario immediately drops her arm.

MARIO *(trying to sound coldly indifferent)* : Oh!

NATALIA *(mortified and stammering)* : I thought you'd understood.

That's why I said that…you shouldn't think…but that if you wanted to keep me company…

MARIO *(aggressively ironical)* : But of course. Your servant.

Mario is about to lose his temper. He leans against the wall now, looking at the girl, and he jokes to hide his disappointment.

MARIO : That's just what I was hoping for. Here we are. May I ask who you're waiting for and when this person will deign to show up?

NATALIA *(ever more mortified)* : No… no special time.

MARIO : That's perfect! Let's hope he takes his time… so we can manage to get soaked too. It's going to rain soon.

Mario looks up at the overcast sky.

NATALIA *(quickly)* : No. It won't rain. It's just very humid. It's always this way at night. Last night, for instance, I… came back here after you'd gone. It was so humid I thought it really would rain. But it didn't.

Mario stares at the girl. Evidently he suspects she's pulling his leg.

MARIO *(sharply)* : I don't think your grandmother can be so severe if she lets you go out alone like that… spend the night out…

NATALIA *(candidly)* : But my grandmother doesn't know.

MARIO : That's the ticket!

NATALIA : Poor Grandmother. She'd really be upset if she knew.

The girl has suddenly become sad; her eyes fill with tears.

NATALIA *(with sudden violence)* : But how about me? I've cried enough over other people's troubles. I have to think about myself too… maybe shed a few tears for myself too.

Mario is struck by her sudden toughness, by the mature woman revealed within the girl. But Natalia has got hold of herself now. She smiles weakly.

NATALIA *(almost beseeching)* : You think he won't come?

Mario is extremely embarrassed. He avoids looking at Natalia.

MARIO *(deciding to leave)* : Listen, miss. I...

NATALIA *(immediately)*: I'm not crazy, don't be afraid. I can explain everything to you, if you like. My story is so ordinary...

An elderly couple is walking along the street toward the entrance to the alley where the girl lives. The man is leading a dog on a leash and walks slowly, his head down. The woman, dressed with some pretentiousness, walks behind him, gesticulating as she speaks excitedly.

NATALIA: My grandmother's a foreigner. I think she used to be rich a long time ago. My grandfather sold carpets. When he died, the women took up mending them. There's not much left of what they used to have. They've sold everything. But we do have a lot of carpets. They don't belong to us.... They bring them to us to fix.... It's quite difficult to do.... We only do the most valuable carpets, the most beautiful ones. We have a room we let out, upstairs in our house. One day a new lodger came to us.

MARIO: Why, was there another one before him?

NATALIA: Of course. But when he left another one came, because we can't make ends meet without a lodger. Giuliana brought him. She works for us fixing the carpets, and she does some housework too. Now she lives in the upstairs room.... The new lodger wasn't from around here. He'd come from another town....

Home of Natalia and her grandmother. Inside. Evening.

An enormous well-lit room, with the rafters of the low ceiling exposed. The floor is completely covered with carpets; rolls of carpets are also propped up against the walls. At the rear, a door. The door suddenly opens.

NATALIA'S VOICE: Since he didn't try to bargain down the price, Grandmother accepted him right away.

A tall man appears in the doorway; the features of his face are not clearly visible.

Natalia's aged grandmother is huddled up in a decrepit old armchair; Natalia sits on a footstool beside her, intently mending a carpet.

NATALIA'S VOICE: But she wanted to know about him, and she asked me...

GRANDMOTHER: Natalia, is he young?

VOICE OF NATALIA: And I didn't want to lie, so I said, "He's not especially young, but he's not especially old either, Grandmother."

At her granddaughter's words, the old woman leans down and whispers grumblingly to her.

GRANDMOTHER: What does he look like? Is he handsome too?

NATALIA'S VOICE *(almost indistinguishably)*: And I didn't want to lie this time either, so I said, "Yes, Grandmother, I think so."

The grandmother leans down and whispers grumblingly in Natalia's ear again:

GRANDMOTHER *(irritated)*: Just think of it! We've got to have a handsome lodger too. Things were different in my time. Don't look at him.

Natalia stares at the lodger. He gets a suitcase down on the carpet-covered floor.

NATALIA'S VOICE: I was sitting there quietly and thinking. Just think, it's Grandmother herself who puts certain thoughts in my head.

GRANDMOTHER: What are you doing there? Get up, hurry up, go to my room and get me the rent book.

Natalia stands up suddenly, evidently forgetting that her skirt is pinned to her grandmother's. Stopping short, Natalia is fearfully embarrassed and mortified. The grandmother has almost fallen out of her chair. The girl leans down and tries to unpin her skirt; her hand trembles so that the operation becomes even more awkward.

NATALIA'S VOICE: I'd forgotten my skirt was pinned to hers. I was so ashamed I burst out crying like a stupid child.

The grandmother shrieks. Natalia weeps. Natalia's crying calms down little by little.

Outside. Night.

Natalia's crying becomes a restrained and somewhat moved laugh. Natalia continues her tale.

NATALIA: From that day on, I used to die every time I heard some noise in the entrance hall. I'd think, "There he is." And if Grandmother had pinned me to her, I'd take out the pin without her noticing it. Sometimes, when I was sure he wasn't home, I'd go up to his room with the excuse of doing some housework. One morning...

Lodger's room in Natalia's home.

The room occupied by the lodger has been partitioned off between two suites, which accounts for its peculiar size and form. The ceiling is low and the furniture consists of only a few essential pieces: a modest iron bed, dresser and two chairs. Most of the volumes contained in a small, well-ordered bookshelf along the wall have bright covers which make it obvious at first sight that they are detective stories. As Natalia is absorbed in leafing through one of these, she is startled by the sound of footsteps. She turns instantly.

NATALIA'S VOICE: ... I suddenly found him in the room with me. He began to laugh and said hello.

LODGER: Hello. How's your grandmother? I see you like my books. Take them if you like. I've already read them all. *(Natalia, still holding the book, is speechless.)* I read them to fall asleep with. It's become a habit by now. Do take them.

They're fun. *(As he speaks, the lodger comes over to the bookshelf, picks out a few volumes, and turns to the girl once again.)* Anyway, you have plenty of time to read. It must be boring to stay in the house all day long. Take these for a start. *(He has come over to Natalia and places the books in her arms, scrutinizing her face more intently now; more kindly.)* You're a fine girl. I'm sorry to see you treated like that. It seems impossible that in this day and age a girl... *(With an abrupt change of tone)* Don't you ever go out? To the movies, for a walk? *(Silenced by timidity and emotion, the girl gazes at the lodger.)* Would you like to go out with me sometime? Tonight. Will you?

The girl continues to stare at him. She takes a few steps backward and shakes her head slightly, still without a word. The young man laughs, takes her hand and pulls her back to him.

LODGER: You don't want to? Or your grandmother won't let you? If that's what the matter is, it's easy enough. Don't ask her and we'll go out secretly.

The girl frees herself almost reluctantly and turns her back to him.

NATALIA'S VOICE: I managed to answer that I didn't want to do anything behind Grandmother's back, and that she'd never let me go out alone with a man.

The lodger laughs heartily. Natalia turns to look at him, beseechingly and a little frightened at the same time.

LODGER: Well, if that's the case let's forget it.

Natalia is about to reply but does not dare. She clasps the books to her breast and rapidly leaves the room.

LODGER'S VOICE: But I'd think about it if I were you.

Natalia runs down the stairs. Halfway down she stops and turns to look back. The lodger is standing in the doorway of his room; he smiles at her and waves. Natalia turns and runs down the remaining steps.

Outside. Night.

Mario's expression reads, "Well, it's easy enough to figure out what his intentions were." Natalia looks at him, realizes what he is thinking, and is almost resentful. Then she looks about and shivers. She shrugs her shoulders.

NATALIA: Do you mind if we walk over that way? *(Smiling as if to excuse herself)* We can walk a bit.... I'm cold.

The two start off toward the spot where the girl had been waiting the night before. The high outlines of a church are silhouetted against the cloudy sky.

NATALIA: At first my grandmother... wasn't at all pleased that he'd lent me the books. She was so suspicious of everything and everybody. She insisted that I read them aloud to her one by one.

Home of Natalia and her grandmother.

The large room covered with carpets. The grandmother is sitting in her armchair intent on unraveling the edge of a carpet. Natalia is huddled on the footstool reading aloud from one of the detective stories lent her by the lodger. Her voice has become monotonous with exhaustion, and the words cannot be well distinguished.

NATALIA'S VOICE: And after a little while she began to love them so that she was always after me to read to her.

GRANDMOTHER *(with extreme interest)*: How poorly you read, Natalia! I can't understand a word! "He tightened the noose and..."?

Natalia stops reading for a moment and passes her hand over her brow. She looks at her grandmother with melancholy and resignation, sighs and raises her eyes. Someone is heard moving around upstairs.

NATALIA'S VOICE: I was tired, tired and irritable. He went out of the house only rarely then. I could hear him moving around in his room upstairs, going downstairs...

GRANDMOTHER *(impatient)*: Well?

Natalia bends over the book again to resume reading. But she immediately looks up again, trembling as she hears the lodger's steps nearing the room and then the door opening.

But the lodger evidently changes his mind and does not enter. The door remains slightly ajar and his steps are heard departing. At once relieved and disappointed, the girl begins to read again. But the lodger now suddenly opens the door and enters the room.

GRANDMOTHER *(to Natalia)*: Who is it?

Natalia continues to look down, even when the lodger has come over to the grandmother and speaks pleasantly to her as he places some books in her lap. The grandmother touches the books.

LODGER: I've brought you some more books. And I also... wanted to know what you've decided...

Only now does Natalia raise her eyes to find the young man watching her and smiling conspiratorially.

GRANDMOTHER *(grumbling with irritation)*: Decided? What was I supposed to decide?

LODGER *(still looking at Natalia)*: I asked the young lady to ask you whether you'd like to go out some evening.

GRANDMOTHER: What? What?

LODGER: I'd like to have the pleasure of inviting you and your granddaughter to the opera some evening.

The grandmother turns to Natalia.

GRANDMOTHER: You never told me. Why didn't you tell me?

Natalia and the young man continue to gaze at each other. The young man smiles at her.

Corner of Natalia's bedroom, with mirror.

Natalia runs to comb her hair before the small mirror on the dresser. She is extremely nervous. A basin of water stands near the mirror.

NATALIA'S VOICE: He went on so long about it that Grandmother finally accepted. I was on pins and needles all day long before we went. For the first time I realized that I wasn't pretty and my clothes weren't right, that I was ugly.

Natalia combs her hair hurriedly. She dips the comb into the water and tries to plaster down a rebellious curl. Then she examines her face in the mirror. She bites her lips to make them red.

GRANDMOTHER'S VOICE: Natalia, are you ready?

Natalia runs out.

Stairway in the theater. Inside. Night.

A crowd of people is pushing and hurrying up the narrow stairs leading up to the balconies of the opera; among them are the lodger, Natalia, and her grandmother, who is leaning on her arm. Natalia continually looks toward him, then turns away as he returns her gaze.

NATALIA'S VOICE: That evening, my whole life... was decided.

Balcony of theater. Inside. Night.

The two women sit side by side in the balcony at the opera. The grandmother listens with extreme attention and does not miss a note of the music. Natalia is smiling happily. Now and then she turns to look behind her, where the lodger is sitting; we can see only his knees and hands. At one point the man's hand moves to rest softly but firmly on Natalia's shoulders.

The girl bends her head until her cheek grazes his hand. Now Natalia has ceased to glance backward. She remains immobile, breathing a little heavily. Then she seems to be conquering her timidity after a long struggle: she leans her cheek more forcefully on his hand, then turns slightly and kisses it. Then she raises her head immediately and looks straight ahead, terrified by her own gesture.

The man's hand now caresses Natalia's neck and shoulder. She continues to look straight ahead. Now she is no longer frightened; she half closes her eyes and trembles with happiness.

Music of the opera.

Outside. Night.

Natalia gives the impression of awakening just now from the spell we have left her under at the opera.

NATALIA: Now I know what you're thinking. That he must have come to visit us more often... every day... after that night. But no, he stopped visiting almost altogether. It was impossible for me to do anything. I couldn't work, I couldn't read. I cried all the time. I tried to figure out why he was acting that way, and I couldn't find any explanation. Then one day, exactly a year ago, he told my grandmother that he'd finished his business in this town and was going away.

Natalia is silent, lost in thought. Troubled, she stares at the canal, sighs, and then raises her eyes to look at Mario, who has not missed a syllable of her story.

NATALIA: What could I do? He was to leave the next day. And I decided…

Stairs leading to the lodger's room.

Natalia and the lodger are locked in a passionate embrace. When Natalia draws back from the man's kiss she seems faint. Only now do we discover that the couple is standing just outside the man's room. He begins to talk softly, pressing her tight against him, and leads her gently into the room, where he sits her down in a chair.

The lodger gives Natalia something to drink. Then he looks at a suitcase standing outside the door. The man looks at the girl with a question in his eyes. She covers her face with her hands and breaks into violent, childish tears. The lodger stands before the pale girl and gazes at her with immense sadness in his eyes. Then he comes over to her and kneels before her, whispering with emotion.

LODGER: Listen, Natalia. Listen to me. It's because I do love you… I don't want to take advantage of you. Can you understand that? I… I… I can't marry you now. I've been in difficulties—understand? A lot of trouble, and that's why I've had to accept a job away from here for a year.

Natalia throws herself in his arms again. She cries and laughs at once, and he tries to calm her down.

NATALIA'S VOICE: I almost went crazy. I told him I couldn't go on living with my grandmother any more, that if he didn't take me away with him I'd run away all the same... but that I wanted to live with him, because life meant nothing to me without him. I was being tortured by both shame and love.

After this outburst the girl gradually calms down.

LODGER: Come on... let's go out...

NATALIA'S VOICE: We walked around the neighborhood for a long time, along the canals. We didn't even notice the people looking at us. He wanted to calm me down... he wanted me to think clearly.

Outside, along the canals. Night.

NATALIA'S VOICE: We came by here too. He told me again that he couldn't take me with him then... he couldn't marry me then... but he swore I was the only woman who could make him happy.

The lodger and Natalia walk along the canal in a nocturnal setting very similar to the present scene.

LODGER: Listen to me, Natalia. I have to go away for a year. And I can't ask you to promise me anything. I don't want you to promise me anything. I don't want you to be unhappy because of me. You have to be free. When I come back next year, if you still love me then, I swear to you, we'll be happy.

NATALIA'S VOICE: You want to test me, I told him. But I'm not afraid. I'll wait for you.

Outside. Night.

Natalia speaks to the young man, whose back is to the camera.

NATALIA: I'll be here to meet you a year from now... at this very time... and you'll still love me... and I'll be yours... yours forever...

With these words Natalia has drawn closer to Mario, almost as if she were addressing them to him, with the same intensity that she must have had with the other man. Mario at once moved and uncomfortable, moves a bit away from her.

NATALIA: He left the next morning... and... I'm here to wait for him.

There is a long silence. Natalia bows her head.

MARIO *(violently)*: But this story is absurd!

To recover from the emotion the girl's closeness and her confessions have provoked in him, Mario raises his voice and speaks with irritation and extreme agitation.

A pair of lovers who have been kissing in a dark corner not far from Mario and the girl turn in alarm.

MARIO: I... I may be ingenuous. But... but not to this point. You want to make me believe...

The girl gazes at the young man with disarming simplicity.

NATALIA: I don't want to make you believe anything. I've told you my story. It's an ordinary sort of story, I know. All girls...

MARIO *(interrupting her)*: All girls what? You mean all girls are crazy?

Natalia is truly astonished and anguished by the young man's reaction.

NATALIA: I don't understand. What's so strange about what I told you?

MARIO *(decisively)*: It's that... either you're crazy or you're making up fairy tales!

Natalia looks seriously at the young man without answering.

MARIO *(trying to control himself)*: You tell me you're waiting here for a man... who left here a year ago and whom you haven't heard from since.

NATALIA *(as if it were the most natural thing in the world)*: Yes.

MARIO: And where did this gentleman go? To the moon?

NATALIA: I don't know. It's not important.

MARIO: What d'you mean it's not important? Why hasn't he written you, at least? You can mail a letter anywhere in the world. Did you know that?

NATALIA *(impatient)* : But we'd decided not to write. I told you that, I think.

MARIO *(ironical)* : Fine. Fine. A fine decision. So you don't even know where he went?

NATALIA : No.

MARIO *(expecting to be contradicted)* : And I suppose you don't even know what kind of work this man does.

NATALIA *(with simplicity)* : No.

MARIO : That's perfect. *(Ironical)* But... you're sure he exists?

Natalia looks reprovingly at Mario. It has begun to drizzle. The couple who have been kissing nearby now passes by them.

MARIO *(still ironical, but now melancholy as well)* : Let's go; you'll get sick out here. And I'm... not anxious to catch a cold myself either. Let's go, please.

NATALIA *(sincere)* : I... I don't understand. You think I've made it all up, and that I'm crazy?

MARIO : Look, I don't even know what I think. *(Losing patience)* Can you possibly be so ingenuous as not to realize that that man...

The young man shrugs his shoulders to express his opinion of Natalia's inamorato. Then, still vexed, he raises the collar of his jacket, puts his hands in his pockets, and starts off. The girl follows him.

NATALIA : You're mistaken.

MARIO : Listen. Forget it. I'm a man and... I can judge. He'll never come back.

It is drizzling. Mario takes Natalia's arm and runs with her to the shelter of an overhanging cornice. The girl follows the young man without resisting. But as soon as they are safely sheltered she frees herself from his hand and looks at him seriously and challengingly. A few yards away an old man has also taken refuge under the overhang.

NATALIA: You're mistaken. And the truth is that he has… come back. *(More timidly)* I mean he's back in town.

MARIO *(surprised)* : Eh? *(Looking around ironically)* So where is he?

Mario's glance rests on the old man standing nearby, and he jokingly raises his eyebrows, as if to say, "Is this the fellow?" Natalia does not respond to the joke.

NATALIA: I heard it today from Giuliana, our old helper. He's come back and I know where he's staying too.

MARIO *(loudly)* : And you say he's not a cad?

NATALIA *(softly)* : No, I think… because he wanted me to feel free…he'll try first to find out whether I…whether I… still…

The girl turns toward Mario but meets the old man's stare. Embarrassed, she stops. She watches the rain, and little by little, trying to control herself and not be noticed, she starts to cry. But Mario does notice. He comes closer to Natalia and puts a hand on her shoulder.

MARIO: Please don't cry. Don't cry. Stop it. Are you offended by what I said? I was joking. I've been indiscreet. That's it, you see, this story is so far from… the kind of person I am… from my way of thinking… But that doesn't mean anything. And if I… could help you… Come on.

Mario looks embarrassedly toward the other man and speaks more softly in order not to be overheard. Natalia, still crying, leans against Mario. The old man looks curiously at the couple and they look at him in embarrassment.

The old man feels de trop. *He shrugs his shoulders, and after a moment's indecision, goes off into the rain. Now that he is free of the other man's presence, Mario speaks more openly and loudly, without fearing to sound like a child.*

MARIO: You feel better now? Good girl. I didn't think there were still girls like you in the world. For me, you see, it's like asking me to believe in fairy tales.

The rain is heavier now. The old man returns hurriedly to his refuge. Mario looks at him and the old man looks back, now almost defiantly, as if

to say, "*It's not my fault.*" *Natalia notices the old man's expression and suddenly smiles in amusement.*

OLD MAN: It's raining....

Mario smiles too. As on all such occasions, an exchange of observations becomes obligatory.

MARIO: It won't last long.

OLD MAN: Let's hope not.

A car passes by and splashes them. The car continues on, leaving the tracks of its tires on the wet asphalt.

Inside café. Night.

The rain has stopped. The café is closed. Wooden tables and chairs are stacked up against the wall under the overhanging roof. One of the tables has been opened and placed with two chairs at the corner of the platform next to the stack of chairs. Mario sits with his elbows on the table and looks at Natalia, trying to hide with a joking tone of voice the interest the girl has aroused in him.

MARIO: I've always been a solitary sort of guy, like you. Not so much here in this town, where I was transferred not long ago and you could say I don't know anyone anyway. But before. Your grandmother keeps you attached to her with a pin. My parents... just the opposite. Out! Get out of here! I was in boarding school as a child. Then always here and there with relatives because it was one mouth less to feed at home. Then the army, then work. I've known a lot of people. Girls too. You see them on and off. Maybe you like them too. Then... you have to move again. And the whole thing starts all over again. That's life. And it's really the best thing in life. You know what I mean?

The young man rests his hand on the girl's.

NATALIA *(perplexed)*: I don't know. It's different for men.

MARIO: These days it's the same for men and girls. You know it too, and the proof is that at a certain point what did you do? When you fell in love you went to him, and you told him so. And that was the right thing to do. But afterwards...

Mario shakes his head in disapproval.

NATALIA: What do you think I should have done?

MARIO: You shouldn't have let him go; you should have made him take you. Or else... make up your mind it was all over. Even when a person says they'll wait... I've said it myself...

NATALIA *(spiritedly)*: Without believing it? *(She laughs.)* I don't believe you. You always try to make yourself out worse than you really are. You're really good, sincere... and I'm very happy we've become friends.

The young man looks at the girl without the courage to lie. He simply withdraws his hand.

MARIO: Me too.

Now Natalia places her hand on his.

NATALIA *(beseeching)*: Give me some advice. You can help me.

MARIO: Who, me? *(Embarrassed, he picks up a spoon and taps it nervously on the edge of a tray.)* What can I tell you? I think... *(The girl's attentive and pleading look makes him change his tone.)* Anyway... this gentleman has left you complete freedom. But, if I've understood correctly, he said that for his part he considers himself engaged. Is that it? *(Natalia nods.)* So? Go find him... talk to him...

NATALIA *(joyously hopeful)*: You go.

Mario looks at the girl in consternation.

MARIO: No. No. What have I got to do with it? But... even without going to him... you could write him a letter.

NATALIA: No, no. I can't. It would be like trying to force him...

MARIO *(still upset)*: Not at all. There're all kinds of letters. The important thing is to find out how you stand, instead of just crying and waiting. You tell him to meet you at a definite time; you say... you only want to... That is, you take the first step and see if he...

Mario takes his pack of cigarettes out of his pocket. It is empty. Annoyed, he throws it on the tray.

NATALIA: You think so? Well, what should I say?

MARIO: It's not hard. *(As if giving an example)* It's very easy: Dear...

NATALIA *(immediately)*: Sir...

Mario looks at her in surprise but is pleased at the implications of her response.

MARIO: That's fine: Dear Sir...

Natalia takes the empty cigarette package, opens it, and spreads out the white paper on the inside.

NATALIA: It would be better to say: Sir.

MARIO: If you prefer; then: Excuse me for writing to you, but you must forgive...

Mario takes the paper from her and a pen from his pocket and begins to write hurriedly, as if trying to discharge a bothersome obligation which has been forced upon him.

Natalia moves closer to Mario and follows with great interest.

NATALIA: No, I'm sorry, it would be better to say: Please forgive my impatience...

MARIO *(writing)*: You're right. No excuses. Forgive my impatience, but for a whole year now I have been living in anticipation...

NATALIA *(not looking at Mario)*: ...I have been living with a happy dream.

MARIO *(impatiently crossing out)*: All right.

NATALIA: Are you sure it's all right? You're the one who has to judge.

MARIO: It's just fine.

NATALIA: Now you have returned and perhaps you have changed your mind about me...

MARIO: ...in which case...

NATALIA: I shall not complain or accuse, because evidently this is my fate, but I should like...

Mario turns the paper over, but the other side of the cigarette package is printed and there is not room to write on it. Mario hands the sheet to Natalia.

MARIO *(in conclusion)*: Then you just say that you want to clarify things and... end it. And then you make an appointment.

NATALIA: For instance: tomorrow evening at the same place.

MARIO: Whatever you like. *(Trying to take Natalia's hand)* Now try to pay a little attention to me, won't you?

Natalia withdraws her hand gracefully, laughing gaily.

NATALIA: You're not going to flirt with me? *(Laughs)* You're looking at me like a man in love. You can't, after all I've told you, fall in love. Anyway you won't have time to; maybe we won't see each other again.

MARIO: Even if we're only friends, it doesn't mean we always have to˙talk about your troubles. Let's talk about mine too.

NATALIA: Do you have troubles?

MARIO: No. But I might sometime.

Natalia laughs in amusement. Then she abruptly becomes serious and looks at the paper in her hand.

NATALIA: If I send this letter and then... I mean... I'd like to be sure he gets it, I mean.

MARIO *(without much interest)*: You should get someone to take it to him personally. Copy it out tomorrow. We'll meet, and then I'll deliver it.

NATALIA *(pleased)*: Would you?

MARIO: Sure. A friend can do a favor, can't he?

Natalia looks at Mario, radiant with gratitude.

NATALIA: And you say you're not good. I'm so happy I met you. You... you can't possibly know...

The girl opens her purse, takes out an envelope and hands it to Mario.

NATALIA *(ashamed)*: Here.

Mario looks at the envelope suspiciously and frowns.

MARIO: What's this? It's written on. *(Beginning to understand)* You'd already...

NATALIA: Yes. It's just like the one you wrote. *(To hide her embarrassment she begins to laugh.)* I... I'm so grateful to you. I trust you... like a brother.

Mario smiles unsmilingly.

MARIO: Oh! Natalia... Natalia...

He continues to stare at the envelope, then slowly puts it in his pocket.

NATALIA: Well... You'll really take it to him?

MARIO: Rest assured. If there's any difficulty I'll let you know.

NATALIA: Oh yes. You know where I live?

MARIO *(smiling)*: Of course.

NATALIA: That's right.

Mario is increasingly vexed. He avoids Natalia's eyes. She looks at him and smiles disarmingly.

NATALIA: When we met the first time, you didn't expect to have to act like an older brother to me.

MARIO: Now that you mention it...

NATALIA: And... are you sorry?

MARIO: A little. *(Smiling with effort)* And for a guy like me that doesn't believe in fairy tales.

NATALIA: You believe in them now?

MARIO: Eh?

With a gesture of embarrassment and impatience he pushes back his chair and almost loses his balance. He stands up to pick up the chair, but now Natalia too has risen to leave.

MARIO: No, no...

Natalia smiles as if to say, "Yes, it's time now," and starts to walk off slowly. Now Natalia turns toward Mario.

NATALIA: Don't come back with me. It's so late.

MARIO: Not at all...

NATALIA: Really. *(Pauses)* But... if there is any difficulty about... *(Natalia motions with her head toward the pocket in which Mario has placed the letter.)* You will let me know, won't you?

MARIO: Of course. *(Hopefully)* And anyway we'll be seeing each other, I hope.

Natalia shrugs her shoulders and smiles endearingly.

NATALIA: You needn't be so pleased about it, because tomorrow I'll either be so happy or so desperate that I won't be very good company either way.

Natalia starts to go off. The prostitute who has passed before shuffles toward them.

MARIO: Wait...

NATALIA *(coming back toward him)*: No. And... I don't like good-byes. Thanks for everything. *(Natalia is already walking off.)* Thank you, thank you, you can't know how much.

Natalia runs off. Mario starts to follow her, then stops. He is also embarrassed by the presence of the prostitute, who has stopped a few feet from him and gazes at him slightly ironically. Mario turns, doubly vexed.

The prostitute walks on again. Mario too starts off and finds himself overtaking her. She looks at him again, takes a cigarette from her purse

and, without speaking, turns to ask him with a gesture for a light. With an impatient gesture Mario puts his hand in his pocket and pulls out the letter and then the matches. He hands the woman the matches and then immediately, increasingly vexed, walks off with the letter still in his hand.

A few steps later he is at the canal. After a moment's hesitation he crumples the letter and throws it into the canal. When he finally brings himself to look at the letter floating in the water, it has already been carried a little distance away by the slow current. Mario shrugs his shoulders and walks off, as the church bells ring the hour.

Mario's room. Inside. Day.

Mario's room is in great disarray. The bed is empty, the dark suit thrown haphazardly over a chair. The landlady is heard knocking on the door and calling in the same monotonous street vendor's voice of the day before.

LANDLADY'S VOICE: Aren't you going to work this morning? It's after eight. The night…

The woman opens the door and looks into the room. Almost at the same moment, Mario appears behind her, evidently fresh from the bathroom, with soap dish and towel in hand.

MARIO: The night what?

The landlady turns in surprise and stares at Mario.

LANDLADY: You know what.

Mario enters the room behind the landlady.

MARIO: You're wrong.

LANDLADY: Eh?

MARIO *(annoyed)* : I said you're wrong. I don't know. I—don't—know.

The landlady is a little offended by Mario's tone.

LANDLADY *(argumentative)*: What d'you think, I want you to tell me your business? I'm not interested, believe me! Anyway I can imagine... I'm old. I know perfectly well what young men your age do when they stay out at night... and have that expression on their faces in the morning...

The woman picks Mario's suit up from the chair.

MARIO *(trying to control his bad mood)*: You can take your time cleaning it. I'm not wearing it today.

LANDLADY *(more kindly)*: Don't you feel well?

MARIO: Me? *(Lying)* I feel just fine.

Mario glances at himself in the mirror.

LANDLADY: Hmmm...

The landlady would like him to confide in her, but Mario is really not very encouraging. He has gone over to the window and looks sadly out.

The landlady is about to leave the room reluctantly, taking Mario's good suit with her. But now Mario suddenly turns around, comes up to her, and takes back the suit.

MARIO: Give it back, maybe I will wear it. I'm going out tonight... I want to have a good time for once.

LANDLADY *(bitingly ironical)*: Ah, because these past nights...

Mario begins to dress rapidly.

MARIO: These past nights... I don't know myself what I was doing. I was dreaming. That's what I was doing. I was dreaming. *(As Mario dresses he seems to be arguing with the landlady, who looks at him without understanding.)* What kind of people live in this town? If anybody'd told me I wouldn't have believed it. I don't believe it even now, understand, but anyway it's none of my business... no, no... *(With a jeering laugh at himself)* I'm not sorry. Sorry, my eye...

Mario speaks very quickly. The landlady looks at him in astonishment. From the corridor are heard the voices of the other lodgers, who call, open and close their doors. The landlady shrugs her shoulders.

LANDLADY *(muttering)*: I'm coming, I'm coming.

She leaves after a last look at Mario, who continues to mutter to himself as he ties his shoes.

MARIO: Little lady, I'm not playing your game. You've got the wrong boy...and I have other things to do...and I should...

Main street. Outside. Night.

Near a movie theater. The street is lit by the many neon signs and is fairly crowded. Mario walks along with his hands in his pockets, with an almost defiant expression on his face as he turns to stare at the single girls strolling by.

Two girls are looking at the photographs displayed in front of the movie theater. They are fairly pretty and casual-looking though not vulgar. Sensing Mario's gaze they laugh and whisper to each other. They enter the theater.

Mario is uncertain what to do. He starts to walk on, then slows to turn around. Suddenly he stops and looks attentively straight ahead, where he thinks he sees Natalia walking among the crowd. The girl is hidden from view by the crowd. Relieved, Mario starts to continue on when he again sees the girl, who has now stopped to look in a shop window.

Natalia sees Mario's reflection in the mirror at the back of the shop window. Under her coat Natalia is wearing the dress she wore the evening she went to the opera with the lodger; her hair has been arranged with particular care. As soon as she sees Mario's image reflected in the mirror, Natalia smiles, surprised and happy, and turns to look at him.

But Mario is no longer there. He has turned away instantly, and quickly tries to make his way through a group of people gathered around a sidewalk toy vendor. The people make way for Mario and look at him in annoyance.

Mario stands in the first row surrounding the toy vendor. He accidently steps on one of the toys on the ground and thus earns the irritation of the vendor as well, who is leaning against the wall with one hand in his pocket, maneuvering the little toys. At intervals he plays a small harmonica. The toys consist of two wooden figures operated by two strings, one of which is attached to a nail in the wall and the other of which is pulled to make them dance. With the same hand the vendor uses to move the toy he is also holding a long wire spring to the top of which is attached an aluminum butterfly. The vendor is decently dressed, wears a hat, and speaks tiredly but pronouncing his words syllable by syllable as vendors do. He continues to repeat the same things without ever looking at anyone in particular.

VENDOR: The dancing dolls, Arthur and Diomira. They can do all the latest steps, even the hardest steps. It's a safe toy; today a fireman bought one. It's licensed; here we have a

policeman who can testify to that. It's a clean toy; I sold
two to the parish priest today....

*Mario turns slightly to make certain he is concealed by the rest of the group.
He sees Natalia passing by without seeing him. Mario watches the vendor.*

VENDOR: Buy the little dancers for your kids; they'll love it. Come
on, dance. If you haven't got kids, buy them for your wife.

*Mario turns again, more courageously this time, even rising up on tiptoe
to look over the heads of the people around him. Natalia is not to be seen.
Reassured, Mario relaxes and listens to the vendor.*

VENDOR: If you haven't got a wife, thank God for it and buy them
for yourself. Come on, dance. Only a hundred lire, not
even the cost of the labor, the whole family dances.

*Mario's expression suddenly changes. Beside the vendor, against the wall,
he now sees Natalia, who is smiling at him.*

NATALIA: Now you're the one who's trying to hide....

MARIO: Me? And... and... why should I?

NATALIA *(laughing gaily)*: Of course you are. I saw you before,
you know....

*They are standing very near the vendor, who continues to recite his pitch,
barely raising his eyes to look at them in annoyance.*

VENDOR: Buy the little toy, the little blue butterfly...

*As she starts to come over to Mario, Natalia grazes one of the toys with
her foot. She immediately stoops to set it upright again and remains a
moment kneeling beside the vendor. When she rises, the butterfly catches
in her hair. Natalia laughs and embarrassedly tries to remove it. The
impassive vendor plays his harmonica. Mario helps the girl remove the
butterfly from her hair.*

NATALIA: But I'm happy to have run into you!

*She laughs. Without looking at them, the vendor stops playing the harmonica
and takes up his patter again.*

VENDOR: Just a hundred lire for the butterfly, not even the cost
of the labor, and if the young lady's your girl...

Natalia turns to the vendor.

NATALIA: No, thank you.

But he does not even look at her. He continues his monotonous patter.

VENDOR: Buy the little toy, the dancing dolls *(et cetera)*.

*Natalia and Mario pass through the group and leave. Natalia rearranges
the locks of hair which have been mussed by the toy.*

NATALIA *(laughing)* : The whole day long I was afraid of seeing
you. Yes, of seeing you come to the house because... well,
to tell me that you'd had no luck. But now...

VENDOR'S VOICE: If you haven't got a wife, thank God for it and
buy them all the same.

*The two young people stop, facing each other, a few paces away. Natalia
smiles as she listens to the voice of the vendor, then she addresses Mario
again.*

NATALIA: Are you annoyed with me? *(Apprehensive)* Or is there
something...

MARIO *(brusquely)* : Of course not. Why should I be? I... didn't
see you, that's all...

NATALIA *(again gay)*: Don't fib. You're just like me... I stutter
when I fib. I noticed it the first night I met you.

MARIO: I was stuttering?

*Natalia nods and laughs. Mario is still more embarrassed and edgy.
Natalia is already distracted and looks about her.*

NATALIA *(speaking rapidly, a little excited)* : I just love this street,
don't you? I love it because... *(Laughs)* I don't know why.

Once I tried to describe it to Grandmother, building by building... even if they all look alike... and the lights... and the stores. Afterward I asked her, "How do you imagine it?" "It sounds horrible," she said. Maybe she's right. But I love it all the same. Which direction are you going?

MARIO: Me?

Mario looks around, then gestures vaguely ahead.

NATALIA: If you'd like I can walk along with you a little way. I've got a lot of free time. My grandmother sent me out on a errand, and Giuliana's home and will put her to bed. I don't want to go home yet. Anyway the time drags so at home. *(The two are strolling along.)* If I told you everything I did today to make the time go by... I even washed all the windows. And meanwhile...

Mario suddenly stops.

MARIO: I'm sorry but I have to leave you. I... I have an appointment.

NATALIA *(disappointed)*: Oh! *(Recovering)* That's why you didn't want...

MARIO *(on edge, looking at his watch)*: Yes. In fact... I'm already late. I'll really have... to leave you. Goodbye.

NATALIA *(still more disappointed)*: Yes, yes. Don't be late on my account. I've already given you so much trouble.

Natalia turns slowly toward a lighted window. Mario remains where he is.

NATALIA *(turning to Mario again, with a timid and beseeching air)*: When did you take the letter? This morning?

MARIO *(not looking at her)*: Uh huh.

NATALIA: And... do you know if he was there?

MARIO *(still avoiding looking at Natalia)* : I think so.

*Now he looks at her. His now very obvious desire to stay with her is strug-
gling with the resentment he feels at her forcing him to lie. Mario comes
up to Natalia and resolutely takes her arm.*

MARIO: Come with me.

NATALIA *(surprised)* : Where?

MARIO: Wherever we like. Didn't you say you're free?

NATALIA: You know. Till ten.

MARIO *(a little equivocally)* : I do know, that's why...

NATALIA: And your appointment?

MARIO: I'll go later on.... I won't go at all. *(Giving it a try)* You
won't go to yours, and... *(The girl laughs as if at a joke;
Mario looks at her and becomes serious.)* Listen, I have to tell
you something....

*The two stroll slowly along. Light and sounds issue from the doorways
of the stores. Natalia, suddenly dismayed, walks with her head bowed.
Mario avoids looking at her and tries to confess his guilt.*

MARIO: Natalia...

*As soon as he begins to speak, the girl places her hand on his arm and
speaks seriously.*

NATALIA *(with an effort)* : Don't tell me, please. *(There is a pause,
during which Mario looks at Natalia in dismay.)* It's what I
think, isn't it? *(Mario has stopped and looks uncertainly at
Natalia, wondering how to interpret her words; she continues,
simply.)* You... want to tell me that I shouldn't keep up
my hopes any more. Well, don't say it, there's no point
to it.

MARIO *(stammering)* : No, that's not quite it. In a certain sense,
perhaps...

NATALIA *(smiling)*: Yes, it is. You're stuttering. *(Brief pause, then seriously again)* Look, I've already told myself, but I haven't been able to convince myself. The other nights... I sensed that I'd be unhappy. But *(Taking courage)* tonight I feel... that everything'll be wonderful, that everything will turn out well. I feel it. *(With a pathetic gesture Natalia opens her coat to show her poor little party dress.)* You see, I'm so sure, so happy, that I even dressed for a ball.

MARIO *(ever more embarrassed)* : Well, I can only trust to your instinct. *(Mario seems to be preparing again to leave her, but now he gathers his courage.)* Maybe everything will end well, perhaps differently from the way you expect. It's the end result that counts. *(Laughs)* Where shall we go?

Natalia has not been able to follow Mario's secret reasoning, but she, too, laughs, immediately won over by the young man's gaiety.

NATALIA *(still laughing)* : And your appointment?

Mario shakes his head, still laughing.

Café and dance hall in the center of town. Inside. Night.

Music, voices, noise. The café area is glaringly lit and is fairly crowded. The small dance room adjacent to the café is less brightly lighted; Mario and Natalia are now entering. The television is on in the café section and the sound of the program is heard along with that of the jukebox in the dance room, creating an unpleasant cacophony at the doorway between the two areas.

Three or four couples are dancing in the modestly furnished room. Natalia watches, enchanted as if she were in a splendid ballroom.

NATALIA: I didn't know they had a dance room too! I've never really been dancing.

MARIO *(gaily)*: Well, I imagine there are nicer ones.

NATALIA: Yes?

MARIO: If you like it, we can stay here.

Natalia barely nods. Then, concerned about the time, she places her hand on Mario's wrist so as to see his watch. Mario immediately pulls back his hand.

MARIO: It's still very early…. *(Natalia looks at Mario as if to assure herself that he is telling the truth; Mario nods and continues, half-joking, half-sad.)* You're having such a bad time with me?

NATALIA *(emphatically and sincerely)*: You're so nice, so good… that I love you… almost as much as him.

Mario frowns; Natalia laughs. Then she immediately continues on into the room, looking at everything with great interest. She speaks softly, as if at a theater.

NATALIA: How beautifully they dance! Can you dance that well too?

Mario shrugs and leans against the wall with something of a superior air.

MARIO *(with a modest, blasé tone)*: I can dance….

NATALIA: I can't.

Natalia has come near Mario, almost leaning against him. Mario watches her and tries his "melancholy" line again.

MARIO: Not that I come very often to this kind of place. Just like everybody else, when I finish work I think of a thousand nice things to do in the evening and all the rest of my free time. Most of the time, though, I end up just all by myself, thinking about lots of things… remembering… In my town I sometimes liked to go out alone to the places where I'd been happy, and I'd try to make the present conform to the past. Maybe tonight too, if I hadn't met you, I'd have ended up going back to where we were together last night, to think about you….

NATALIA *(a little embarrassed)*: Then you're something of...a dreamer too.

Mario nods, smiling modestly and sadly. But the effect is immediately ruined as they are interrupted by a couple who almost crash into them as they whirl about. The man is a thin young fellow who looks insistently at Natalia; she smiles back innocently, admiring his skill in dancing.

The music ends. The dancer turns to look at Natalia as he goes over to the jukebox. Mario does not notice. Now he helps Natalia remove her coat and places it over a nearby chair. As Mario turns to come back to Natalia, the girl sees the thin young man start back toward her after selecting another record. The young man, evidently encouraged by Natalia's admiring gaze, now motions to her to join him on the dance floor.

To Mario's real alarm, Natalia starts to go over to the dancer and accept his invitation, after having flashed Mario a timid smile.

Mario reacts promptly, taking Natalia by the waist and beginning to dance with her.

NATALIA: But I don't know how to dance, I told you.

MARIO *(beginning to dance)* : It's very easy, take my word for it.

NATALIA *(somewhat reassured)* : Well, here goes... it's like walking!

The repulsed dancer looks ironically at Mario for a moment, then picks up his former partner and almost leaps to the center of the room, intentionally brushing Natalia as he passes by her.

Mario throws his rival a look of reproof and warning. The other man's only response is another ironical look at Mario and, as a sort of challenge, he begins to dance with perfect form, like a professional giving an exhibition.

Natalia smiles with pleasure as she watches the dancer. Increasingly indifferent to Mario's hostility, he begins to show off, and is immediately imitated, much less skillfully, by another couple.

NATALIA *(laughing, admiring, and watching the thin dancer)* : How good he is.

Mario glances at the other man, who continues to look at him with an air of superiority as he moves like a virtuoso. Then, with the courage of the timid, Mario, too, begins to attempt to show off: he removes his hand from Natalia's waist and begins to jump about rather awkwardly, staring back defiantly at the other dancer.

After a moment of surprise, Natalia begins to clap her hands with pleasure as she watches Mario, who is dancing like a lunatic, very serious but creating great confusion on the floor. The thin dancer is forced to move back a bit and watches open-mouthed. Though absolutely clumsy and chaotic, Mario's exhibition appears to be a parody of the other man's, and as such delights the few others present.

Natalia, who is the most delighted of all, laughs ever more gaily. Now, as Mario, still very serious and glaring at his rival, slows down, she in turn tries to improvise a little dance, which continues until the end of the record.

In the sudden silence following the end of the music, the thin dancer applauds ironically. Mario, ready to react, approaches him until he is stopped by

Natalia. Panting and smiling, she takes his arm and very gracefully bows before the thin young man to thank him for his applause.

The thin young man is hurt and looks at Natalia in astonishment. She turns proudly to Mario.

NATALIA: Now I can say I've been dancing.

Café and dance hall. Inside. Night.

The brighter lights have been turned off to create an atmosphere more

suited to the slow music now playing. The room is lit only by the horrible
hanging lamps shaped like bunches of grapes. One couple is dancing in a
tight embrace. Mario and Natalia are sitting beside each other on a sort
of bench near the jukebox. Natalia is drinking something with a straw
and with a fairly lazy gesture starts to look at Mario's watch. He imme-
diately pulls back his hand, and his expression answers, "Hey, it's still
early!" as he concludes what he was saying without interruption.

MARIO: Everybody creates romantic dreams in their imagination.
　　　Your thoughts run away with you and... your imagination
　　　boils... like the water in a coffee pot. You don't desire
　　　anything more because you're creating your life, you're
　　　creating it according to your own whim. You understand
　　　what I'm trying to say?

Natalia nods, smiling and serious.

NATALIA: Yes. When I was younger, I used to think... to dream...
　　　as I sat beside my grandmother... for so long! *(Laughing)*
　　　And I always ended up marrying a Chinese prince.

MARIO *(rather surprised and disappointed)*: Eh? *(Recovering)* But...
　　　even certain passions are only the fruit of your imagination.
　　　Like the Chinese prince. Those dreams begin to seem as
　　　if they have something real, something tangible about
　　　them. You end up disregarding real life, because it seems
　　　so dull, so wretched, and you don't believe that some day
　　　you might give all your years of fantasy for just one day of
　　　that wretched life.

NATALIA *(immediately moved)*: That's so true. You've... understood
　　　so many things....

Mario takes her hand.

MARIO *(softly)*: Fantasy is monotonous, it's the slave of shadow, of
　　　thought. The slave of the first cloud that suddenly hides
　　　the sun. It leads you to a melancholy solitude. The years
　　　pass by and suddenly you find yourself asking: where have

my best years gone? Have I really lived? I've gone through this too. Only to discover that there is a real life, eternally young, where no one hour is like another. *(Troubled, Natalia looks at Mario, who is still holding her hand.)* Life, reality, is the happiness I feel now when I'm with you, and I'm sure...

Natalia looks about her, lost. Mario takes the glass from her hand and places it on the bench. With his arm about her waist, he invites the girl to get up and dance, holding her tight against himself.

Natalia's cheeks are flaming; her eyes are troubled. She continues to look about her as if seeking to escape; she tries to smile, jokingly referring to her lack of skill in dancing. But Mario's own agitation, as he holds her delicately and forcefully close to himself, forces her finally to lower her eyes, agitated in turn.

MARIO *(whispering)* : Natalia...

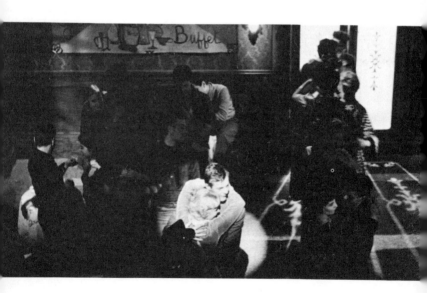

Natalia suddenly breaks away from Mario and moves rapidly toward a corner of the room where there is a window. She tries again to smile. But her eyes are still troubled, her face aflame. She passes her hand over her cheek as if to erase the blush. Nearby, Mario looks at her with love in his eyes. She opens the window.

MARIO *(as if commencing a speech)* : Natalia...

Among the confused voices in the street they suddenly hear a woman's voice.

WOMAN'S VOICE *(shouting)* : Gino! Ginoooo! *(Natalia avoids Mario's eyes.)* Gino! Go call Papa! Tell him it's way past ten o'clock!

Natalia's expression suddenly changes. Without a word, almost as if she's forgotten Mario's presence, the girl turns from the window and runs toward the door.

Mario starts to call her back but instead hurries to pick up her coat and motions the waiter over.

Outside. Night.

Natalia has stopped at the edge of the sidewalk and waits impatiently to be able to cross. As soon as the street is clear she darts across and is already some distance away when Mario comes out of the café and starts to follow her.

MARIO : Natalia!

Natalia crosses the street flanking the canal. Mario catches up with her and puts the coat over her shoulders, speaking forcefully, breathlessly, and almost harshly.

MARIO : Natalia, wait! I have to talk to you!

Natalia's eyes are filled with tears and she is extremely upset. She slips the coat on awkwardly as she continues along.

NATALIA: Go away, go away.

MARIO *(forcefully)*: No, listen, Natalia, I love you. I love you. Listen, Natalia...

By now they are near the girl's rendezvous and can see that no one is waiting at the bridge. But Natalia does not even look at the spot; extremely agitated, if not angry, she turns on Mario.

NATALIA: Go away! Go away! I don't want him to find me here with you! He won't come if you're here.

MARIO *(getting angry in turn)*: But he won't come, can't you under-

stand? Anyway what meaning would it have, a meeting
like this that you've begged for? Let sleeping ghosts lie.
You've understood it too. What counts is that you and I...

NATALIA *(not even listening to him)* : Go away! Go away! I... haven't
been unfaithful to him. It's not true! Go away!

MARIO *(exploding)* : You're crazy, that's what you are. Damn the
moment I first met you. When I think of the time I've
lost thinking about your silliness I could kick myself.
Damn! Damn!

*The young man crushes his head between his hands and looks at the girl
with such wrath in his eyes that he seems about to hit her. Perhaps to overcome just this temptation, he starts away, venting his anger verbally,
and crosses the street.*

MARIO: If they're not whores, they're out of their minds. They belong in a straitjacket. That fellow had the right idea... enjoyed himself as long as he wanted to and then...

Another area outside. Night.

Mario has crossed the street and hurries away furiously. As he reaches the other sidewalk, near the corner of an alley, the aging prostitute whom he has run into before comes toward him. She smiles, pleased to see him.

PROSTITUTE: Hello, handsome! Always alone and always in a hurry!

Mario stops short and raises his hand as if to give the poor woman the blow he has not given Natalia. She looks at him in fright and astonishment. This expression brings Mario to his senses.

PROSTITUTE *(her voice very prudent now)*: I'm not going to eat you up. *(Taking courage)* I was saying, if you're all alone you could come with me....

MARIO: That's right, better you, look...

The young man has taken the prostitute by the arm and drags her along with him, walking rapidly. The prostitute is still a little frightened; she clops awkwardly along on her too high heels, trying to keep up with him.

PROSTITUTE *(laughing and breathless)*: Hey! Crazy! Slow down, slow down. Oh... *(Laughs)* Where're we going? To your place?

MARIO: Wherever you want.

PROSTITUTE: This way, then. Stop. Let's cross.

The prostitute is no longer afraid of Mario and is very pleased to have found a client, whom she leads toward the place where she usually entertains her clients.

PROSTITUTE: You know where we're going? *(Laughs)* You'll see,

you'll like it. Hey, can't you slow down a little? That's
it; good boy. Look! You've made me twist my heel.
*(She raises her foot to show it to Mario—pretending to sulk like
a child.)* I'll make you pay for it, you know. Bad boy. *(She
slips her arm under Mario's and presses close to him.)* What a
nice fellow you are! Handsome! Umm! You know I like
you? I like you! Careful, it's slippery here.

*The two have reached a ramp leading down below a bridge. Mario looks
straight ahead, expressionless. His anger gone, he feels all the absurdity
of this situation.*

MARIO: Where are we going?

*Behind them is a tavern; before them, the darkness of the ramp, toward
which the woman now points.*

PROSTITUTE: There. I always go there. *(Catching herself)* Let's
go there.

MARIO *(stopping)* : No.

PROSTITUTE *(irritated)* : So where do you want to go?

MARIO *(edgy)*: Nowhere. Excuse me. Goodbye.

*Mario starts to turn away but the woman immediately takes his arm,
trying to overcome her terror that the young man will leave her.*

PROSTITUTE *(laughing, nervous)* : What's the matter? You don't like
it there? It's nice there, but if you want…

MARIO *(interrupting her)* : That's not it. I don't want to.

*Mario walks away. Now the woman has understood that the adventure
has evaporated, she can no longer control herself. Her smiling face becomes
infuriated and she seems even older and more worn out.*

PROSTITUTE *(raising her voice)* : Come here. *(Mario does not stop,
he barely shrugs his shoulders; her voice even louder)* Come here!
What do you think you're doing, giving people the run-

around? *(Shouting)* Thief! You'll pay me, understand? Pay me!

Mario turns with an annoyed expression:

MARIO: Cut it out! No one's done anything to you!

A man (the lodger) comes along the street. The prostitute approaches him resolutely, raising her protesting voice even higher.

PROSTITUTE: He's trying to cheat a person like me, the coward. Because I'm all alone...

The lodger stops in surprise and looks first at the woman and then at Mario.

MARIO: Cut it out, I told you.

Evidently the woman has approached the lodger believing he is someone she knows: another man who now actually does appear. He is a man of extremely equivocal appearance who approaches slowly and menacingly. He is evidently her protector:

MAN *(to Mario, pointing to the woman)* : If she says you owe her something, then you do, and I advise you...

Everything happens very suddenly. Mario looks from one man to the

other, evidently convinced (not altogether mistakenly) that he is being framed. With all his unresolved anger he throws himself upon the passer-by and punches him in the face, then snaps around and punches the second man with equal violence.

MARIO: Crooks, cowards!

The lodger, taken by surprise, stumbles backward but immediately recovers and throws himself on Mario, trying to immobilize him. The prostitute starts to shriek in fright.

Mario twists free.

LODGER: What do you want from me?

MARIO: Coward. You don't know, do you?

He immediately starts lashing wildly out again. The woman's protector gets into the brawl too, but when things appear to be becoming serious he limits himself to shouting insults and to an attitude of self-defense and of preparation for retreat.

MAN: Thief!

Consequently he throws a warning glance at the prostitute, who begins to back off, still shouting and protesting.

But from the door of the nearby tavern, from which the woman's protector had just come, a number of clients appear, mostly sailors and stevedores, attracted by the shouts and noise. Their intervention makes it impossible for the woman and her protector to escape. Mario and the lodger are separated by force. The prostitute now protests in a completely different tone of voice.

PROSTITUTE *(protesting)* : What are they doing? What's going on? How awful!

The explanation for her sudden change of expression and tone is made clear by the appearance of a policeman, who has turned a corner from the dark alley and appears suddenly in the midst of the brawl.

POLICEMAN: What's going on here?

His appearance produces an immediate transformation in the behavior of everyone present. Many try to slink away; among these are the woman's protector whom, however, Mario blocks.

MARIO *(pointing to the lodger and the protector)* : They work together and they were trying…

LODGER *(interrupting violently)* : I don't know what he's talking about and I don't know anybody here. He attacked me.

PROSTITUTE *(moaning)* : I don't know anything about it. What's going on? I don't feel well.…

The prostitute turns to the onlookers, seeking solidarity.

MAN *(trying to free himself from Mario's grip)* : This guy's crazy. Let go of me!

Disheveled, the three men stare angrily at each other. The policeman whistles energetically to call for reinforcements. In the meantime he takes the passer-by by the arm; the man tries to wrench himself free, protesting indignantly.

LODGER : Will you try to understand I have nothing to do with it? He's the one.

POLICEMAN *(ironical)* : Don't get so excited. You'll have plenty of time to explain your side of it. *(To the prostitute)* Hey you, stick around, stick around… you've got a place to sleep for tonight anyway.

Wavering on her heels, the prostitute comes up to the policeman. She seems even more aged and squalid. With a pitiful smile she turns to one of the onlookers, than begins to laugh childishly as the policeman whistles again.

PROSTITUTE : Just think, the one time I find myself a customer…

Outside near the police station and adjacent streets. Night.

Two policemen lead the prostitute and her protector out of the police station, in front of which another policeman is standing guard in the cold.

The prostitute, increasingly exhausted and squalid, assures herself with a rapid glance that the policemen are not watching her. Then, still stumbling on her high heels, she tries to catch up with her protector and to touch his arm to elicit a smile of pardon with a piteous smile of her own. But the man barely glances balefully at her.

MAN *(whispering)* : Leave me alone or I'll murder you.

The group disappears in the dark at the corner of the building, and immediately we see the headlights of a car and then the sound of the motor starting. As it turns, the car's headlights light up the sentinel and the door of the police station for a moment. Mario and the lodger are coming out now, one a few steps behind the other. A policeman comes after them with some identification documents.

POLICEMAN : Just a minute. Whose are these?

Mario and the lodger stop and look at the documents. Mario takes them and puts them in his pocket. His glance meets the lodger's. The two men barely nod goodbye. Both are distracted, irritated. Mario still bears the obvious signs of the battle.

MARIO *(expressionless)* : I'm sorry. Forgive me.

The lodger barely shakes his head and starts to extend his hand, but Mario has already turned and gone off. The lodger is uncertain whether to catch up with him or not; then, again absorbed in his own thoughts, he too goes off, avoiding going in the same direction as Mario.

As soon as he has crossed the street and is out of the police station area, Mario stops to examine his badly damaged suit. Then slowly, as if instinctively attracted by something (but without any voice or sound arousing his attention), Mario raises his eyes. A few steps away, humiliated and abased to the point of seeming smaller than she really is, with her face half-hidden by the raised collar of her coat, is Natalia.

Mario goes toward her, and for a long moment they look at each other in silence. When Natalia speaks her voice trembles.

NATALIA: He didn't come. You were right. He didn't come. *(After a pause, more softly)* Forgive me for having offended you before.

Natalia smiles in the desperate attempt not to cry. Mario avoids looking at her. He assumes a certain nonchalance and tries to rearrange his hair and his torn jacket as best he can.

MARIO: Well... you can't say either of us has had much luck tonight, eh?

NATALIA: You would never have been able to do such a thing, would you?

Mario is so touched that his expression suddenly hardens.

MARIO: Natalia, I have to make a confession: I threw away that letter. Understand? I didn't take it. Because... I fell in love with you at first sight, and I couldn't.

Natalia gazes at Mario, stupefied, then is suddenly troubled.

NATALIA: You...

MARIO: Yes, I did it. So...nothing's changed. Are you happy now? *(Desperate)* And...everything'll end well, you'll see. Try to forgive me. Maybe you'll be able to when you're happy, won't you? *(Mario smiles bitterly.)* You should have known better than to trust a guy like me. And I told you so too: never trust anybody. *(Trying to joke, with great effort)* Especially a man in love. Now be happy.

Mario notices that Natalia is crying desperately.

MARIO *(desperately)*: Natalia, what can I say? I'm guilty. I'm asking you to forgive me. I'll try to make good, shall I? Look, I love you so much I want you to be happy. I'll go to him. I'll explain.

Natalia tries desperately to fight down her tears and shakes her head.

NATALIA: No.

MARIO: You don't want me to? Why? What difference does it make if I do tomorrow what I didn't do yesterday?

Natalia again shakes her head.

NATALIA *(her voice breaking with sobs)*: That's just the point. What difference does it make, yesterday or tomorrow? What counts... is that he didn't come. I'm glad you didn't take the letter. I thank you for having spared me that last humiliation.

Mario takes Natalia by the shoulders and holds her tight.

MARIO: No, Natalia, I told you not to trust the judgment of a man in love. You're really just a child! Everything I said doesn't count… because I was just thinking about myself. I told you not to believe in fairy tales, and I was beginning to believe in one of my own. I felt just like you did, last year, when you went to him with your little bag.

Natalia gazes at Mario, touched by his generosity. Then her expression suddenly becomes serious; for the first time it is that of a mature person.

NATALIA: I've loved him for a whole year, and I've never, never been unfaithful to him, not even in my thoughts. He's despised all this.

She has stopped with her face against the wall. Her expression is strained and now she scratches her fingernail violently along the crack between two bricks.

NATALIA: God be with him. I want to forget him. But I still love him. But I'll get over it, I must get over it… because now I've seen the truth. I've seen how he's deceived me. But you…

MARIO: Natalia…

Natalia passes her hand over her face.

NATALIA: It'll pass. It must pass.

MARIO: I'm just an ordinary sort of guy, insignificant. But that's not the point. *(Stammering)* I… I… I can't even say what I want to. I… it's true… I did think that in a certain sense you didn't love him any more, and… and then I'd have… I'd absolutely have made it so that you… could love me… Oh! *(Interrupting himself and suddenly changing his tone, annoyed with himself)* Why am I saying this to you? *(Changing tone and decision once again)* Natalia, if one day, even in the distant future…

Natalia overcomes her emotion. She breathes deeply, as if definitively to cancel out her anguish.

NATALIA *(with nervous excitement)* : Yes, I wish... If despite everything... you feel that your love is so strong...

MARIO *(with anxious hope)* : Yes, yes, that's just... what I mean.

NATALIA : If you really think you can love me as much as you say,
then I swear that my gratitude...

*Mario stops listening. He embraces Natalia. The two begin to walk
along the canal.*

MARIO : Natalia, it's not just that you pity me, is it? You do love
me, too, a little, don't you?

NATALIA : I don't know.

MARIO : But later on?

NATALIA : Maybe. You have to be patient. Let's let time go by.

The two stop, facing each other.

MARIO : Of course. Of course, I... I... don't ask anything more.
But if you feel you'll be able...

*Mario takes Natalia by the shoulders and speaks to her feverishly, at the
acme of joy. She is obviously dismayed by the young man's behavior, which
is in stark contrast with his words; she tries to pull back but does not
succeed.*

MARIO : I'll... wait for you as long as you want. I'm so happy,
Natalia, so happy because I'm sure. Understand, Natalia?
I'm sure. Come, come, Natalia, come with me, come,
come...

*Mario is so happy that he does not notice Natalia's discomfort, as she tries
with an effort to smile. He pulls her down a ramp toward a rowboat tied
up at a little bridge. He stumbles on a little step but recovers his balance
immediately.*

NATALIA *(laughing nervously and again upset)* : Where are you going?
Let me go; I'm falling!

Mario gets into the rowboat and forces Natalia to follow him. Then he unties it and takes up the oars.

MARIO: Come, come with me! Get in, get into the boat, come on.

NATALIA: But we can't, it's not ours....

MARIO: It doesn't matter!

Mario begins to row vigorously as Natalia, sitting facing him, pulls her coat more tightly around her.

MARIO: I want to take you to a place where I once saw some couples kissing, and I thought: when I have a girl we'll come here, all by ourselves....

The boat goes under a bridge; Mario stops rowing. Natalia looks around her.

MARIO: Here it is, here we are.

Natalia laughs.

NATALIA *(ironically)*: All by ourselves...

A group of bums is sleeping along the quay in the light of a little fire. Natalia looks at them. Mario turns to look too, then turns to Natalia.

MARIO *(laughing)*: It's because you're not really my girl yet. When you are, there won't be anyone here and... no one will bother us.

NATALIA: Ssh.

MARIO *(with an effort)*: All right, I won't say another word about it until you want me to.

Natalia puts her finger to her lips and looks about.

NATALIA: Sssh.

Mario goes to sit beside the girl. The boat floats slowly ahead.

MARIO: But look, it's my duty to tell you this: I'm poor. Very poor. I have a job—I can do better, of course—but...

well, that is... with you behind me, I will certainly do better.

Mario and Natalia embrace. Mario turns to Natalia with new fervor. Her head lies on his shoulder; her eyes are closed as if she is sleeping.

MARIO: I... I'd like to make you go to sleep like those characters in fairy tales who sleep and sleep and wake up only the day they will be happy. *(Natalia smiles, with her eyes still closed, as if to herself.)* But it'll happen to you too. One day you'll wake up and you'll see it's a beautiful day, with the sun. And everything'll be different, new, crystal clear. And what seemed impossible before will become simple, the obvious thing to do. Don't you think so? I'm sure of it, and it'll be soon, maybe tomorrow. Look! Look, Natalia, what a sky! It's gorgeous.

Natalia opens her eyes and slips from Mario's embrace with an expression of marvel on her face.

NATALIA: Oh!

Mario too is surprised. Snowflakes begin to fall, at first just a few and then more and more thickly.

MARIO: What's happening? It's snowing!

Natalia is delighted.

NATALIA: Oh! Oh! It's snowing!

Mario jumps gaily to his feet.

MARIO: It's snowing, it's snowing!

Then, calling to the bums sleeping under the bridge, he grabs an oar and pulls the boat over to the quay.

MARIO: Hey! It's snowing!

Natalia claps her hands, enchanted.

NATALIA: Oh! How beautiful it is! It's snowing! It's snowing!

They laugh.

Square high over the city.

Natalia and Mario approach one of the benches set among the trees on the piazza, from which the entire city is voisible. The snow is still falling.

MARIO: I tell you it's true!

NATALIA: No...

MARIO: It is, believe me. That is, I...

NATALIA: Look! Look! Oh!

Natalia picks up some snow and begins to make snowballs which she throws at Mario. Mario defends himself, then counterattacks. He suddenly stops, opening his arms and looking around.

MARIO: I swear to you! I'm another person. Oh! Oh! Believe me. I'm another person. It's because I'm sure... I don't know... Well, I've understood the whole thing, even if I can't explain it.

The snow continues to fall. Natalia continues to throw snowballs at Mario. Mario continues his speech with fervor.

MARIO: You see? Before this city seemed so gloomy, so sad. It was my own fault, because look, all of a sudden everything's become so gay. We only have to... to want it ourselves. That something inside me wants it... *(Then he catches Natalia and drags her with him toward a tree, which he leans against, shaking a thick white shower of snowflakes down on her.) …* and the girl I love becomes my wife, all dressed in white.

Natalia shakes off the snow, leaving Mario's side. He follows her. The snowfall has ended.

NATALIA: Oh! Oh, what a pity. It's all over already.

She shivers. Mario takes off his coat, shakes it out, and forces her to put it on.

MARIO: No! No! It's still…

NATALIA: No, no, no.

MARIO: Yes.

NATALIA: Thanks.

Mario presses her to him.

MARIO: Just think, everybody's sleeping in the city. They don't know yet. Soon they'll begin to wake up. They'll open their windows and they'll say… they'll say…

NATALIA: "What a beautiful day."

Mario hugs Natalia closer.

MARIO: Is that what you'll be saying too?

Natalia breaks away from Mario and starts off.

NATALIA: Yes… yes…

MARIO: Will you really, Natalia?

The two embrace.

NATALIA: Yes. Come on, let's go.

Natalia breaks away again and runs away. Mario catches up with her. They laugh.

A distant whistling is heard through the still air. Natalia stops suddenly, as if struck. Mario nears her.

MARIO: What is it?

Natalia shakes her head. Mario embraces her. The two walk off down the hill leading to the city.

Outside. Dawn.

It is now dawn and the street lamps are off. Coming down the hill, Natalia is suddenly startled. In the background, on the bridge, a dark figure (the lodger) is strolling slowly. Natalia presses against Mario, forcing him back against a decrepit wall.

NATALIA: Oh...

MARIO: Who is it, Natalia?

NATALIA: It's... him... it's him. Oh!

Natalia breaks away from Mario's embrace and moves a few steps toward the lodger.

LODGER: Natalia... is that you?

Natalia stops a moment. Mario is still standing almost petrified against the wall. Natalia begins to run again, crying out and letting Mario's coat fall from her shoulders. She reaches the bridge and throws herself into the lodger's arms, then breaks away and runs back to Mario. She takes his arms and pulls him to her.

NATALIA: I... I... I've been deceiving you and myself. For a moment I believed that you and I... *(She hides her face on Mario's breast.)* God knows what I wouldn't do for you now. Try to forgive me.... I'll always be grateful to you.

MARIO: Go to him. Go to him. Don't be sorry. I... I was wrong... to try to make you doubt. Go to him. And God bless you for the moment of happiness you've given me. *(Natalia* kisses Mario.) It's not a little thing. *(Natalia breaks away from Mario and runs toward the other man, who awaits her.)* Even in a whole lifetime...

He clutches his shoulders with his hands. His face is covered with tears. He bows his head on his breast.

Natalia runs toward the bridge. She embraces the lodger. Arm in arm they cross the bridge toward the Sport Café and stop, embracing again.

Mario stands stock-still in the background. Natalia and the lodger break

their embrace and walk off. Mario starts to walk over to pick up his coat. He shakes it and puts it over his shoulders. He walks on, stopping a moment to look at the rendezvous window.

As Mario reaches Via Grande, still walking slowly, the stray dog comes up to him and greets him happily. Mario continues on, followed by the dog.

THE END.

Rocco and His Brothers (1960)

Credits

Producer:	Giuseppe Bordogni
Director:	Luchino Visconti
Screenplay:	Luchino Visconti, Suso Cocchi d'Amico, Pasquale Festa Campanile, Massimo Franciosa, Enrico Medioli, based on the book by Giovanni Testori, *Il Ponte della Ghisolfa*.
Director of Photography:	Giuseppe Rotunno
Camera Operators:	Nino Cristiani, Silvano Ippoliti, Franco Delli Colli
Editor:	Mario Serandrei
Art Director:	Mario Garbuglia
Music:	Nino Rota
Costumes:	Piero Tosi
Sound:	Giovanni Rossi

Rocky cliff overlooking the sea. Dawn.

Wind and torrents of rain. The sea is wild and stormy. The waves crash against the rocky coast.

Four black figures stand at the edge of a cliff jutting out over the sea. Two are holding up a coffin; the other two, shorter in stature, stand a few paces behind. Battered by the wind and the lashing rain, they stand immobile for a moment, then the two coffin bearers lift their burden and tip it over the edge.

The coffin falls slowly through the air and is swallowed up by the violent waves, as the four watch in silence.

Now the first man steps forward, his face streaked with rain and tears. He controls his sobs with an effort as he speaks.

SIMONE PARONDI: This is Simone. Vincenzo's the one who should be talking to you; he's the oldest son. But he's far away... and he doesn't know. If you hadn't died in the winter we'd have taken you to Bernaldo, where the cemetery is. But now there's mud and landslides and there're no roads....

The second coffin bearer comes up beside him. His expression is more tightly closed as he speaks:

ROCCO PARONDI: This is Rocco. We're broken and grieving for you. But there are other people at the bottom of the sea, all your friends....

With these words Rocco crosses himself, followed by Simone and the two younger boys who have been standing behind them: Ciro, aged sixteen, and Luca, twelve. The two boys pull their jackets more tightly around them as they shiver in the cold.

The ceremony is over. Simone and his brothers start back home. We see them struggling through the mud down a steep path. In the distance the village appears, white against the black sky. As they walk along, the credits begin to appear, continuing as the four pass through the narrow muddy streets of the village and reach the square.

Village square. Dawn.

A line of farm laborers stands along the wall before the run-down employment office, waiting to be chosen for the day's work. In the background is the small church, from which someone is removing the signs of mourning. A squalid little man emerges from the employment office.

MAN: Nicola Mancinelli's vineyard's to be hoed. Three days' work.

The laborers remain silent for a moment, as if each man were making his own calculations.

FIRST LABORER: Ten kilometers to walk and ten back.

MAN: Well?

FIRST LABORER: It'll take six hundred lire.

A long pause; the faces are closed and hostile. End of credits. The first men in line see the four brothers passing and take off their caps; the others follow suit. Having been interrupted by the passage of the four brothers, the labor auction is now resumed.

SECOND LABORER: Five hundred.

Another pause. Then, his voice bereft of expression, another laborer makes an offer.

THIRD LABORER: Four-fifty.

The group's silence is prolonged after this figure. Then the employment man concludes the bargaining.

MAN: All right, it's yours for four-fifty.

He goes off with the laborer. The other men go back to leaning against the wall. One comments.

FOURTH LABORER: It must be in the books somewhere...that we have to die hungry.

Rosaria Parondi's house. Inside. Dawn.

The title appears: THE MOTHER. A line of black-dyed clothing is being hung up, still dripping, by Rosaria: already aging, harrowed by her trials, her eyes reddened in the pain-racked face. She wears mourning black. She extracts another of the dyed garments from the steaming pot. The interior of Rosaria's house suggests the epitome of an existence of bare survival. The room, with its several beds, serves for sleeping, eating, and cooking. No windows; the light filters through the door. The furnishings are poor and typical. Besides the beds and a few broken chairs, there is an old dresser, adorning which is a figure of Saint Nicolas, protected by a glass bell. Other images of saints stand with tiny oil lamps before them; a few pots and strings of tomatoes and green peppers hang on the walls. On the floor, in a corner, some apples and potatoes and a couple of large containers filled with tomato paste. A round table stands in the center of the room.

A peasant woman sits at the table writing, with difficulty, the letter which Rosaria is dictating as she hangs up the clothes.

ROSARIA: My son, since this awful thing happened I've been thinking always about just one thing. Your father was always stubborn as a mule; he had to die on the land that gave us only misery and ruined his health. I always tried to convince him you were doing well; let's all go to Vincenzo's, I always used to tell him. And he wouldn't...

Rosaria's expression undergoes almost imperceptible transitions from conventional pain to passion, to an appeal for pity, to rancor, to imperiousness. In contrast, the other woman's face is fixed in an appropriate expression altered only by the suffering caused by the effort of writing. Rosaria continues.

ROSARIA: Now he's dead, I have to decide everything by myself. Because my other boys have grown up too; who knows how far they could get in a bigger town, especially Simone, you should see how handsome and strong he is now.

Through the open door we see Rocco, sitting on a old chair in the road. A very young girl (Imma) leans back in a chair against the wall of the house opposite; her legs dangle lazily.

ROSARIA: Only Rocco can't realize we have to leave here.

They gaze at each other in silence.

Outside Rosaria's house. Day.

Rocco and Imma, who is sewing, continue to gaze at each other without speaking; in the background we see and hear Rosaria through the doorway of her house, dictating her letter.

ROSARIA: The truth is that he's stuck on the girl across the street, Micuccio's daughter, and when we talk about going they sit around all day looking at each other. Not even if it was the end of the world...

Imma suddenly interrupts her work and cuts off a lock of her hair with the scissors. She crosses furtively over to Rocco, her gestures timid as if she fears being observed. She touches Rocco's hand, which has not moved. The lock of hair passes from her hand to his. The two youngsters stare at each other with great emotion. Then Imma bends over Rocco and rapidly snips off a lock of his hair. Rocco opens a little bag hanging around his neck and hides the two locks of hair, his and Imma's, inside it.

Field. Day.

A small field apparently very arid and sterile. Simone and the buyer walk along the roughly marked-out boundary line. Ciro and Luca, sitting on a low wall, follow the movements of the two men with a curious and melancholy air.

At the end of the field, Simone and the buyer shake hands and exchange the bill of sale and the money.

ROSARIA'S VOICE: ... We'll be able to sell the land and leave. I know, it's worthless, it's barely enough to pay for the train. But what should we keep waiting for here?

Train. Outside. Night.

The train races along through the night. A very rapid sequence of signs and stations. Other trains pass by at top speed.

Train. Inside. Night.

The inside of the compartment occupied by Rosaria's family. Their luggage is modest: thin cardboard suitcases, large bandannas containing enormous loaves of bread. The boys and their mother sprawl upon one another as they doze: the image of a compact, self-contained family.

La Lombarda Gymnasium, Milan. Outside. Evening.

As we continue to hear Rosaria composing her letter, we finally see her son Vincenzo, who is coming out of a small boxing gym.

ROSARIA'S VOICE: ... Now listen to me, Vincenzo. You've done well for yourself. Now it's your brothers' turn. We'll be coming, sooner or later....

Vincenzo walks up the stairs from the basement gym; behind him we see the confusion of figures and the movements of the boxers, and hear the almost imperceptible sound of voices, the rhythmic thud of the equipment. The atmosphere of this squalid evening training center is charged and somewhat surrealistic.

As he emerges into the cold winter air, Vincenzo pulls up the collar of his cheap shiny coat and rubs his bare hands together. He passes along the chain of basement lights, low and square and strongly lit from the inside, which afford fragmentary glimpses of the gym activity through the frost-decked panes. The confused murmur of voices is heard at brief intervals.

OCTOBER 1955.

Central station of Milan. Inside. Evening.

A northbound train pulls into the smoky gray Milan station. Like a multitude of ants, the passengers swarm out from the myriad train doors now flung open and move toward the exit through the confusion of noise and the bustle of trainmen, porters, food vendors, passengers for other trains, etc. Little by little a more compact group becomes discernible on the platform beside a third-class car. The five figures huddle close together, their modest baggage piled at their feet.

The crowd thins out. Only this group remains there, uncertain and lost. Now we can see them better: a middle-aged woman surrounded by three young men and a child. Finally they make up their minds to ask some information of a station employee or policeman. Laden with its numerous bundles, the group eventually moves slowly off toward the exit through the gigantic halls of the station.

Milan Station. Outside. Night.

The family cautiously crosses the outer atrium of the station through the confusion of cars and taxis, and struggles on toward a bus stop. Besides their luggage, they are carrying some food which was to be eaten during the trip or offered as gifts: the large loaves of bread in bandannas, a few chains of dried figs.

Interior of Milan bus. Outside. Night.

The fantastic lights of the city are visible through the steamed-up windows of the bus as it crosses Milan. The family has a deformed and fleeting vision of what seem colored, wavering streaks of lightning.

The Giannellis' home. Inside. Night.

Smiling and embarrassed, Vincenzo sits in the dining room of the Giannellis' house, with Ginetta beside him. He wears a brand-new suit, with a black felt button in the lapel as a sign of mourning. The Giannelli parents are sitting at the center table with several relatives who have come to congratulate the young couple.

MOTHER GIANNELLI: They want to decide everything for themselves. Who listens to parents any more?

Ginetta's hand seeks Vincenzo's; he squeezes it a little awkwardly. Ginetta is a little brunette girl, neither beautiful nor ugly, but with a pleasant and fresh face.

VINCENZO: We have to get along by ourselves! I can't imagine going back down there. We want to live here. Right, Gina?

Gina has gotten up to pour drinks from a tray set out on the table with liqueur and glasses.

The two Giannelli sons are standing near the radio: Alfredo, twenty-five, and Bruno, seventeen. One of the relatives approaches the older boy, who has a more bourgeois air about him and seems to be keeping aloof from the festivities.

RELATIVE: So aren't you thinking of getting married too?

ALFREDO: Not on your life! It's enough that one person in the family should be going through this silly business, isn't it?

His laugh is forced as he looks toward his sister and future brother-in-law, toward whom he wishes to express his disapproval.

Ginetta places the bottle of liqueur back on the tray.

GINETTA: He thinks they'll have to support us. *(To her brother)* We'll never ask you for anything. Don't worry.

She sits down again beside Vincenzo.

The doorbell rings at length. Everyone turns toward the door.

BRUNO: That's Aldo. I'm going to the movies, Ma.

FATHER *(out of temper)* : Every single night? Don't you ever get tired of your movies?

A COUSIN *(trying to keep the occasion cheerful)* : For goodness' sakes! I went Sunday, to take little Francesco, and I went right to sleep!

A confusion of voices is heard from the little vestibule.

A COUSIN: I slept right through it. Grandma, he says to me...

VOICE OF BRUNO: Vincenzo... Come here a minute!

Everyone turns to look toward the vestibule, where they perceive Rosaria and her four sons, who have just entered. Vincenzo jumps up and rushes to the door.

VINCENZO *(shouting)* : Ma!

Immobile, Rosaria waits for him. She opens her arms and gathers Vincenzo to her breast.

ROSARIA: My son!

She bursts into tears. Vincenzo, surprised but happy, turns from her and welcomes his younger brothers with affectionate slaps. He lifts up little Luca and kisses him on the cheeks.

Mother Giannelli has come up to Rosaria.

MOTHER GIANNELLI *(with an impulse of sincere welcome)* : Rosaria!

There is enormous confusion as the guests rise to greet the new arrivals. Father Giannelli helps Rosaria set down her bundles. Vincenzo helps his brothers with the suitcases and packages. Alfredo looks curiously at Rosaria's boys, so encumbered and shy.

Rosaria is now seated; the Giannelli's and their relatives surround her.

Rosaria dries her eyes, sighs, and searches for Vincenzo as she begins to speak.

ROSARIA: What a terrible thing happened to us. Oh, my handsome
boy... *(The chorus of women hovering about Rosaria makes
appropriate exclamations.)* But you've stopped dressing like
a waif?

*Vincenzo overcomes his embarrassment, takes Ginetta by the hand to intro-
duce her to his mother.*

VINCENZO: Sure, but tonight... *(Smiles)* This is Ginetta. I wrote
you we were getting married... so you've come just in time
to give us your blessing.

Rosaria examines Ginetta and shakes her head sadly.

ROSARIA: Getting married? You're already so rich you can take
care of your little brothers and your children too?

*Ginetta is embarrassed by Rosaria's comment. She smiles briefly as she
looks at Vincenzo, who only now seems to be realizing the significance of
the situation. He turns to his mother with a questioning tone.*

VINCENZO: Ma? Why didn't you tell me you were all coming?

Rosaria's eyes fly wide open.

ROSARIA: We did write you!

VINCENZO: When Father died you wrote me...and I told you
first I had to see if there was work...for them...and then...

*He looks at his brothers, who are staring at him without missing a single
word.*

MOTHER GIANNELLI *(exclaiming)*: I thought you came for the wed-
ding!

ROSARIA: I've got too much pain to think about celebrations.

Father Giannelli breaks in.

FATHER GIANNELLI: They've just decided everything all by themselves.... But tell me, did you just come right from the station? Where are you going to sleep?

ROSARIA: I can tell you that my son won't make me sleep in the street. He's the head of the family now.

The Giannellis exchange a look of astonishment.

MOTHER GIANNELLI: Donna Rosaria, don't take offense, maybe we should get things clear right away. You have to think of your sons, that's as it should be. But I have to think of my daughter.

GINETTA *(raising her voice)* : Ma, what kind of talk is that?

ALFREDO *(raising his voice)* : Let her go on. Mama's right....

GINETTA *(as above)* : You already know what she's going to say.

ALFREDO: I'm not stupid and she's right.

They are all speaking very excitedly now. It is more than obvious that the discussion will end up in a quarrel.

GINETTA *(shouting)* : And don't shout!

ROSARIA *(her voice piercing)* : Vincè, my son, take me away from this house! Right now!

VINCENZO *(stupefied)* : Ma! What are you saying? What are you shouting about?

GINETTA: My God! My God! Calm down. *(Shouting)* Have you all gone crazy?

ROSARIA: Nooo! I'm not crazy! I understand everything! *(Pointing to Vincenzo)* You understand too, they want to keep you from doing your duty to your mother and the little ones. Not even a little respect for the poor dead man. Brutes! I don't ever want to see them again. Let's get right out of here. *(Ginetta tries to break in.)* You be quiet too! You're birds of a feather... all the same.

VINCENZO: Mama! What's got into you?

ROSARIA: Let's go. Boys, pick up the bags. God will repay you! Because God is just! And merciless.

Enraged, Father Giannelli makes the sign of the horns to ward off her curse. Ginetta takes Rosaria's arm.

GINETTA *(pleading)*: Please calm down. Please understand. No one wanted to offend you.

ALFREDO: Gina, stay here!

VINCENZO: Let her alone!

Alfredo drags Ginetta back. She screams with pain. Vincenzo is about to hurl himself on Alfredo.

ALFREDO: You think you can scare me, you ass?

MOTHER GIANNELLI *(to Vincenzo)*: Get out of here!!!

ROSARIA *(dramatically, to Vincenzo)*: Do you hear her? Now do you understand?

Rosaria drags Vincenzo and the boys out.

Building site. Outside. Night.

A red lantern hangs on a cement pillar next to the watchman's shed. A large mongrel dog, chained to a pole nearby, barks without respite. The shed door opens and the watchman appears, his face still enveloped in sleep. He is a man of about forty.

VOICE OF VINCENZO: Armando! It's me.

WATCHMAN: Eh?

He tries to see, but the darkness is too profound. He then lifts the red lantern off the pillar and shines its light on the face of the visitor.

WATCHMAN: What's going on? You scared me. Come on in, it's cold outside.

Watchman's shed. Inside. Night.

The two men enter the shed, which is furnished with only a cot and a wooden bench. The watchman lights the acetylene lamp standing on the bench. A violent light flares up, emphasizing Vincenzo's pallor and his expression of dismay.

Vincenzo gestures as if to say it would take too long to tell the whole story. He sits on the end of the cot. The watchman sits down too, wraps himself in his blanket and lies down, curled up against the cold.

VINCENZO: If you don't mind, I'd like to stay here.

The watchman shrugs. He would like to go back to sleep.

WATCHMAN *(struck by Vincenzo's expression)*: All right by me... You haven't got yourself in trouble, have you?

Vincenzo shrugs. He himself doesn't know how to describe what's happened to him.

VINCENZO: My mother and my brothers have. They've come like a storm. I have no more room and no more girl. And I've got all these people to take care of.

WATCHMAN *(amused)*: Your room and your girl are the same thing?

Vincenzo gazes at the watchman, slow to catch the joke.

VINCENZO: You can joke about it. But what am I supposed to do with this family? They're five people, understand? Where can I put them? Where can I get the money for an apartment?

The watchman yawns. He has lost interest in his friend's predicament.

WATCHMAN *(yawning)*: That should be the only problem. There's no shortage of places....

VINCENZO: If you can pay.

WATCHMAN *(bored)* : Do what everybody else does. You take a place in some low-rent project, and if you can, you pay for a couple of months. Then you stop paying, and after another month you'll be evicted. Then they send you to the city housing for the evicted, where you don't pay anything and they even heat the place free. In Milan they don't leave anybody in the middle of the street.

VINCENZO *(interested)*: Could we get in there right away?

WATCHMAN *(yawning)* : Oh no. You have to be evicted first!

Lambrate, on the outskirts of Milan. Low-rent housing project with internal courtyards. Outside. Day.

Before the basement apartment which Vincenzo has been able to find, the entire family is busy unloading the necessary minimal furnishings from a hand cart. The brothers have already undergone a subtle transformation since the evening of their arrival in the city. They unload the cots, mattresses, and so forth with a cheerful air. The concierge observes them and exchanges comments on the new tenants with a neighbor woman who leans out from a first-floor window.

CONCIERGE *(with a disdainful gesture)* : Africa...

NEIGHBOR: Where are they from?

CONCIERGE *(still scornful)* : Lucania... You know even better than I that they don't even take them into consideration for these apartments if they're not from the South.

NEIGHBOR: At least this is a fine-looking family: all boys, and the only female is the mother!

CONCIERGE: Well, as far as that goes, I've seen plenty of fine-looking families that when the time comes... D'you want to bet that these people will get their eviction notice too, after

a month, or two at the most? They're all the same! Southerners!

The brothers pass in and out with their burdens, gay and full of enthusiasm.

Home of Rosaria and her sons. Inside. Night.

*The basement apartment Vincenzo has rented for his family consists of
a bedroom, a kitchen, and a toilet. Copper pots and pans hang on the
kitchen wall. Chains of tomatoes are festooned from the ceiling. The four
older brothers sleep in the bedroom, Luca and the mother in the kitchen.
Vincenzo and Ciro sleep in opposite directions on the same cot. Nearby stands
a large sack of garlic. The place is barely lit by the dawn light filtering
through the windows.*

*The distant sound of voices in the courtyard now disturbs the absolute
silence in the apartment. Vincenzo stirs in his sleep, then awakens. He listens
intently for a moment, then jumps out of bed and goes to open the window.
The courtyard of the building is covered with a thick blanket of snow, which
has fallen during the night. The snow continues to fall. Thick greasy
streams of smoke gush forth from the chimneys beyond the courtyard walls.
A man standing in the courtyard is shouting to another at a ground-floor
window. Without closing the window, Vincenzo goes to awaken his brothers,
kicking at the cots and stripping off the blankets.*

VINCENZO: Simone! Rocco! Ciro! Wake up! There's work for
you today!

The brothers shiver and turn, open their eyes and look toward the window.

BROTHERS: What's up? You out of your mind? Let me sleep!

Rosaria comes to the door of the bedroom.

ROSARIA: It's snowing! It's snowing hard!

LUCA *(jumping out of bed)*: Snow!

VINCENZO: Hurry up or you won't find a place. It's a bad snowfall.
And the Milanese can't stand to see snow in the streets.

(He climbs over one of the cots to get to the toilet; he stumbles, losing his balance.) Hurry up, come on, sleepyheads!

LUCA: Ma, is it night or day, Ma?

ROSARIA *(shouting)*: It's day, day. You'll all be coming back to-night with money or I'll disown you.

The boys rush about dressing, washing, fixing up their lunches, etc.

ROSARIA: Little Rocco. You've been sick. Put on two of my sweaters.

ROCCO *(reluctant)*: But Mama, why do I have to wear women's sweaters?

Simone bursts out laughing.

ROSARIA: Don't listen to him, listen to your mama. Nobody can see them under there anyway.

One by one, bundled up in their sweaters and coats, the brothers kiss their mother and file out of the house.

Entranceway and courtyard. Dawn.

Crowds of men pour out of the doorways opening onto the courtyard like swarms of bees, exchanging greetings and comments. Someone calls out.

NEIGHBOR: Simone!

SIMONE: What?

NEIGHBOR: You fellows coming too?

SIMONE: Where are we supposed to go?

NEIGHBOR: To the bureau.

SIMONE *(addressing another man)*: Where is it?

The other man shrugs his shoulders sleepily and stamps his feet against the cold.

SECOND NEIGHBOR : Who knows?

The men all go on toward the entrance.

Outside the entranceway. Dawn.

A taxi pulls up before the apartment building and a young woman gets out: Nadia. She is well-dressed, almost sophisticated in appearance. Her clothing, and in particular her makeup, are in sharp contrast with the setting: the sooty-black buildings and the gray dawn light. The men leaving the courtyard go off without noticing the taxi and the woman.

CABBIE *(skeptical)* : Here?

Nadia pays her fare and looks around. She walks toward the entrance of

the building where the Parondi's live. In one hand she is carrying a package containing a half-full bottle of champagne and some cakes; in the other, a large handbag. She is a little awkward on her high heels as she walks through the snow, and in fact she is a little tired and chilled through.

Stairway of Rosaria's apartment house. Day.

Somewhat out of breath, Nadia goes up the last few steps, fastidiously avoiding the dirty and wet parts of the stairway. She rings a harsh-sounding doorbell on the top floor. After a moment a very plain little woman opens the door.

NADIA *(serenely)* : Hello, Mama.

She plants a nonchalant kiss on the woman's cheek. The girl's appearance frightens the mother, and her words are fearful and a little mysterious.

MOTHER: Holy Virgin, is it you? Get away quick before your father comes back.

As the astonished and still incredulous mother watches, Nadia pushes the door open with her foot.

NADIA: I got lonely for my mama and papa.

MOTHER *(immobile)* : Are you in trouble? Again?

NADIA: What d'you mean, trouble? *(Laughs)* I brought you some cake. Happy?

The mother glances worriedly at the cakes which Nadia puts in her hand and lifts the bottle to measure its contents. They are evidently the remains of a party interrupted at its high point.

Nadia enters the house and stretches, sensual and bored.

NADIA: I'm going to sleep!

Street near the cathedral. Day.

The team which includes Rocco, Simone, and Ciro is shoveling snow on a street in the center of Milan. It is hard and exhausting labor, but the Parondi brothers, bundled up against the cold, are working enthusiastically, almost gaily. Simone wipes the sweat from his forehead.

SIMONE : I wish the boys down home were here... Domenico, Fiorino... *(Gesturing scornfully as he remembers)* They all say there's no point in leaving, coming here, it's the same story up here too. And meanwhile there they are, lined up against the wall, out of work... and they wait ...but what are they still waiting for?

Two elegant ladies pass by in their furs. Simone watches them and points them out to Rocco.

SIMONE : They're different up here too.

Another street in downtown Milan. Day.

A municipal water truck passes by, squirting water to wash away the last of the snow. Ciro has left the group and stopped before a store window, where a sign reads: "Teenager Wanted for Errands. Maximum 16 Years Old. Apply Here."

SIMONE *(calling)* : Ciro!

Ciro runs back to his brothers.

CIRO : Hey, listen, Simone, I just saw something. Should I apply? They want... *(Pauses)* what does "teenager" mean?

SIMONE : Come on... *(Mimicking)* "teenager."

The shovelers continue their labors.

SIMONE : Anyway, you see? This is the place to come if you're looking for work. Who are all these people? Not all of them were born rich!

One of the shovelers answers Simone.

SHOVELER: See that wine shop over there? The owner came from my brother-in-law's town. He was as hard up as a man can be down there. But now when my brother-in-law comes he pretends he doesn't know him. *(He spits angrily.)* It's all a question of luck.

SIMONE: Luck comes if you make it come. Vincenzo'll never make it. I've already figured that much out.

ROCCO: Why not? He works. He's helped us. He's fixed us up with a house. What more should he do? Now it's up to us.

Simone continues to look around at the tall buildings of downtown Milan.

SIMONE *(gloomily)*: Right, it's up to us. Wait till I get my bearings. It can't be that we have to work like animals here too, run here and there for a day's wages....

Street in downtown Milan. Day.

It is now eight-thirty: stores are opening and employees are hurrying to their offices. The buses are slow and overcrowded because of the heavy snowfall. A file of buses discharges hurried and agitated groups of passengers at the bus stop. Ginetta gets off one of the buses, accompanied by her older brother, Alfredo. Followed by Alfredo, she reaches the service entrance of the department store where she works, and where a number of other employees are converging. Ginetta greets the other salesgirls cordially and dismisses her brother with some annoyance.

As Alfredo walks off, Vincenzo appears from behind a newspaper stand. He watches Alfredo until he is out of sight, then hurries toward the department store service entrance.

VINCENZO *(calling)*: Ginetta!

Ginetta turns and gazes happily at Vincenzo. Then, with a worried expression, she comes back toward him.

GINETTA: Look out! Alfredo's...

VINCENZO: I saw him. He's gone.

They gaze at each other. Ginetta lowers her eyes.

GINETTA *(her voice trembling)* : You haven't been to see me....

VINCENZO *(bitterly)* : I can't come to your house. Someone's always with you when you go out. I work when you work. I could come this morning only because I had the bad luck...

GINETTA: What's happened?

VINCENZO: I was sure they'd be working on the building, so I didn't go shoveling and so I've lost my day's pay in both places. What can a man do? If they don't give you legal residence here you can't get steady work...and day laborers can work only when the sun's out.

GINETTA: Papa says the times are finished when they gave a southerner residence if he just asked for it; he'd put his cross on a piece of paper and become a Milanese.

VINCENZO: But I hope...

GINETTA: You were born hoping. But is that enough?

VINCENZO: But we might make it, you know. We have a house, my brothers are beginning to find day work...

GINETTA *(painfully)* : Yes, yes, I know. But my family doesn't want to hear another word. How can we start a new life?

Vincenzo seeks his words with effort. He is very embarrassed, but he wants to get it all out.

VINCENZO *(carefully)* : Mama says that a man that really wants a woman... a man who's really a man... well, he takes her.

GINETTA *(lowering her eyes, diffident)* : What d'you mean, takes?

VINCENZO *(increasingly embarrassed)* : Takes her, like you take a woman, without asking her permission or anybody else's.

Ginetta sorrowfully points to the crowd of salesgirls, all fairly well dressed and chic, now entering the department store.

GINETTA: Oh Vincè! Can't you understand we're not in Lucania any more? *(Here eyes darken and deepen with thought.)* You have to ask my permission.

VINCENZO *(intensely)* : Well, I'm asking you.

The last salesgirls hurry through the entrance. Ginetta is about to enter too.

GINETTA: So long...

VINCENZO *(taking her hand)*: Well? *(Ginetta starts to run off; Vincenzo catches her hand again.)* Do you love me?

Ginetta smiles and runs into the store. She turns to gesture: "See you this evening."

Courtyard, storage room, and stairway. Inside. Outside. Evening of the same day.

Vincenzo and a man of about sixty, Nadia's father, meet before the storage room under the stairs, where they are putting away their bicycles. Since the doorway is quite narrow, Vincenzo allows the older man to pass through first.

VINCENZO: You go on first.

NADIA'S FATHER: Thanks.

He enters and puts away his broken-down bicycle, then reappears and starts up the stairs.

NADIA'S FATHER: Good night.

VINCENZO: Good night.

Vincenzo enters the storage room but noisily knocks over two or three other bikes as he tries to put away his own. Concerned, he turns on the weak light of an overhead lamp and looks through the door toward the stairs. But Nadia's father seems not to have noticed. He continues whistling up the stairs.

Relieved, Vincenzo picks up the bikes one by one and lines them up. Suddenly, violent shouts are heard from the top of the stairs. A door is opened and violently slammed shut.

VOICE OF NADIA'S FATHER *(shouting)* : I'll kill you! I'll kill you!

Stairway. Evening.

The sound of high-heeled shoes racing down the stairway. A door is heard opening again. The threats are more audible now.

VOICE OF NADIA'S MOTHER: Guglielmo! Come back inside. Let her alone. *(Crying)* Let her alone!

Vincenzo can hear no more.

Storage room. Inside. Evening.

A woman flies into the storage room and closes the door behind her. It is Nadia. Panting and disheveled, she does not even try to pull her bathrobe, which is untied, around her. Her body, partly revealed by her short slip, makes an immediate impression on Vincenzo, who remains stock-still in astonishment before her.

VINCENZO *(stammering)*: What's going on?

In answer, Nadia motions him to silence.

VOICE OF NADIA'S FATHER: Get out! Get out of my house!

VOICES OF NEIGHBORS: What's going on? ... They gone crazy? ... Damned southerners!

VOICE OF NADIA'S FATHER: Leave me alone. I don't care if I go to jail.

Vincenzo and Nadia remain in silence until the shouting upstairs finally dies away. Meanwhile, the girl is squeezed tight against him, for the storage room is really too small for two people. And Vincenzo is very much disturbed by this contact. Nadia notices and draws away from him.

NADIA: I'm sorry.

VINCENZO *(stammering)*: What's going on? Who is it?

NADIA *(with an ironical little laugh)*: My father. We don't get along very well.

VINCENZO: But you live here? I've never seen you before.

NADIA *(whispering)*: I wish I could. But they don't want me. Did you see how they treat me?

Vincenzo gazes at her, increasingly disturbed.

VINCENZO: Don't cry.

Nadia is far from crying, and looks at Vincenzo in surprise. But she takes up the suggestion.

NADIA *(lowering her head)*: That's not easy.

She sniffles. Vincenzo starts at her, his gaze and his voice trembling.

VINCENZO: But why?

NADIA *(sighing, half in self-mockery)*: The usual thing, the usual business about honor. Yes, the honor of the poor... that is, the honor of girls. They're so concerned about that kind of honor. *(Rebelling)* And what's a poor girl supposed to do? Wipe herself out? Disappear? To please them? *(Shaking her head)* If every woman who... *(Smiles, almost cheerfully)* Well, let's forget that....

Vincenzo tries to smile and joke, too.

VINCENZO *(smiling)*: Yes. Only the men'd be left... *(Smiles again, coarsely wicked)* with nothing to do! *(He adjusts her bathrobe over her shoulders.)* ...But what'll you do now?

NADIA: I'm leaving. Before they start up again.

VINCENZO: Like that? Come to our house. My mother'll give you something to put on.

NADIA: Thank you.

She kisses him on the lips.

VINCENZO *(disturbed)* : What did you say?

NADIA: I said thanks. *(Vincenzo tries to kiss her again but Nadia slips out of the little room, adding:)* Let's go.

Rosaria's house. Night.

As Vincenzo and Nadia enter, Rosaria and her sons are each bent over plates of lentils, removing the pebbles and grass. Nadia gazes at them all, then speaks in a thin, weak little voice.

NADIA: Good evening.

They look up in astonishment.

ROSARIA *(extremely alarmed)* : Vincenzo, what have you done? Then they were screaming about you?

VINCENZO *(embarrassed)*: Of course not, Mama. This young lady's had some difficulty. You have to help her out, Mama. Lend her something, I don't know, a coat...

Vincenzo's brothers are all on their feet now.

Nadia appraises them one by one with an expert eye.

NADIA: I'm sorry... to give you trouble...

ROSARIA *(much perplexed)* : Who's got a coat? *(To Vincenzo)* If she can get along with your father's...

VINCENZO: Anything, just hurry, Mama. You see she's cold....

Rosaria gets up and goes off grumbling.

ROSARIA: Let's see...

She disappears. The boys observe the girl, so different from themselves. Simone has a particularly pleased expression, Rocco smiles, Ciro frowns, and Luca is ecstatic.

NADIA: All your brothers?

VINCENZO: Yes.

Simone stares at Nadia, unable to tear his eyes away.

SIMONE: You're Milanese, miss?

NADIA: Let's say from Lombardy. *(Her caressing glance again sweeps over the group of boys.)* ... And you're from the South, aren't you? But what are you doing in Milan?

She inspects the Parondi kitchen, where newspaper clippings of Vincenzo in boxing outfit are nailed to one wall. Simone shrugs his shoulders.

ROCCO: Today we shoveled snow.

NADIA *(laughing loudly)*: Oh no! What an idea!

Simone looks reprovingly at Vincenzo.

SIMONE: He took us. We've been here a month. We still haven't found steady work.

NADIA *(coyly)*: Smart boys like you find what they want to. You just have to move around. *(Pointing to photograph)* Which one of you boxes?

Simone looks meaningfully at Rocco.

SIMONE: Him. *(After a pause)* He used to but he's given it up.

Rosaria re-enters carrying a sweater, a dress, and an old coat. A cloud of dust rises as she throws them down.

NADIA: That's a pity. I know a champ! *(Laughs)* I can't remember his name. He's got a car big as this house. No snow shoveling for him!

SIMONE *(turning to Vincenzo)*: You see? He's the one who doesn't want us to start....

ROSARIA: Then start on your own, don't wait for him! Don't you hear what the lady says?

VINCENZO: That's just what they say. I started and I stopped. Two

thousand lire once in a blue moon, that's what I earned...
boxing.

NADIA *(amused)* : Because you're not a champ.

VINCENZO : Right. But it's not easy to become a champ.

ROSARIA : Who says Simone and Rocco won't make it even if you
didn't? They're younger, stronger!

VINCENZO : It's enough to have one man in the family getting his
face bashed in.

Nadia laughs in amusement.

ROSARIA : I don't think anyone could bash Simone's face in!

LUCA : Mama's right, Simone's stronger than you.

*Rosaria nods meaningfully at Simone. Vincenzo goes to the door opening
on the stairway, opens it slightly and peers out the crack, listening.*

ROSARIA *(to Nadia)* : Miss, we need this stuff....

Nadia takes the clothing in her arms.

NADIA : I'll bring everything back tomorrow. You can trust me.

She looks worriedly at Vincenzo, mutely querying him.

VINCENZO : That's good: the cop's here, the one that lives upstairs.
He's a friend. He's taking your father back in.

*Nadia must remove her bathrobe in order to change, but the eyes of the men
are still fixed upon her.*

ROSARIA *(intervening)* : You can change in the bathroom.

NADIA *(relieved)* : Thanks.

*As everyone watches her, she goes to the bathroom and closes the door
behind her. Rosaria immediately explodes at Vincenzo.*

ROSARIA *(exploding)* : Where did you get the idea of bringing
her here? How do we know who she is, what she's done?

ROCCO *(ecstatic)* : She's beautiful!

ROSARIA : All goose pimples...bad complexion... How do you look at women? What do you look at 'em with, I ask you?

VINCENZO : She's got goose pimples because she's cold.

ROSARIA *(tenacious)* : No. Her skin is really ugly... northern skin.

Vincenzo is still peering out the door.

Entrance and stairway. Inside. Night.

He sees a policeman coming back down the stairs. The policeman sees Vincenzo and nods cordially to him.

Rosaria's home. Night.

VINCENZO : Hello, sergeant. Good thing you were here. Listen... *(A sharp noise is heard inside the bathroom.)* Maybe you should take that poor girl home.

Another sharp noise from the bathroom. Everyone exchanges glances. Vincenzo realizes something is not right.

VINCENZO *(embarrassed, trying to erase his last words)* : Good night, sergeant.

The sergeant salutes, somewhat surprised. Rocco runs to fling open the bathroom door. He looks inside; no one is there.

ROCCO *(turning to the others)* : She's gone...

VINCENZO : Impossible.

ROCCO : She's gone! She must have climbed out the window. She's gone out that way.

They all run to see. Simone stares maliciously at Vincenzo and addresses him point-blank.

SIMONE: You're sorry, aren't you?

Simone laughs jeeringly; Rosaria rapidly intervenes.

ROSARIA *(smiling)*: Vincè, maybe you noticed Ginetta's not the only woman in the world?...

Gym. Inside. Evening.

This gym is the most squalid conceivable. A large, humid, dirty cellar. The clientele is equal to the situation. For the most part they are rowdy young men in ragged woolen undershirts and shorts, doggedly working out on the rough board floor, concentrating all their will to success and well-being into the movements of their arms and legs. In one corner is the gym's great white hope: a young man with a crafty, evil expression. The gym's trainer stands near the ropes of the ring observing the workout. Beside him is another boxer, an older man who serves as the gym's second trainer.

Vincenzo and the young boxer finish a round and rest against the ropes. The trainer makes some technical observations to the young boxer. Vincenzo awaits the next round with the absent and passive air of a "punching bag." At a certain point his attention is attracted toward the entrance to the gym. In the glare of the ring lights he cannot see well; he squints and finally recognizes his three brothers—Simone, Rocco, and Ciro—standing just inside the door. Vincenzo jumps down from the ring and runs toward them in embarrassment.

The bells rings; Vincenzo must go back for the next round. He is uncertain what to do. He would like to send his brothers away. He hesitates until the trainer has to call him.

TRAINER: Vincenzo!

The trainer turns and sees Vincenzo with his brothers, all bundled up and hovering there timidly.

TRAINER: Who're these guys? Christmas bagpipers from the sticks?

As he starts back to the ring, Vincenzo answers.

VINCENZO: I'm sorry. They're my brothers. They decided to come on their own.

TRAINER (indicating the locker room): It's all right by me....

Simone, Rocco, and Ciro start timidly for the locker room. Vincenzo climbs back into the ring and resumes boxing.

TRAINER (monotonously): Left... left...

Behind the boys working out more or less clumsily, Simone, Rocco, and Ciro reappear very timidly in their shorts and undershirts.

MARCH 1956.

Building site where Vincenzo is employed. Day.

Spring: the muddy ground that Vincenzo crossed the night he slept at the site is now dry and covered with patches of grass. The building is now well toward completion. Luca runs toward the building, stopping now and then to reconnoiter the route he must take to reach the workmen.

LUCA *(cupping his hands)* : Vincenzo! Vincenzo!

Luca begins to run again. He goes in one direction, then turns and runs to the other side, bumping against a man carrying a sack of cement. It is Simone.

LUCA: Where's Vincenzo?

Simone gestures upward. Luca starts running again, turning to shout in great excitement, as if announcing the greatest news in the world.

LUCA: The eviction people are here!

VOICE OF VINCENZO: Luca! Luca!

Luca turns to look up toward the scaffolding. He runs again, as if following a kite, toward Vincenzo's voice.

LUCA *(shouting happily)* : The eviction people are here! Mama wants to know what to do! Can you come home?

Vincenzo leans out from the scaffolding, hanging onto a rope.

VINCENZO: I can't. Go look for Rocco. Be careful, eh? Do it right!

Municipal housing for the evicted. Inside. Dusk.

The communal kitchen is at the end of a vast corridor on which open the large rooms, each sheltering an entire family. Small electric stoves, one for each family, are lined up on a long counter in the kitchen. Rosaria is being shown around by a custodian.

CUSTODIAN: This is your stove.

He shows her how to operate it. Then he points to the sinks. Many of the women are already busy in the kitchen. All look at Rosaria without great curiosity. Small children are playing everywhere in the kitchen and the hall.

Rocco is wandering happily about in the hall, surreptitiously peering into the rooms. Then he goes to his mother to tell her, happily, his impressions.

ROCCO *(softly, excited)* : You should see what beautiful furniture they have in one of the rooms down there. It's just like they told me. People stay here and save, and when they're finally given a house they're all ready.

ROSARIA *(to Rocco)* : He says we have to go see the director.

Rocco and Rosaria go along the hall. He is a little embarrassed. Vincenzo runs up.

VINCENZO: He says you have to go to the director.

He walks along the hall beside Rosaria, Rocco going ahead.

ROSARIA: Right now? Will you come too?

VINCENZO: No. I want to go see if I can talk to Ginetta. I want to tell her the good news.

ROSARIA *(hostile)* : Can't you forget about her? I thought you were interested in somebody else, anyway.

VINCENZO: Me?

ROSARIA: Well! You brought her into the house, and she even took my shawl.

VINCENZO: You'd have liked it if I took up with that one? Don't you know who she is? The cop that lived in our house there in Lambrate told me all about her. She's a...

The shouts of the children cover Vincenzo's last words. Rosaria is scandalized. Vincenzo comes to a door and opens it without hesitation. A man and a little girl are eating at a table; a woman is in bed, evidently ill. Vincenzo immediately closes the door.

VINCENZO: I made a mistake. But where are we? *(He goes back to the door before the one he had opened, looking in.)* I'll be right back.

This is the room which Rosaria and her sons have been assigned. Inside, Rocco and Luca are helping Ciro stretch an old blanket across a cord, to divide the room in two.

CIRO: If we can get them to give us one of the Romita Plan apartments, they've got three rooms, bath, and kitchen.

A woman appears in the doorway with a child in her arms. She looks tranquilly into the room at the new arrivals.

CIRO: We can rent out one room....

He beckons to Rocco to help him.

The child in the woman's arms has begun to whimper. Rocco sees the woman and smiles politely. She turns her back but remains there, rocking the child wearily in her arms.

Simone enters the room, turning to look at the woman and then coming up to his brothers with an expression of comic horror.

SIMONE: What a mess.

ROCCO: But it's free. Can't you understand that? We don't even pay for the electricity.

SIMONE *(laughing)*: Who's objecting?

The blanket has collapsed. Ciro patiently begins to stretch the cord again. Simone hops nimbly over it, falls on Rocco, and begins to box with him.

ROCCO: Cut it out!

SIMONE: Come on! Let's see your right....

Ciro nails up an advertisement for a professional school for mechanics.

Gym. Inside. Dusk.

Simone is taking his first try at the gloves with the trainer. It is late spring now: all the windows of the gym are wide open, and the patches of damp and dirt on the cellar walls show up more hideously than ever.

TRAINER: Right. Left. Keep your arms up higher, kid.

He parries Simone's blows easily, standing still in one position. Then he turns to look toward the entrance. Taking advantage of the trainer's momentary distraction, Simone lands a hard punch and the trainer wavers back. He avoids falling only with a certain effort, and protests angrily.

TRAINER: Oh! You gone crazy?

Simone stops, embarrassed. He, too, looks toward the door, where an extremely well-groomed man in a light-colored raincoat is now entering. This is Morini, a boxer who has retired only a few years earlier.

TRAINER *(greeting Morini)*: Look who's back!

Morini answers with a little wave. He stares at Simone: a serious and attentive stare which embarrasses Simone. Morini comes slowly up to him.

Rocco is exercising before the gym's one mirror, whose surface is bisected by a long crack. He sees the reflection of Morini's tall figure talking to the trainer, his eyes still fixed on Simone.

MORINI: New?

Morini speaks softly, with a typically hoarse voice.

TRAINER: He's been coming here three months now. But he's a real roundhouse punch.

Morini comes over to Simone and suddenly whirls him around, raises his arms, tests his muscles, pulls back his lips.

MORINI *(smiling)*: You've got the teeth of a wolf, but there's too much nicotine. If you want to box, no cigarettes. *(To the trainer)* If he stays here, no offense meant, after a year he'll still be where he is now.

The trainer is somewhat mortified at Morini's words. He and Morini leave Simone and go into the trainer's office. Rocco runs to Simone, who has climbed into the ring and is fastening his protective sparring belt. Rocco beckons to his brother and Simone leans over the ropes to listen to him.

ROCCO *(gesturing toward the office)* : He wants you to go to Cecchi's gym, did you understand? Where they have all the professionals, the champs!

Simone looks toward the open door of the office.

SIMONE: Let's hope the trainer says okay. *(Immediately menacing)* But even if he doesn't, who gives a damn? I'll go all the same. Apparently they think I have the stuff. They never wanted Vincenzo.

ROCCO *(pleased)* : That's true.

Simone suddenly has another thought and looks at his brother.

SIMONE: What about you?

ROCCO: You have to worry about me now? *(Laughs mildly)* It means I don't have the stuff.

Rocco is suddenly silent; he raises his eyes and sees Morini before him. Simone too, still leaning over the ropes, looks at Morini.

MORINI *(to Simone)* : Age?

SIMONE: Twenty-one.

MORINI: Army?

SIMONE: Look, I've been deferred because of an accident.

He points to a long scar on his leg.

MORINI: We can fix that. Do you really want to work hard?

The word "work" puts Simone on his guard.

SIMONE: Work where?

MORINI: Training. In the gym, in Cecchi's gym. Train to win, of course. We wanted some young guys to set up a team. You're not really young, and you've started late, but I'd like to try all the same.

Simone glances at Rocco. He smiles, with an imperceptible wink.

Arena and locker room entrance. Inside. Night.

Evening of the interregional amateurs' bouts. The hall is full of enthusiastic, quarrelsome, noisy aficionados of this type of encounter. Voices, shouts.

Two young men are fighting in the ring with more rage than competence. At the entrance to the locker room, some of the boxers due to fight later in the evening are looking out into the arena following the bout. Vincenzo is standing near ringside, looking toward a group of people sitting elsewhere in the hall. As is usual for this type of occasion, the arena is full of smoke and we can barely make out, behind the smoke screen, Ginetta, seated with her brothers and other friends and relatives, all southerners.

The match in progress draws to a close amid general disapprobation. Vincenzo makes his way past the ring toward the locker room. At the entrance to the locker room, Vincenzo finds Simone. Vincenzo is much more wrought up than his brother. He embraces Simone.

VINCENZO *(stammering)*: The Giannellis are here. Just think, if you win we might even make peace.

SIMONE: Oh, fine! And I'm supposed to get my face bashed in to please the Giannellis.

VINCENZO: I was just saying.

Simone claps his hand on his brother's shoulder. The two boxers who have just finished their bout return to the locker room, followed by the boos of the crowd. Cecchi comes up to Simone, then calls the seconds, one of whom is Vincenzo himself.

CECCHI: Let's go.

As he passes by to enter the ring, Simone is greeted by his first trainer.

TRAINER: Don't make me look bad, will you? *(To Cecchi, aggressively)* I was the one that taught him, remember.

The fighters are representing the various regions of Italy, and the audience too is divided by regions. They call out to their champions in their local dialects, waving posters embellished with provincial references. Simone's appearance with the word "Lombardy" on his robe provokes a sudden explosion of shouts, boos, and invective cutting through the applause of the Milanese for Cecchi's protégé.

VOICES: Murder 'im! Traitor! You sold out!

Vincenzo looks about in alarm as he tries to identify the point of origin of these cries.

TRAINER: Those are your fellow Lucanians.

VINCENZO: I know! I know! If I could get at them...

TRAINER: What can you do about it? Calm down, now.

Simone is in his corner, intent on the prebout preparations.

VOICES: Sellout! Traitor! How much did they give you? Stick with who pays you, traitor!

Vincenzo, increasingly alarmed, looks around the room and now sees Ginetta's brother shouting excitedly.

VINCENZO: That bastard. He's got it in for me, that guy.

Meanwhile, Simone's opponent has climbed into the ring.

REFEREE: Simone Parondi of the "Lombardy" team from Milan... Lombardy... *(Boos)* against Vitolo of the "Virtus" team of Potenza... Lucania.

A Lucanian battling for Lucania! The Lucanians in the audience go wild.

VOICES: Come on, Vitolo! Give it to him, Vitolo! Give 'im a new face, that traitor!

The boy is dark and thickset, much shorter than Simone, all muscle, bullnecked. His expression is closed and primitive, but very young. The bell rings for the first round; Vitolo runs to the attack with great ingenuousness. He guards badly and Simone is able, after a couple of straights to the face, to send him to the canvas. Vitolo remains down until the referee has counted nine seconds, then gets up still raring to go.

Applause for both boxers. Simone goes back to his corner. Between the first and second rounds the southerners' booing of Simone and encouragement of his opponent increase.

VOICES: Come on, Vitolo! Kill 'im! Come on, murder 'im! Down with Simone!

The second-round bell silences the excited audience, and the sound of the blows and the panting of the boxers is clearly audible. Simone's opponent returns to the attack, but Simone guards well and parries with his gloves until he is able to send Vitolo to the canvas once again. This time the Lombards cheer for Simone.

VOICES: Give it to 'im, Simone! Come on! *(To Vitolo)* Wake up, baby-face! Go back to your nurse, runt!

Vitolo rises with difficulty. The referee has just finished counting and Simone attacks again. A feint, a one-two, skillful parry and a lightning punch, and Vitolo, hit straight-on without time to get up his guard, ends up on the floor again.

Simone stands with his gloves hanging by his sides. Vitolo lies still on the canvas and the menacing noise of the crowd increases. The referee stops the fight and proclaims Simone the winner by a technical knockout. He raises Simone's arm.

REFEREE: Simone beats Vitolo by a technical knockout in the second round.

The referee's voice is drowned out by the insults shouted by the southerners:

VOICES: Coward! Disqualified! Disqualified! He faulted him! Traitor!

Boos. Simone leaves the ring through a tempest of insults and boos, and goes to the locker room.

Locker room. Night.

Simone is alone in the locker room. The cries of the audience watching the last match can be heard outside. He comes out of the shower and dries himself, combs his hair and puts lotion on it. He takes off his boxing outfit and begins to put on his undershirt and trousers.

Morini appears suddenly at the end of the locker room and quietly approaches Simone, watching him as he dresses among the rows of benches and lockers. Simone becomes aware of his presence but does not turn. Simone continues to button up, pulls his belt as tight as possible, and starts to take his shirt when Morini's voice interrupts him.

MORINI: Bravo!

SIMONE: It was easy. He went down early.

Morini looks him up and down with a mocking smile. He touches Simone's purple trunks, hanging on a hook.

MORINI: Purple, eh? The color of champs and of prima donnas. *(After a pause)* I'll see you outside. I have to talk to you, Apollo. We'll eat, we'll celebrate your first victory. Then… there's so much to do….

And in his usual brusque fashion, Morini turns his back on Simone and walks away. Simone remains still, musing in silence. Then he knots his tie. Luca appears at the locker room door, shouting excitedly.

LUCA: Simone! They're fighting outside!

Arena exit and adjacent streets. Outside. Night.

Near the exit of the boxing arena, a small group of Lucanians who have been waiting there to insult Simone have come to blows with his Milanese supporters. Ciro, Rocco, and Vincenzo are there, about to enter the fray. Part of the audience which is still filing out of the building stops to watch disapprovingly. Insulting cries accompany the blows.

VINCENZO: Cowards!... You're jealous!...

VOICE: Farmers!...

Luca runs up and immediately joins the battle.

LUCA: Farmers yourselves!...

LUCANIAN: Where are you from? Renegades! You still stink of the train! Go back home!

Someone grabs Vincenzo's neck from behind; he frees himself with effort and when he turns, he finds his assailant to be Alfredo, Ginetta's brother.

VINCENZO: You! We've got some business of our own to settle!

ALFREDO: Let's settle it right now!

Vincenzo is about to fling himself on Alfredo but Ginetta, standing nearby with the other brother, immediately intervenes.

GINETTA: No! Vincenzo, please! Let him alone!

VINCENZO: It's time to settle this. What did we ever do to him? He's got to stop it! What's he got against us?

Ginetta holds him back as Bruno restrains Alfredo.

GINETTA: You're right. But see what happens? Let me take care of it. You'll see what I can do!

Alfredo has freed himself from his brother's hold in the meanwhile and slaps Ginetta. Vincenzo can no longer control himself and the two men join battle.

A car honks repeatedly as it tries to make its way through the crowd, which is forced to divide in two. In one of the groups, Rocco, Ciro, and Luca are giving their all. Ciro's lip is already swollen and little Luca covers an aching eye with his hand.

Two policemen arrive and separate the contenders with an effort. Simone appears at the exit of the arena. Amused, he stops to watch the end of the fight as if it in no way concerned him. As the groups shift positions, Simone sees and recognizes Nadia, standing nearby. Their eyes meet. Nadia laughs at the situation as she looks at him. Simone smiles back and approaches her.

SIMONE: Hello.

NADIA: Recognize me?

She slips her arm under his and they walk off together. As they walk along the sidewalk, they pass a parked car. It is Morini's. Simone does not notice him and the couple continues on. But Morini watches Simone and Nadia through the windshield. Under the impression that Simone is deliberately ignoring him, Morini flashes the headlights to attract his attention. But Simone does not notice, and as the couple walks off into the dark, the picture is superimposed with the word: SIMONE.

Nadia's bedroom. Night.

Simone is lying on the bed with his hands crossed behind his head. Nadia sits beside him on the bed, smoking. Simone's figure is almost completely in shadow, like a massive sculpture in dark marble; Nadia's is in full light. She wears a very skimpy lace slip. She smokes greedily, with lengthy inhalations, and turns slightly to blow the smoke in Simone's face.

NADIA *(continuing a conversation)*: …So you've decided to go in for this boxing all the way. Like I do my profession. For this, of course. *(Gesturing to indicate "money")*

SIMONE: Yes. But I love it too.

NADIA *(amused)*: Oh? Really?

She laughs. She lets her head fall back and stretches her arms.

NADIA: If that's the way you look at it, I "love it" too. You bet!

As she moves, her cigarette falls to the floor on Simone's side. Nadia leans over to pick it up, stretching out over Simone. She remains lying over him for a moment.

NADIA *(suddenly serious)* : No. I don't like it. *(She gets up slowly.)* Or do I? How should I know? *(Shrugs)* When I want to, I like it.

Simone takes the girl by the arm, about to ask her an obvious question which Nadia immediately forestalls with a malicious little laugh as she frees her arm.

NADIA: What about your brother?

SIMONE: Which one? I have four of them.

NADIA: That dope, the one that called the cop that night. What a day that was! The snow, my father... I ought to've left... *(She interrupts herself, laughing.)* But that wasn't the end of it: your kind brother went on for some time, having the cops look for me. Poor boy! Maybe he thought he was doing me a favor. But I can't stand cops. *(She laughs ironically, looking at Simone.)* Ever since I was a little girl...

Nadia throws away the cigarette and gets up. As she passes before the mirror, she looks with some satisfaction at her body, barely covered by the filmy lace slip.

Nadia's bedroom is furnished with a few cheap but extremely pretentious Venetian-style pieces. There is a tiny adjoining bathroom. The wardrobe which Nadia is now closing contains a very few dresses, with a jumble of stockings, cosmetics, and two handbags on the shelf. She passes her hand lovingly over the painted side of the wardrobe.

NADIA: Beautiful, isn't it?

Simone pulls himself up on his elbows, gazes at the wardrobe, and nods in assent, convinced. Then he looks admiringly all around the room. It is clear that Simone finds everything enchanting.

SIMONE: New?

Nadia responds with a shrug. She reopens the wardrobe to take out a jar of cold cream and some tissues, then comes back to the bed and begins to spread cold cream over her face.

NADIA: Two years ago I had a more beautiful place. Then I had some trouble. But just wait a little while and you'll see how I fix myself up again. *(She wipes off the cream.)* There was wall-to-wall carpeting. *(Yawns)* Listen, I'm going to sleep now and you'll have to leave.

Simone passes his arm around Nadia's side.

SIMONE *(softly)* : Nooo!

NADIA: Yes! I like to sleep alone. *(Laughs)* What d'you think! That's why I left home. *(She turns toward Simone, speaking vivaciously to distract herself.)* When I was little, my father got sick and had to stay ever so long in the hospital! So me and my mother went to live with my aunt and uncle. It was just after the war. Everything was so hard for us. They put us into a room, a sort of room.... I don't remember just how many we were. *(Laughs)* "Overcrowded living quarters." Like your house, if I'm not mistaken. Mornings when there wasn't any school, we all used to play in the courtyard. For my age, I was... *(Gestures)* well, you know... and I didn't feel like playing kid games.... There was a dentist that lived on the ground floor. I can almost see him now. *(Laughs)* He must not have been much good because he never had any patients and he was always looking out the window. One day he calls me over.... *(a brief pause)* Afterward, of course, I preferred to go at night. When everybody was asleep at home, I'd sneak out. At least we were only two in the bed.

Nadia is amused at her own story.

SIMONE *(disturbed)*: How old were you?

NADIA: Thirteen. *(Her tone changes.)* That's just a story; it's not true at all. When I was small we had a fine house. The trouble came later. At that time... I even had a governess.

SIMONE: What's that?

NADIA *(laughing heartily)* : A governess. You don't even know what that is? What fun is there in telling you stories? *(Laughs)* Oh, just look how cheery I am tonight!

Simone tries somewhat awkwardly to embrace the girl, but she pushes him away.

NADIA: Go on, leave. It's late. *(She laughs, still watching Simone.)* What do you want? *(Meaningfully)* Again? *(She tries to free herself from Simone's embrace, but now it is only a game; no longer laughing.)* But no more after this, eh? You'll leave...

Simone tightens his embrace until the girl lies back. She stretches her arms, lazy and voluptuous.

NADIA: Well, anyway, I like you. Too bad you're... a little too unpresentable... because if not...

Street near the Naviglio canal. Day.

Ciro directs a car as it backs into a parking space. A southerner of about forty is superintending the operations from a distance. It is clear that Ciro is an employee of this self-authorized parking attendant, who watches cars in a particularly busy part of the city. After parking the car, the driver gets out and finds Ciro smiling reassuringly at the door.

CIRO *(indicating the dirty windshield)* : Clean 'em off?

The client hurries away. Ciro remains a moment by the car, then runs to rejoin Luca, who is sitting on a little wall overlooking the canal. Luca hands Ciro the sandwich he has evidently left behind to run to assist the client. On the wall beside Luca is a package of textbooks and some sheets of paper (advertisements for night schools) which Ciro picks up and studies attentively as he chews his frugal meal.

LUCA: Here. I've brought you the night-school ads. *(He points to one of the sheets, which reads: "Night Courses for Technicians.")* But you have to have a grade-school diploma to register.

CIRO: So? I have it, don't I? *(Luca extracts a package of bubble gum from his pocket and offers a piece to Ciro.)* Will you stop throwing money away?

LUCA *(resentful)*: I didn't buy it! Simone gave it to me.

CIRO: Ah! *(Chewing)* Did Simone go to work this morning?

LUCA: He was still asleep when I left. But he never goes in the morning.

CIRO: I'd still like to know what kind of work he does.

LUCA: Better than anybody else, because yesterday too he gave Mama two thousand lire.

CIRO: What about you?

LUCA: I deliver the customers' packages. I have to go now.

CIRO *(examining the papers)*: Wait a couple of years and I'll show you how to get ahead.

The parking attendant whistles. Ciro puts the sandwich down and runs to help a client pull out his car. Luca watches Ciro for a moment, then looks down at the stagnant water in the canal, at the passers-by, and finally at the sandwich. After making certain that Ciro does not see him, Luca takes a huge bite out of the sandwich and then puts it back on the wall. He jumps off the wall, picks up his packages, and goes off.

Café. Inside. Dusk.

Ivo is laughing heartily as he leans against the billiard table. The café is comprised of a single, rather large room. The front section, containing the bar, is brightly lit by neon tubes. The back area, where the billiard table stands, is very dimly lit. Although the café is located near the center of town, its clientele is rather on the shady side and is particularly active in the evening. There are always people in the billiard area even when the front room is empty.

The clientele is composed for the most part of young habitués of bookie joints, of the gyms on the outskirts of town, etc. They rarely play billiards: the table is used primarily by the older men, seamy-looking failures who are always on the lookout for business deals and always the butt of the younger customers' humor. Among the latter is Simone, who takes the cigarette from Ivo's lips, takes a drag, and then replaces it before going over to the telephone. He calls out to the waiter.

SIMONE: Switch the line over here.

WAITER *(from the bar)*: And you give me the twenty-five lire!

SIMONE *(to Ivo)* : Give 'im twenty-five lire.

IVO *(resisting)* : You're broke already?

Simone grimaces as if to say, "Obviously."

IVO: Then what?

SIMONE: You said you were bringing me another carton. So I gave the money to my mother.

IVO: To Mother. But you're going to have to start getting emancipated.

YOUNG MAN AT THE BILLIARD TABLE: How wise we are tonight! *(Approaching the two)* If you're interested, Vaghi, that fellow from Bovisa, has a whole carload of Swiss stuff at his place.

IVO: Just the right man! He wants cash first!

ANOTHER YOUNG MAN: What d'you want? For him to risk his neck for your pretty face?

SIMONE *(impatient, to the waiter)* : Well, the telephone?

WAITER *(mimicking)* : Well, the twenty-five lire?

As Ivo goes to pay the waiter, he turns to Simone, protesting.

IVO: Who d'you have to talk to anyway?

Simone has taken from his pocket a rumpled scrap of paper with a telephone number scrawled on it in wavering calligraphy. Ivo hands the waiter the money and now protests anew as he sees the note in Simone's hand.

IVO: The same one! But this time you'll come clean!

Simone has dialed the number and waits as the telephone rings. Ivo hurries to his side and lays his head on Simone's shoulder to listen in. Simone tries unsuccessfully to push Ivo away.

The ringing is interrupted.

NADIA'S VOICE: Hello?

SIMONE: It's me.

A dry click follows immediately as Nadia hangs up. Ivo laughs jeeringly.

IVO *(laughing)* : You make such a nice impression. "It's me." Slam. There's no hope for you, women just don't like you.

Simone hangs up the telephone. His expression is gloomy. Observing him, Ivo realizes that this is no time to joke.

IVO: Well? Do we go see this Vaghi? Maybe we can persuade him to give us a carton on credit. We'll take it, we'll sell 'em in the Concourse, and then...

SIMONE *(gloomily)*: You go to Vaghi. I have to go to the gym.

IVO: At this hour?

SIMONE: At this hour. Why? Don't you approve?

Ivo smiles slyly at Simone.

Street and entrance to Nadia's apartment building. Dusk.

The concierge of the building is polishing the brass door handles when she hears someone pass by her and turns.

CONCIERGE: Hey, you there. Where are you going?

Simone is already near the stairs and turns only slightly.

SIMONE: Balzani. Third floor.

The concierge comes toward Simone, still holding the dirty rag.

CONCIERGE: She's not home.

SIMONE: She's home, she's home.

CONCIERGE: I say she's not. Come on down, please don't go up.

SIMONE *(lying badly)*: But I just talked to her ten minutes ago and she said she'd expect me here!

The concierge looks suspiciously at Simone, then shrugs her shoulders and starts toward the courtyard.

CONCIERGE: Well, let's see, eh?

Simone does not even wait for her to reach the courtyard before he races up the stairs. The concierge does not immediately notice his absence. She mutters as she continues toward the courtyard.

CONCIERGE: They could take care of their dirty business by themselves....

When she realizes Simone is not following her, she remains for a moment undecided whether to call up from the courtyard or simply extract herself from the whole business. She decides on the latter course, shrugs her shoulders, and returns to her work, though she does glance up the stairs as she passes by.

Landing and Nadia's apartment. Dusk.

Simone rings Nadia's doorbell, his index finger pressed steadily on the button. Sound of doorbell.

Exasperated at not obtaining any answer, Simone begins to beat on the door with his fists. He stops only to ring the bell once more. He stops ringing only to start banging again. He is about to give up and starts to turn toward the stairs, unleashing a final kick at the door.

The door now opens and Nadia appears, wearing a very short and very provocative robe.

NADIA: Will you cut that out?

Simone is embarrassed, as if caught out. He has suddenly lost all his self-assurance.

SIMONE: I called you, and you... Maybe you didn't recognize me.

NADIA *(coldly)*: I recognized you, all right. That's why I hung up. Now get out of here!

She starts to close the door. Humiliated, Simone suddenly reacts and quickly prevents Nadia from closing the door, almost falling on her.

NADIA *(enraged)*: What do you want?

SIMONE: You've got someone here, haven't you?

Without waiting for an answer, Simone races toward Nadia's bedroom.

Nadia's bedroom. Dusk.

The room is in disorder but there is no one there, or in the bathroom or the kitchenette, which Simone also looks into.

NADIA: All finished? Shall we go now?

Simone comes humbly back to her.

SIMONE: I've looked for you for days. I've come here morning and night. I've telephoned....

Nadia looks at Simone less angrily now, even amused.

NADIA: You could have saved yourself the trouble. Because if I wanted to see you I know where to find you.

SIMONE: But what's happened, Nadia? Why don't you want to...

NADIA: Want to what? *(Laughs)* What's got into you, little boy? I've got things to do, you know. *(Good-naturedly)* So long. Come on, get out. It's all right.

SIMONE *(pleading)*: But why? Why are you sending me away?

Nadia's moment of kindness has passed; she is again angry and nasty to the point of raising her voice.

NADIA *(shouting)*: Will you leave me alone? What have I got to do to get rid of you? Give you an inch and you all want to take a mile. Get out of here and don't call me and don't come back again, and I mean it. Understand?

Simone allows her to push him out. The door slams violently behind him.

Cecchi's gym. Inside. Evening.

This gym is quite different from the one where Simone and Rocco made their debut. It is a fairly small area but well lit, perfectly equipped and scrupulously maintained. The young men training there are few but of a class superior to that of the boys working out in the slum gym. And above all, they are all, without exception, much more expert.

Cecchi and the trainer stand near Simone, who is working out at the punching bag. Evidently the trainer has made some observation which has set Cecchi off, and he is now sharply reproving Simone.

CECCHI *(to Simone)*: If you keep on this way you'll be finished before you even get started, let me tell you. Instead of making progress you're going backward, like a crab. You've fallen off in everything, you have. You have no will, you have no enthusiasm, you haven't got any wind either; you haven't got a thing.

Simone continues to punch the bag stubbornly.

SIMONE *(gloomily)*: Who says so?

CECCHI: I say so. I wasn't born yesterday.... Oh! *(Cecchi is forced to step aside to avoid Simone, as he revolves around the bag.)* But remember that you found the door open when you came and you can find it open to get out too. *(Simone continues to punch the bag angrily.)* Understand?

Simone stops and is about to answer when his expression suddenly changes. At the top of the stairs leading down into the gym, he sees Nadia.

Laundry. Inside. Day.

The preceding scene vanishes in a cloud of steam. We are in the back room of the Widow Donini's laundry. As the steam thins out, we see a girl in a white smock and cap intent on operating one of the two electric washing machines. She flips through a handful of receipts pinned to her smock.

GIRL *(in a sharp, querulous voice)*: Listen... are you sure you know how to read? I don't know, since you came here there's always such a mess.

VOICE OF SECOND GIRL: Don't listen to her. It's always been like this.

The second girl too appears from behind a cloud of steam, which rises from the machine where she is pressing a pair of trousers. Between the two girls stands Rocco, a basket of packages at his feet. Evidently one of the packages is unlabeled. Rocco holds it in his hand as he silently questions first one and then the other girl.

SECOND GIRL *(calling)*: Bring me the receipt book.

A third girl appears from the front of the shop, on the street. Unlike the other two, her smock is of black satin. She is small and blond.

GIANNINA *(holding out the receipt book)*: Here, but it's impossible to figure it out.

She comes up to Rocco and the first girl, to look inside the package. A fourth girl, Ida, appears in the back room, also in a black smock.

IDA: Shhh! The boss is upstairs and has a headache! *(Ida, too, comes up to Rocco, who patiently continues to hold the cumbersome package; to Rocco)* You don't remember the name of that lady that's some kind of relative of the boss's?

Rocco shrugs his shoulders.

GIANNINA: How should he remember if he's only been here a month?

ANOTHER GIRL: Even if he stays around a year... Sleeping Beauty!

Ida, try giving him a kiss, you never know, maybe he'll wake up.

Ida smiles at Rocco, who seems more embarrassed than ever. The girls burst out laughing. Then they hear the shop bell ringing.

GIANNINA: Oh, heavens, customers!

Simone appears at the street door, looks inside, and then emits a long tuneful whistle to summon Rocco. The girls exchange glances, amused and surprised.

GIANNINA: Who's that?

ROCCO *(embarrassed)*: It's my brother.

He replaces the package in the basket and starts toward Simone.

ANOTHER GIRL: Bring him back here or go out in the street. The boss doesn't want any relatives in the store.

Rocco nods and goes toward the front, but Ida is already bringing Simone into the back of the store. She looks at Simone with a certain sly intent, immediately shared by the other girls, with the exception of the first, who picks up Rocco's package and places it on a table where a large number of men's shirts and other finished items are neatly stacked. She then returns to the washing machine.

SIMONE: Hello, everybody.

He is in an excellent mood, and even his eyes are laughing. His hair has been combed carefully and sparkles with brilliantine. He carries his gym bag and amuses himself by twirling it about as he looks at the machines, pretending not to notice the girls' stares.

SIMONE *(whistling in admiration)*: Wow!

The girl at the steam press removes another pair of perfectly ironed, steaming trousers.

SIMONE *(laughing)*: That's just what I need! *(To Rocco)* You didn't tell me what a great place this was. You just put the stuff in there and...

IDA *(coyly)*: Didn't you read it outside? People can come in here, undress *(Indicating a tiny curtained-off dressing room)* and just a couple of minutes later they go out looking like a new person.

SIMONE: That's just what I need. Can you really do it right away?

He tosses away his bag and begins to take off his jacket. The girls laugh.

ROCCO *(embarrassed, coming over to Simone)*: It costs a lot of money.

Simone begins to unbutton his pants.

SIMONE: I can pay.

Another curtain, of the same material as that forming the dressing room, conceals the stairway leading to the second floor. It is suddenly pulled aside and the owner, Mrs. Luisa Donini, appears. Upon seeing her, the girls slip silently back to their jobs. Luisa is about forty and cannot hide it, despite the pancake makeup with which she has carefully veiled her face and neck. She is dressed in black and wears flashily vulgar jewelry.

Rocco picks up the basket of packages, and only Simone remains in the center of the room, in shirtsleeves and with his trousers half-unbuttoned. There is a moment of silence. Everyone seems to be awaiting an outburst from Luisa, who is frowning as she stands there, hands on hip.

Then Simone suddenly bursts out laughing, breaking the ice.

SIMONE *(laughing)*: They tell me they can make even me look elegant in five minutes. Is it true?

Luisa looks at Simone and smiles as she comes toward him.

LUISA: Why not? Step right in.

She goes over to the dressing room, beckoning to Simone to enter and undress. Reassured, two of the girls go over to Luisa, too, one to take Simone's trousers and Giannina to ask about the package. Luisa motions them back to their places.

LUISA *(to Simone as he enters the dressing room)*: Give them to me. *(To Rocco)* Are you still here?

GIRL *(pointing to the dressing room)* : It's his brother.

LUISA: Ah!

GIANNINA *(to Rocco)* : Show Madame that package.

Rocco puts the basket down again and goes to get the package.

GIANNINA *(to Luisa)* : The ticket's missing. But I know whose it is. It's that lady, that relative of yours....

LUISA *(wearily)* : Mrs. Brighetti. Via Pirandello seventy-three.

She takes a pencil from her pocket and writes the name and address on the package.

Simone leans out of the dressing room in his undershirt, holding out his trousers and shirt. Two coins roll out of the trousers pocket. Luisa stops them with her foot and Rocco bends down to pick them up.

LUISA *(to Simone)* : Not the shirt. *(With a little laugh)* We can't do miracles.

SIMONE *(with comic disappointment)* : That's a shame!

LUISA: I agree. But the quality wouldn't improve anyway. *(She hands the shirt back to Simone and the trousers to the girl, with a regal gesture; to Rocco)* Go on, go on, you're late already.

Rocco nods and starts to obey.

SIMONE: Wait a minute! Where are you going, dopey?

Simone leans out of the dressing room and stops Rocco. He pulls the curtain about him to cover himself as best he can. The girls laugh, amused.

SIMONE *(to Luisa)* : I wanted to talk to him. The rest came afterwards.

LUISA *(amused)* : Pardon me!

But she does not stir. Rocco and Simone look at each other, embarrassed. Then Simone decides to speak anyway.

SIMONE: Can you lend me some money? You've been paid for
the week, haven't you?

*Rocco looks at Luisa, who stands there smiling and impassive as if she has
not heard, although she continues to watch them.*

ROCCO: Tonight, I think.

SIMONE: Look, I need it right away. I'm going out of town. Tell
them at the gym. I'll be away two days. *(Laughs)* Out of
town, understand? Out of Milan!

LUISA *(still watching Simone)* : Rocco, don't lend him anything.

Simone plays the part of the victim.

SIMONE *(smiling at Luisa)* : Oh! You really don't like me, do you?

LUISA *(amused)* : I'm defending your brother. Because one has
to protect oneself against people like you.

SIMONE *(to Rocco)* : Well? All right?

Rocco looks at Luisa as if to say, "It depends on her."

LUISA: How much do you have to give him? Half your pay? Yes?
Minus what he has to pay here...

*Rocco nods, then picks up the basket and starts for the door. He turns to
Simone.*

ROCCO: When'll you be back? Does Mama know?

*Luisa goes over to the pressing machine to pick up Simone's trousers.
Simone is still looking out of the dressing room. Just beside him is a large
pile of freshly laundered white shirts. Simone reaches out and rests his
hand lightly on one of the shirts, as if caressing it. Then he looks around
to make certain no one is watching. No one is. He rapidly picks up one shirt
and draws back into the dressing room, closing the curtain.*

*Through the opening we see Simone rapidly measuring the collar of his
own shirt against that of the clean one. They are very similar. He bends*

down rapidly and places the fresh shirt in his gym bag, then straightens up and puts on his own shirt.

Luisa is approaching the dressing room with Simone's freshly pressed and still steaming trousers.

LUISA: Look here, they look like new.

She looks at Simone, who looks back innocently.

LUISA *(with a critical tone)* : The shirt certainly leaves something to be desired.

Simone continues to button up and brazenly indicates the table on which the freshly laundered articles are stacked up.

SIMONE: One of those would do the trick.

LUISA: They're Dr. Fossati's. *(Sighs)* Oh, heavens, for that matter they'd look better on a fellow like you. *(Sighs)* But that's life. We get nice things only when they're no good to us any more.

The girl at the pressing machine overhears and smiles ironically, winking at Giannina.

GIRL *(singing softly)* : Red moon, looking at me...

Cecchi's gym. Inside. Evening.

TRAINER: Can we please shut that door?

The trainer, Morini, and the gym directors are standing around a visiting boxer. The trainer is evidently repeating a frequent refrain as he turns toward the door, where Rocco stands, shifting his gym bag from one hand to the other and speaking to Cecchi in great embarrassment.

ROCCO: He doesn't feel well and he says that he may not be able to come tonight and tomorrow.

MORINI *(slowly)* : He's not feeling well? But he was in the Concourse at three…

Rocco turns toward Morini, who has left the group near the ring and is coming in his direction.

ROCCO *(embarrassed)* : Well, I don't know.

MORINI *(not turning to Rocco)* : If you don't know, I do. And I know something else too. *(Morini is heading for the stairs, and only when he arrives and leans against the bannister does he turn to Rocco, shouting with such rage that Rocco lowers his eyes.)* Damn me and damn the day I brought your brother here.

CECCHI *(conciliating)* : Really, up to now I can't complain.

MORINI *(still shouting)* : That's not true; you have complained and you've got plenty of reason to. I brought him and I regret it now. But before anybody else tells me I prefer to say for myself that I made a mistake.

Morini leaves, followed by the rather ironical stares of some of the athletes. Cecchi, too, knows how to interpret Morini's outburst. He watches him go out, sighs, and then looks attentively at Rocco.

CECCHI: Your brother's got a good body. And he hits well too. But he's slow. He needs more training than another man would that's less gifted. So I say, shouldn't we do something about it before it's too late?

ROCCO: Are you asking me?

CECCHI *(a little out of patience)* : Yes you! From now on you come here with him, and you can keep an eye on him. You come together; you leave together. You're a good boy, that's easy to see. You won't have to pay, don't worry. But you have to stand watch over your brother. Keep him from certain company… women, for instance.

ROCCO *(increasingly embarrassed)* : But I… *(As if finding a valid justification)* But I have to go into the service soon.

CECCHI: When?

ROCCO: I don't know. Soon.

CECCHI *(increasingly impatient)*: All right. But until then come here and keep after your Simone. *(He goes off, then looks back at Rocco with some sympathy; to himself)* It won't do any good but we've got to give it a try.

EASTER 1956 (APRIL).

Bellagio. Lake Como and wharf. Day.

A lovely sailboat skims over the lake on a beautifully sunny day.

Bellagio. Street and entrance to pension, near large hotel. Day.

Nadia and Simone walk along arm in arm before a large luxury hotel. They are forced to step aside as a bus passes by, loaded with tourists singing at the tops of their lungs. Nadia looks at the bus in annoyance.

NADIA: You can't really say we're the only ones who thought of coming here. *(Pauses)* It's easy enough to understand— two holidays in one: Easter and Sunday.

SIMONE *(laughing)*: But Easter's always on Sunday.

NADIA: Oh really?

SIMONE: Of course. They have a procession in my home town. They start ringing the bells at Saturday noon.

NADIA *(distracted)*: I'm afraid this town of yours is a great bore.

She gazes fixedly at the gardens of the great hotel, where a number of expensive cars are parked. The tables on the terrace are set for dinner;

the diners are very few and the waiters very many. Simone follows Nadia's gaze.

SIMONE: What's this?

NADIA: A hotel, can't you see?

SIMONE: A hotel?

NADIA: A hotel, a good hotel. *(Lying)* I stayed here once. You should see what rooms! Nothing like where we are now. You know it costs more than ten thousand a day just for the room?

SIMONE *(terrified)*: Oh?

NADIA *(ironical)*: Oh. You have a lot to learn, little boy.

SIMONE *(to himself)* : Ten times thirty... *(Out loud)* Then according
to you a person can spend three hundred thousand a month
just to sleep?

*They have reached the small building in which their pension is located.
A bus is parked in front and groups of tourists wait outside for the tables
to be prepared for dinner.*

NADIA *(annoyed)* : Look at that! *(They pass through an unimpressive
little front garden.)* But we'll eat in the room, eh?

SIMONE: What'll we eat? We don't have anything.

NADIA *(laughing)* : They'll bring it up. *(Ironical)* Really rich
people are like the poor : they eat where they sleep. *(Laughs)*
Like you at the welfare housing.

Bedroom at the Bellagio pension. Day.

*The room is in stupefying disorder. The bed has been shifted under the
window in order to get the sun. The little table on which dinner has been
served is in the center of the room. A tray with coffee cups, a bottle of brandy,
and liqueur glasses rests on a chair near the bed. Simone and Nadia are
sunning themselves; they are lying face down, side by side, across the
bottom of the bed. They are resting their heads on their arms, like sun-
bathers at the beach.*

SIMONE: They'll be paying me a lot for this next bout. But I'll really
break through when I turn professional. I've made my
calculations: after one year.

NADIA *(not very interested)* : I know. But how much will they pay
you?

SIMONE: I don't know... a lot! *(He kisses her bare arm, which rests
on his, and nibbles tenderly at it; sighing.)* But I really have to
go into strict training for these matches. It'll be tough for
you too.

NADIA: For me? What have I got to do with it?

SIMONE *(awkwardly)*: Well... when you're in training you can't...

She turns over, covering her breast with a corner of the sheet. Her voice is still calm, her eyes half-closed as she basks like a lazy cat in the sun.

NADIA: Listen, my boy, there seems to be some misunderstanding here.

A silence. Nadia seems totally absorbed in measuring the length of Simone's hair, stretching the locks out against his forehead.

NADIA: We're not married, you know. Do I have to explain this to you every time we see each other?

Simone looks at the girl as if trying to make out whether or not she is joking.

NADIA: We might see each other again. But there's no obligation, no set plan. It might just happen, that's all. *(Laughs ironically)* Look, that's what happened this time. I had to get out of town for a couple of days, and with someone who wouldn't attract attention. *(Laughs)* After an affair it's always a good idea to get away from it all.

She looks at Simone, amused by the horror she reads in his expression. Then she laughs heartily, sincerely amused.

Rosaria's room at the housing for the evicted.

Deafening noise of children running, playing, shouting, and wailing. An air of festivity in Rosaria's room. Following the Lucanian custom, baskets of basil have been placed before the statuettes of San Rocco and San Luca, encased in their glass bells. Candles set before the sacred images are girdled with many-colored ribbons. The colored Easter eggs, each enclosed in a small castle-like cage of sweet cake, are set out on a plate. A palm leaf stands in a vase. The Easter dinner is over. A platter in the center of the table contains the leftovers.

Sitting around the table are Rosaria, Rocco, Vincenzo, Luca, and Ginetta, who sits very politely with her hands crossed in her lap, her head lowered, her eyes slightly reddened by tears. Ciro's place is empty; the plate has not been used. We immediately have the impression that the dinner conversation has not been very lively.

Ginetta glances from beneath her lowered eyelids at Vincenzo, as if urging him to something. Vincenzo catches her look and starts to say something.

VINCENZO: Mama, I... *(But Rosaria is unencouraging, hostile; Vincenzo's courage deserts him.)* What's the matter, Mama?

Rosaria looks at Ciro's empty place.

ROSARIA *(almost to herself)* : Nothing... I was thinking about Ciro. He doesn't love his family any more. He's selfish....

ROCCO: But... they have to work on holidays too, where Ciro works. He told you he couldn't come.

ROSARIA *(bitterly)* : Not even on Easter?

VINCENZO *(meaningfully)* : Well, what about Simone?

ROSARIA: What's Simone got to do with it? Simone's grown up; he's got a life of his own. *(She exaggerates proudly.)* He's made a name for himself. He has to keep up with so many things.

Vincenzo had been about to ask his burning question, but after his mother's speech he changes the subject.

VINCENZO *(conciliating)* : Well, it's a nice day. *(To Ginetta)* Let's take a nice walk, and we'll take Ciro his cake and the Easter egg. *(To Rocco)* You know where he works?

Rocco nods.

ROCCO: At the entrance to the Como thruway.

LUCA *(happily)* : Can I come too?

ROSARIA: No, not you. You stay here with me.

LUCA: Why? What am I supposed to do here all day long?

ROSARIA: You stay here and keep me company. Because it's Easter. *(Grumbling)* A son that doesn't eat at his mother's table on Easter… *(To Luca, her mood changing)* Find me a clean piece of paper to wrap the things up in.

As Luca runs to rummage through some drawers, a heavy silence settles over the room, as if something is about to happen. Rosaria clears the table. The others get up. Luca brings the paper and Rosaria begins to wrap up the remaining sweets. Vincenzo and Ginetta gaze at each other for mutual support. Then Vincenzo speaks.

VINCENZO *(suddenly taking courage)*: Mama, Ginetta and I have to get married!

Rosaria freezes for a moment. Then she continues wrapping up the sweets in silence. She seems not to have heard.

ROSARIA: Tell Ciro to eat them, and that I'm sending them to him.

A very expressive glance passes between Vincenzo and Ginetta.

VINCENZO: Ma, did you hear what I said?

Rosaria turns and hands him the package. She is cold as stone.

ROSARIA *(her voice trembling)*: Vincè, what are you asking me? *(Louder)* What are you telling me? *(She indicates Ginetta for the first time, alluding to the Giannellis.)* After what happened with them, if you want my consent… *(Melodramatically)* you'll have to bury me first. *(She gestures broadly toward Ginetta.)* It's just a pity for this poor girl who doesn't have much to do with it.

But Vincenzo touches Ginetta's head and finds the strength to go on.

VINCENZO: No. I'm marrying her, Mama. I'm telling you I'm going to marry her.

Rosaria shrieks in answer.

ROSARIA *(shouting)* : You're treating me this way? My sons treat me this way? Can a person stand such injustice?

She strides up and down the room, prey to an exaggerated agitation.

ROCCO *(trying to stop her)* : Calm down, Mama. Ginetta's a good girl. Why shouldn't Vincenzo marry her?

ROSARIA *(impersonally)* : If Vincenzo wants to do just what he wants to, it means he hasn't got a mother any more. *(She throws herself on her home-town saints—blooming there for Easter—and groans.)* I've brought them up, I've taken care of them, I've watched over them, these sons of mine... And now must they raise their heads? *(She continues to address the saints, as everyone listens in an atmosphere charged with apprehension; looking at the saints.)* Vincè, open your eyes, open your eyes. "Two eyes have gazed upon you—three want to help you—Saint Anne, Saint Lena, Saint Mary Magdalen..."

VINCENZO: Mama, what are you exorcising for? *(Embarrassed pause)* It's too late... *(Resolutely)* now.

GINETTA *(imploring)* : Vincenzo, let's go. Let's go....

Rosaria turns toward them in great agitation.

ROSARIA *(extremely worked up)* : Why? What's happened?

ROCCO *(trying to restore peace)* : Mama!

ROSARIA *(shouting)* : You brazen things, to bring this shame on me too...

Ginetta is backed against the wall like an animal ready to flee.

VINCENZO: It's my fault.

For the first time, Vincenzo has a fleeting moment of energy. But Rosaria is immovable, hard.

ROSARIA: No. *(Granitic, she speaks slowly.)* I say that when a girl dishonors herself the guilt is all hers and not the man's.

Weeping, Ginetta rushes out. Vincenzo, overcome, looks about him and then races after her.

Service station where Ciro is employed. Highway on the outskirts of Milan. Day.

Ginetta sits on a folding stool not far from the gas pump. Her head is lowered and she is silent and sad. Vincenzo and Ciro are sitting on a bench beside her. Ciro holds the package of colored eggs they have brought from home.

CIRO *(pointing to the highway)* : It's different at night. Just trucks, trucks, trucks, one after the other.

The highway is crowded with passenger vehicles on holiday outings.

VINCENZO *(as if he has not heard)* : Starting tomorrow I'm going to look for another job. The way things are it won't be enough any more just to work by the day.

GINETTA *(shaking her head)* : Great families we have. They let you down just when you need them, and they insist they're in the right anyway.

VINCENZO *(reflecting)* : I'd like to find a steady job, with a paycheck at the end of each month, and a pension. *(To Ciro)* Ginetta and I are going to live by ourselves.

Ciro is still absorbed in his own thoughts, his elbows planted on his knees.

CIRO *(following his own train of thought)* : I wish we could buy a truck some day. *(Shakes his head, reflecting.)* A truck we'd all have a share in, you know. I still don't know how, of course...

VINCENZO: Ciro, with the troubles we've got now...

Ginetta seconds Vincenzo with a gesture.

GINETTA: We have to live day by day.

CIRO: And we want to keep on this way forever? *(A car pulls up to the gas pump and sounds its horn.)* Excuse me, there's a customer.

He gets up but is intercepted by a very young girl, as pretty as all lower-class northern girls are. The girl, Franca, has come from the little office of the service station and runs to the pump to serve the customers.

CIRO: What... are you doing?

Franca nods at him and nonchalantly operates the pump. Ciro sits down again and Vincenzo tries with some effort to be cheerful.

VINCENZO *(to Ciro, benevolently)* : I didn't know you'd taken on an assistant...

His jest barely succeeds in evoking a weak smile from the mournful Ginetta.

GINETTA: Who is she?

CIRO: She's the boss's daughter. *(With conviction)* They're good people, real Milanese...

VINCENZO *(with an older-brotherly tone)* : And she's here all the time?

CIRO *(continuing to minimize)* : No... today. They're here because of the holiday, to keep the father company.

He waves as Franca re-enters the office.

Laundry. Outside. Night.

Rocco pulls down the overhead sliding door of the store. His employer watches from inside. Rocco then runs into the next doorway, from which he reappears a moment later with his bicycle. The girls come out after him, chatting and straightening their clothing and hair. The pressing-machine girl runs toward a boy waiting for her on a motorcycle.

Only now do we realize that we are observing the scene from Simone's vantage point in the doorway of a café located almost directly opposite the laundry. Simone waits for Rocco to leave, then hurries across the street toward the store, only to stop in apparent disappointment before the locked door.

Simone pretends not to see the two girls talking only a few feet from the adjacent entranceway. He begins to hammer on the door.

SIMONE: Rocco!

The two girls notice Simone and approach him, trying to be helpful.

GIANNINA: He just left. Not even five minutes ago. Didn't you see him?

SIMONE: If I'd seen him…

Sound of store door opening inside the sliding door.

VOICE OF LUISA *(from inside the store)*: What's going on?

SIMONE: It's nothing, ma'am, nothing at all. *(Talking against the sliding door)* I'm Rocco's brother. I wanted to leave some stuff for him. But I'll come back tomorrow. *(Turning to the girls)* Could I leave it with the concierge?

GIANNINA: You can leave it right in the store. Go through the courtyard.

Simone rushes to the adjacent doorway. From inside the store, Luisa continues to speak.

VOICE OF LUISA: What is it?

GIANNINA: Nothing, ma'am, nothing. *(Slyly)* He's going through the courtyard now.

Ida looks reprovingly at her friend; then the two girls hurry off arm in arm.

Courtyard. Night.

Simone enters the courtyard and looks around for a moment to get his bearings. He goes over to a little door and knocks discreetly.

SIMONE: May I?

The door is immediately opened by Luisa.

SIMONE: Good evening. Please forgive me.

LUISA: Oh, it's you.

Simone glances rapidly around to be sure no one else is present. Then, he speaks, in an excessively humble tone of voice and avoiding the woman's eyes.

SIMONE: The girls told me it was still open so I thought I could leave this package. I didn't think you were here. *(He looks straight at her, as if he has suddenly taken courage and made a weighty decision.)* But I prefer it this way. Here, and... please forgive me.

Luisa takes the package which Simone hands her. She is very surprised.

LUISA: What is it?

SIMONE: Look.

She hesitates before opening the package, and Simone takes it from her, pulls out a white shirt and shows it to her.

SIMONE *(aggressive)* : It's a shirt that has to be washed. But it's not mine. It's one of those good ones that were lying on that table the other day. I took it and I wore it one day. *(Ironical)* I don't think I did it any harm. You said yourself it would look better on me than on its owner, remember?

As Luisa takes the shirt, Simone grasps her hand. She stares at him in ever-increasing astonishment. Something in Simone's aggressive abasement disorients the woman, who jerks free from his grasp and reacts with a sudden nervous, hysterical explosion.

LUISA: Are you out of your mind? I think you must be out of your mind. *(Shrilly)* Do you think the likes of you has never been seen before? You come in here, you clown around, you ask for special treatment…. *(She waves her hands as she strides up and down the room.)* Oh yes you did. And then you go and take advantage just like a common thief, a mean, sneaky…

SIMONE: I didn't mean to steal.

LUISA: And I'm perfectly free not to believe you. Because a person that would take advantage of the trust of a person that's been kind to them, or you might say even generous… *(To Simone's great consternation, Luisa begins to weep.)* What do I mean, generous! Stupid, stupid. That's the real truth. Because I am stupid. I'm always ready to believe everybody and to help everybody.

Simone judges that this is the right moment to step in. He comes over to the woman with a smile. She attempts, though now with some effort, to keep up her severe tone of voice.

LUISA: It's a never-ending struggle for a woman all alone, you know. To have to be on your guard all the time, against everything and everybody.

Simone draws ever nearer. Now he suddenly takes her by the shoulders, pulls her to him and kisses her.

LUISA *(breaking away)*: What are you doing?

Simone kisses her again. The woman surrenders to his embrace.

Laundry. Inside. Early morning.

The store is not yet open but Rocco is already at work cleaning with exemplary scrupulousness. He is now kneeling down and wiping the floor around the machines. The only light filters in from the courtyard door.

VOICES OF GIRLS: Good morning. Hi.

Rocco looks toward the clock, which reads eight-thirty. He hurries to finish, stands up, and goes to rinse out the rag in a pail of water. One of the girls (Ida) crosses the back room toward the dressing room with her smock over her arm.

IDA *(to Rocco)* : You work too hard! You don't have to wash the floor every morning.

Another girl (Giannina) enters hurriedly; she too heads for the dressing room.

IDA *(annoyed)* : Hey, wait a minute. I'm first.

GIANNINA: Why can't I come in too? *(Irritated)* Some behavior! I'll change right here. Who cares? *(To Rocco)* Shoo, shoo…

She begins to slip off her dress. Rocco turns away in embarrassment and removes the pail.

Suddenly, Luisa is heard shrieking on the second floor. She is making a terrible scene. The two girls and Rocco look toward the stairway leading to her apartment. The third girl, oldest of the employees, now entering the shop from the courtyard, stops as if paralyzed, her eyes fixed on the curtain concealing the stairway.

THIRD GIRL: Holy Mary! What's going on this morning?

Giannina is the first to recover. She pushes Rocco toward the front of the store, unconcerned about his seeing her in her slip.

GIANNINA *(to Rocco)* : Put that stuff away and go unlock the front door. It's eight-thirty. Move! Can't you tell we're in for a storm?

Rocco nods and starts to take the pail out into the courtyard. But before he reaches the door, he is halted by the sudden appearance of Luisa, totally disheveled and still in her bathrobe. The girls are transfixed.

LUISA: My jewels have been stolen. The pin, the one I always wear, my pearls, everything, everything….

The girls gather around her, expressing their regret and asking for the details.

IDA: When did you notice they were gone?

GIANNINA: But you had them yesterday.

THIRD GIRL: But I don't think I saw them yesterday either.

Rocco is still standing there; without answering the girl, Luisa turns to him with a voice trembling with emotion.

LUISA: You understand, Rocco?

Rocco shrugs and nods as if to say he has understood. His reaction exasperates Luisa, who continues to stare at him.

LUISA *(crying)*: I'm going to tell the police. Even if it means a scandal. I don't care. What have I got to lose anyway? The police, I'm going to call the police!

Rocco is consternated. He again nods seriously.

ROCCO: Certainly, ma'am. That's what you should do.

LUISA *(to Rocco)*: Do you have a telephone in your house?

ROCCO *(ever more amazed)*: In our house? And what house? I live at the welfare housing.

Luisa disappears up the stairs. Rocco turns to the girls.

ROCCO *(wonderingly)*: What's she taking it out on me for?

Rosaria's room at the housing for the evicted. Night.

The room is dimly illuminated by the light filtering in from the hall through the frosted-glass pane over the door. Rosaria is sleeping in a cot near the door, in the little room partitioned off by the blanket hung by Ciro. Luca's empty pallet lies beside her cot.

Luca is still awake, curled up at the foot of Rocco's bed on the other side of the blanket. Rocco is lying on his bed in his undershirt and trousers; Vincenzo's and Simone's beds are empty. Ciro, lying on another cot, has been listening attentively to what Rocco has told him.

CIRO: Why should she suspect you?

ROCCO: I don't know. She didn't take her eyes off me all day long.

CIRO: She's crazy.

ROCCO: She is crazy. But finally even the girls noticed it.

CIRO *(scandalized)*: Tomorrow morning we'll go talk to the cops.

They hear a voice calling from the hall, and echoing throughout the length of the vast building.

VOICE OF CUSTODIAN: Parondi! Parondi's wanted in the office.

Rocco jumps up.

ROCCO *(horrified)*: She's reported me. They're coming to arrest me. Ciro!

Ciro motions him to silence so they can hear. They hear Rosaria getting up and opening the door.

VOICE: Vincenzo.

Rocco and Ciro get up and go toward the door, where Rosaria is talking to the custodian.

ROSARIA: Vincenzo's not here. *(To Rocco)* He says they want Vincenzo.

Ciro and Rocco exchange glances.

CIRO: Vincenzo?

ROCCO *(to Rosaria)*: I'll go see.

The brothers exchange glances again.

CIRO: I'll come with you.

ROSARIA: What can they want at this time of night?

CIRO *(to tranquillize her)*: It's not so late, Mama; it's not even ten.

ROSARIA: Will you go?

Rocco nods as he slips his jacket on over his undershirt.

ROCCO *(softly to Ciro)*: You'd better stay here. For Mama. *(To Luca)* You keep quiet, understand?

Luca is standing up on the bed trying to pull his heavy wool shirt down over his legs. He has obviously not understood anything of what is going on, but he does understand that it's something important and this is enough to upset him.

Rocco leaves the room and Rosaria returns to bed.

ROSARIA *(calling sleepily)*: Luca! Come to bed!

Street in front of the building. Night.

Rocco is accompanied to the entrance by the night concierge, who points out a small car parked about fifty yards down the street. Rocco leaves the building and the concierge closes the door.

As he nears the car, Rocco slows down and stoops a bit to see who is inside. Inside the car is Nadia, who is looking into the rear-view mirror and putting on her lipstick. As soon as he recognizes Nadia, Rocco's apprehensions dissolve. He knocks on the car window. Nadia turns and looks at him without recognizing him.

NADIA: But you're not Vincenzo.

ROCCO: No. Vincenzo's not home. But he should be back pretty soon.

As his initial fear vanishes, Rocco is assailed by another, which he immediately tries to dissipate with the information:

ROCCO: Vincenzo's engaged. And now he's...with·his fiancée.

Nadia opens the car door.

NADIA: Lucky him. Get in a minute. *(Rocco is uncertain.)* Come on! Aren't you another one of the Parondi tribe?

ROCCO: Yes. I'm Rocco.

NADIA *(ironical)* : What lovely names you all have! Get in; you'll do just as well.

Rocco gets in, continuing to look at Nadia in great amazement. With an impatient sign, she leans across him to pull the door shut. Rocco shrinks back against the seat with such vehement terror that Nadia bursts out laughing and turns to look at the boy.

NADIA: What are you afraid of? Oh! What beautiful eyes we have! What did you say your name was?

ROCCO: Rocco.

Nadia's moment of amusement seems to have passed, as she clumsily starts the motor.

NADIA *(irritated)* : If I don't get some practice I'll never learn how to drive.

The car jerks forward.

ROCCO *(timidly)* : Where are we going?

His terror again provokes Nadia's laughter.

NADIA *(laughing, and alluding to Simone)* : Where I'm sure I won't run into anybody I don't want to. *(Nadia is a terrible driver and is now forced to keep her eyes straight ahead and both hands clutching the steering wheel.)* Look and see if this is one-way.

ROCCO: Even if it was, I don't know what the symbols mean.

NADIA: It's one-way. Everything is forbidden these days.

With some difficulty Nadia manages to turn the car into a large tree-lined boulevard. She parks in a fairly dark spot. As soon as she has pulled up the emergency brake, she opens her handbag and takes out something which she puts in Rocco's hand.

NADIA: Here. Now listen. I wanted to talk to Vincenzo because I know him already. But as I said, you'll do just as well. You know what that stuff is?

Rocco looks in fascination at the jewelry in his hand. He knows perfectly well where it comes from, but he cannot understand how Nadia has come by it.

NADIA: Your brother Simone says he bought it. But he stole it, sure as there's a God. I don't know from whom, and I don't give a damn either.

Rocco is about to say something but immediately catches himself.

ROCCO: But...

NADIA: I've got enough worries of my own and I don't want to run any risks for stuff like this. Understand?

ROCCO: No.

NADIA *(impassive)*: That's a good start.

ROCCO *(in a strangled voice)*: But why did he do it?

Nadia looks at Rocco in amusement, with a long, ironical gaze.

NADIA *(slowly)*: To go to bed with me, dear. Seems I'm worth it. *(Rocco stares at Nadia with so lost an expression that the girl cannot help laughing.)* What's the matter? Don't you believe me?

Apparently Nadia only now notices that Rocco has no shirt on under his jacket.

NADIA *(putting her hand on Rocco's neck)*: What kind of outfit is that?

Rocco pulls up his jacket collar.

ROCCO: I was in bed.

NADIA *(gaily)* : Sweet boy! Oh what a devil you are! *(Rocco pulls back instinctively; Nadia continues, half-amused, half-irritated)* Take it easy. I'm not going to eat you up. *(Her tone suddenly summary)* Listen, pretty boy. You give that stuff back to your brother and tell him I've left town and not to look for me because he won't find me. Understand? Tell him: Nadia's left town and she says, "So long." *(Rocco stares at Nadia with an attentive and pained expression.)* You know, I could have held on to these knicknacks but... Listen, will you stop looking at me like that? What is there to stare at?

ROCCO: Nothing. You're very... kind. But I can't believe that Simone...

NADIA: Believe it, believe it. And now good night, pretty boy. It was nice of you to say I'm kind. That's already something. *(Softly)* Forgive me if I don't take you back home. So long.

She leans over to open the door for him. Rocco again pulls back as if to avoid contact.

NADIA *(feigning indignation)* : Hey, no! You have to stop being so scared. Here...

As she leans back up and Rocco starts to step out of the car, Nadia takes him by the jacket and kisses him on the mouth. Then she sits up again, laughing, and checks her lipstick in the mirror, as Rocco gets out. She pulls the door too sharply, immediately starts the motor, and drives off.

Rosaria's room at the welfare housing. Night.

Simone and Vincenzo have come home by now, and all but Simone are asleep. He turns apprehensively as he hears the door creak open. To reach his bed Rocco must climb over the one where Simone is lying. Simone gives Rocco a particularly worried look, but Rocco avoids looking at his brother.

Vincenzo awakens too and shakes Ciro.

VINCENZO *(softly, to Ciro)*: He's back. *(Softly, to Rocco)* But they were looking for me, not you, weren't they?

Rocco curls up on his cot, beside Simone's.

ROCCO *(softly)*: For me. I had to go to the store because... they needed the keys to the meters.

CIRO: They needed the keys to the meters?

ROCCO *(innocently)*: Yes.

He takes off his jacket.

CIRO: And what about the theft?

ROCCO: She found the jewelry again. It hadn't been stolen.

CIRO: Then she really is crazy.

ROCCO: That's what I told you. *(Pause)* I quit.

CIRO: You did? But it's a good job.

ROCCO *(lying down)*: No. It wasn't a good job any more.

Simone has been lying still listening to all that has been said, his eyes fixed on Rocco, who feels his gaze and avoids turning toward his brother.

VINCENZO: You could have waited till you found another job.

ROCCO *(softly)*: I have. I just got my draft notice yesterday. With all those goings-on with that crazy woman, forget all about it. I'm going into the service.

He lies still, his hands crossed behind his neck. He feels Simone's eyes still on him. Vincenzo has already curled up and gone back to sleep; Ciro now does the same. There is a moment of silence. Then, without turning, Rocco whispers to Simone.

ROCCO: Simone… *(Simone does not answer but gazes at his brother with an alarmed expression, intended to convey the existence of a defensive explanation.)* I have to tell you something. When I came home from the store I ran into a young lady outside here. The daughter of those people that lived on the sixth floor at Lambrate, remember? She said to tell you she was leaving town and doesn't know when she'll be back.

Simone raises himself on one elbow with an increasingly worried look.

SIMONE: When did you see her? Where?

Rocco curls up to go to sleep, turning his back on Simone.

ROCCO: I just told you.

SIMONE: But where's she going, did she tell you?

ROCCO: No. She didn't tell me.

Simone suspects that Rocco knows much more than he is letting on, but he judges it unwise to question him further. He continues to stare at Rocco in the vain hope of getting an answer. Rocco does not move. Simone lies back down again and unsuccessfully tries to evoke his brother's confidence with a violent and vulgar effort.

SIMONE: How do you know that whore? I wonder what she wants with me? Who knows what ideas she's got in her head? She's as bad as they come. And she plays the great lady, too. But let her go to hell. I haven't got time to waste with dolls like her. If I see her again I'll look away and spit on the ground three times. If you see her again, tell her that.

Rocco seems not to be listening: his eyes are wide open in the dark and he is lost in his own thoughts. Superimposed on the scene appears the word: ROCCO.

APRIL 1957.

Panorama of a provincial city. Outside the army barracks. Day.

Off-duty soldiers are drifting out of the main entrance to the barracks. They pass before the orderly officer and the inspection sergeant, who observe their uniforms attentively, sending some of the men back. Among the soldiers is Rocco, who takes a letter from his pocket as he leaves the building, and reads it slowly as he walks along. Other soldiers pass ahead of him on the sidewalk.

ROSARIA'S VOICE: The reason we couldn't write you before was that we had so much to do, because finally they've given us a house....

Large low-income housing project. Outside. Day.

A large apartment building, new and fairly handsome. It is located on the far outskirts of Milan, and the street in fact wanders off into the meadows behind it. The store windows all along the building sparkle in the sun, and before them passes Rosaria, carrying her shopping basket. Her appearance is smarter and more middle class now, and she stops to look in all the windows with great interest.

ROSARIA'S VOICE: We know everybody in the buiding now because everybody knows Simone won the Genoa bout and they all treat me with a lot of respect....

STOREKEEPER *(standing in his doorway)*: Hello, Mrs. Parondi.

ROSARIA: Hello.

Rosaria continues her inspection of the store windows, walking along somewhat haughtily.

ROSARIA'S VOICE: My son... This was a blessed year except for the misfortune of Vincenzo marrying that girl and going away to live, and you in the service... and Simone can't take a regular job because of his training. But pretty soon the day will come when he'll pay off all his debts to his brothers, with the career he's going to have...

Motor room, Alfa Romeo automobile factory. Day.

A small group of workers is being instructed by a technician. Among them is Ciro, the youngest of the group.

VOICE OF ROSARIA: Ciro quit his job at the Tranversi Garage because he got into Alfa Romeo, now that he has his diploma from night school. At home we have only his salary that we can count on steadily, and with all the expenses... If you have anything left over from your pay send it because you must not spend very much....

Tree-lined boulevard in the provincial city. Day.

As Rocco is absorbed in reading the letter, a passing soldier claps him on the shoulder. He is a jovial Tuscan.

TUSCAN SOLDIER: Coming to the flicks?

ROCCO: I can't.

TUSCAN SOLDIER: Got something better to do?

ROCCO: No, nothing.

He replaces his mother's letter in his pocket.

TUSCAN SOLDIER: So?

ROCCO: I haven't got the money.

Railroad station post office. Inside. Day.

Rocco checks over the postal money order form he has just filled out and counts out the few thousand lire he is sending. Then he steps up to the window and hands form and money to the clerk.

As she takes them and begins to attach the required stamps to the form, Rocco leans on the counter and looks toward the adjacent room, which is the main hall of the railroad station itself. The station is not crowded, and Rocco sees a girl standing before the board listing train departures. She is wearing a tightly belted raincoat and now bends down to pick up her suitcase. Rocco gazes attentively at the girl.

POSTAL CLERK: Here's your receipt.

Rocco swings back to take the receipt and immediately starts out of the post office.

Railroad station hall and café. Inside. Day.

As he leaves the post office, Rocco turns again to look at the girl, who is now heading slowly toward the ticket window. Their eyes meet. Rocco recognizes Nadia; immediately embarrassed, he hurries his step as if pretending not to have seen her. He is almost at the exit when—sure he has not been recognized by Nadia—he turns once more, warily, to look toward the ticket window. The girl is no longer there.

He starts for the exit again, only to find Nadia watching him from the side opposite that toward which he had looked.

NADIA: Ah, I was right. It really is you.

Nadia is very much the worse for wear. She is extremely pallid and her expression is harsh.

NADIA *(unsmiling)* : What are you doing here? They've fixed you up fine!

Rocco gives her an embarrassed military salute.

ROCCO: I'm in the service.

NADIA: I see. How long have you been here?

ROCCO: I've already done almost fourteen months.

NADIA *(laughing ironically)* : What a coincidence. So have I. More or less. And right here in the same town.

Rocco looks at Nadia without understanding.

NADIA: Buy me a coffee? I've got an hour to kill.

Rocco is even more embarrassed.

ROCCO: I... have to go back to the barracks.

NADIA: Well, so long then. *(She seems simply disappointed to have been deprived of a small amusement; nothing more.)* Keep up the good work.

She does not even wait for Rocco to answer before starting slowly off toward the café. After a moment's hesitation, Rocco starts after her.

ROCCO *(timidly, stammering)* : I don't have to go back right away.

NADIA *(beginning to be amused)* : So?

ROCCO *(very simply)* : So I'd be very happy to keep you company. But I can't offer you anything.

Nadia bursts out into gay laughter.

NADIA: I'll pay for you then, silly! Sure! Know what we'll do? We'll rent a carriage and take a nice ride around the town and we'll have our coffee in a less horrible place. My train's at six. We've got an hour. *(Before Rocco has time to answer, Nadia starts for the exit.)* I'd like to have a look at this town, after being here so long....

Piazza with large café. Outside. Day.

Rocco and Nadia are sitting at a table in the café. A soldier passing by recognizes Rocco and turns, looking insistently at him. But Rocco does not even notice him, absorbed as he is in listening to Nadia, who sits with her elbows propped up on the table and her head cocked to one side in a habitual position with makes her hair fall over her forehead.

NADIA: You really didn't understand? Of course. Thirteen months and eight days. *(Sighs)* Because they wouldn't give me a conditional sentence. Because I was a repeater.

*She takes a package of cigarettes from her bag and offers one to Rocco.
He does not accept. Nadia lights hers.*

ROCCO: Was it... very bad?

NADIA *(harshly)* : Yes. *(Rocco lowers his eyes; she recovers.)* No, not
    really. The time goes fast when the days are all alike. You'd
    think it was just the opposite. But that's the way it is. But...
    (Trying to joke) Hey! Wake up!

She looks at Rocco.

ROCCO *(lowering his eyes)* : And now what?

NADIA: Now? Now I'm going back to Milan. The only good thing is that the money we earned on a certain deal... *(Ironical)* hasn't been spent. So I have nothing to worry about for a couple of months. *(Rocco gazes seriously at Nadia, which attracts and embarrasses her.)* What's the matter? You're so upset that someone's been in jail? *(Bitterly)* Look, it happens all the time. *(Laughs)* I'm not the only one in the world. Maybe I'm the only one you've seen.

ROCCO *(immediately, kindly)* : No, no. I've got a friend in my home town, really more than one friend... young men, poorer than you can even imagine. They gave us the mirage of a little land to farm, land that breaks your arms to work it, and you had to walk half a day to get to it. Some of my friends tried to protest but they handcuffed them all and took them to jail in Matera and in Potenza. That's the way things are down where we come from.

Nadia seems not very interested in Rocco's tale but is touched by the passion with which he tries to explain it to her.

NADIA: I know. That's why you all escape to the North.

ROCCO: I wish I'd stayed there, though.

NADIA: You don't like Milan?

ROCCO: Yes, but... It's down there, in our own town, that we should be able to live! We were born and raised there.

NADIA *(a bit ironical)* : I understand....

ROCCO *(smiling in embarrassment)* : I think I don't feel right in the city because I didn't grow up in it. When I say me, I mean my folks, my people. Some people get right into the swing of it and they learn what the others want from you right away.

Not me. Because I think that's not the way it should be. I'd like to want a car, for instance, but not before I'd wanted and had everything that comes first.

NADIA *(laughing tenderly)* : And what comes first?

ROCCO : Work. Being sure you can eat every day. A house. I can't explain very well.

NADIA : Indeed you can't. I hardly understand. But that's all right. *(She taps her spoon against the cup to call the waiter; she looks at Rocco, curious about the boy.)* And what do you think about me?

ROCCO *(defensive)* : What should I think?

NADIA : Oh, I don't know, I'm asking you! Come on. I'm not the kind that feels offended. You can be sincere all the way.

ROCCO *(relieved)* : I thought of one thing when I saw you that time.

The waiter has come over; Nadia pays for the two coffees and the waiter loads the cups on the tray. Rocco is again embarrassed by his presence.

ROCCO : I thought: how old is she?

NADIA *(laughing heartily)* : That's all? Twenty-five. What's that prove?

ROCCO *(simply)* : You asked me what I thought.

NADIA : You're right. If that's all.

ROCCO *(extremely embarrassed)* : Are you offended?

NADIA *(a little irritated)* : About what?

She opens her handbag and looks for something inside. She takes out a comb, but this may not be what she was looking for: hers is a purely nervous gesture. She passes the comb through her hair. She replaces it in the bag. Then she looks at Rocco, feeling his gaze weighing on her.

NADIA *(sharply)* : Why are you looking at me like that?

ROCCO *(softly)*: I'm sorry. *(Lowering his eyes)* I don't know why, I feel so sorry for you.

NADIA *(jeeringly)*: Oh, oh! What a nice compliment!

ROCCO *(immediately, stumbling over his words)*: It's not because of that. I mean because you were in jail. Even the first time I saw you, and then again when you came that time about Simone. I don't know why, I've always had the impression you were unhappy....

NADIA: You're wrong.

ROCCO: Of course. And I don't know you and I can't judge. It's a stupid impression. Maybe because you have an aggressive way of looking at people, but... it's as if you were always afraid.

Rocco is twisting his hands as he speaks. When he raises his eyes again he is silenced by astonishment. Nadia is weeping silently and uncontrollably. Now that she realizes he has seen her, she makes an irritated gesture.

NADIA: Don't pay any attention. I'm just tired. After all, I haven't been very cheerful these past months here. And I don't believe there's anything particularly pleasant waiting for me now either.

Nadia is so nerve-racked that she drops the handkerchief she has started to take out. Rocco bends down to pick it up, and as he offers it to her he squeezes her hand.

ROCCO: Why do you talk like that? Everybody can have the kind of life they want to, if they really want it.

NADIA *(trying to laugh)*: What did you say? You know you're a funny boy. *(Still weeping)* It's better if you keep your mouth shut, much better. You see what happens to me if you talk?

ROCCO *(extremely embarrassed)*: You want me to leave?

NADIA *(drying her eyes and smiling fairly calmly now)*: No. Stupid. Come back to the station with me. But don't talk about me any more. It's a subject I don't like.

Nadia gets up from the table; Rocco follows. She looks intensely at him.

NADIA: If you were in my shoes what would you do?

Rocco is so astonished by the question that Nadia laughs, but she immediately stops as Rocco answers softly, after a pause.

ROCCO: I'd have faith. I wouldn't be afraid and I'd have faith.

NADIA: In what?

ROCCO: I don't know. In everything.

They gaze at each other. Rocco blushes at his own courage and is profoundly disturbed by Nadia's sweet, disarming gaze.

NADIA *(trying to joke)*: Even in yourself?

ROCCO *(softly, still looking at her)*: Yes.

NADIA *(disturbed)*: Will you come see me when you get back to Milan? Maybe you can teach me not to be afraid...

Rocco smiles.

OCTOBER – NOVEMBER 1957.

Church on the outskirts of Milan. Inside. Day.

The four Parondi brothers and Ginetta are gathered round the baptismal font. Ciro is to be the godfather. The lovely traditional custom of these southern folk calls for the child to be carried by its mother along the line of guests, stopping before the intended godfather. In this ceremony it appears almost as if the infant itself chooses its godfather of its own accord.

VOICE: And the child chooses his godfather...

Ciro takes the infant in his arms. The priest begins the ritual. He pronounces the formula of baptism and names the child Antonio.

*Luca stares in fascination and some fright at a fresco in the baptismal'
niche of the recently constructed chruch. Extremely modern, the fresco re-
presents Christ with Saint John the Baptist. Neither of the two can have
much to thank their painter for. Luca pulls Simone's sleeve to show him
the painting. Simone looks too, frowning. He is wearing a flashy checked
jacket.*

The priest has completed the rite.

VINCENZO *(softly, to Ginetta)* : Let's go. It's over.

GINETTA *(softly)* : What are we supposed to do?

VINCENZO *(softly)* : I don't know. Are we supposed to pay?

Ciro gravely hands the screaming infant back to Ginetta.

GINETTA *(softly, to Vincenzo)* : Ask Ciro. He's the godfather.

Simone and Luca start off toward the church door. Vincenzo whispers to Ciro, who makes a reassuring gesture. Then with the air of a paterfamilias, Ciro turns to the priest, thanking and dismissing him. After making the sign of the cross, Ciro turns to join his brothers and sister-in-law as they leave the church.

Rosaria's new home. Inside. Day.

Rosaria is busy rearranging Simone and Ciro's bedroom, into which she now brings another bed, stopping to calculate where to place it. She suddenly stops to listen. Then she rushes to the entrance—upsetting the pail of water for washing the floor—and flings open the door. Rocco is pushing the button that sends the elevator back downstairs (a modest elevator, almost a dumbwaiter, but an elevator nonetheless).

ROSARIA: Rocco! Mama's little Rocco!

Rocco comes to embrace his mother. She passes her hand over his hair and squeezes his arms. Then she starts back into the house.

ROSARIA *(speaking rapidly in her excitement)*: I was just fixing up your bed. Because we just bought it yesterday and they only brought it last night. So between one thing and another... You look wonderful, you know? So wonderful, my son. Look, look, we still don't have much furniture, of course.... *(Pointing)* San Rocco's still there, on the dresser....

The statuette of San Rocco, which we have seen before, contrasts with the modern squalor of the place. And the contrast is heightened by the fact that the figure has been decorated for the occasion with a blanket of braided flowers. Before it is the basket of ex-votos (small crude wax heads, legs, and hands).

ROCCO: You look great too, Mama.

He says it without conviction, as he observes the mother's whitened hair, her lined face, and the indefinable change in her expression. Rocco caresses her head, her face.

ROSARIA: Not so good. I've had such trouble with my teeth. I can't even tell you. *(Looking about)* You like it, don't you?

ROCCO: Isn't anybody home? I was so happy to be coming on Sunday because I thought everybody'd be home. I even wrote you. *(Trying to hide his disappointment)* I was thinking Ciro might even come to the station.

ROSARIA: They'll be back at noon. *(Still looking around, disappointed by Rocco's lack of interest in the house)* Don't you have anything to say about the place? Just look what's in there! Open the door!

Rocco opens the door of the tiny bathroom. He smiles to please his mother.

ROCCO: It's nice.

ROSARIA *(still moving around excitedly)* : Now you tell me where you want the bed. I sleep there with Luca and you three here. Ciro's been so wonderful, you know? *(Rosaria feels obliged to give Rocco some explanation, and now she turns her back to him as if anticipating his reaction.)* They've all gone to Vincenzo's son's baptism.

ROCCO *(surprised)* : And you didn't? *(Rosaria does not answer; Rocco comes up to her.)* Why didn't you go?

ROSARIA: You were coming.

ROCCO *(sensing that she is lying)* : But you could have left a message and I'd have gone too. Where is it? We'll go right away.

ROSARIA: It's too late.

ROCCO: Mama, are you still mad at Vincenzo?

ROSARIA: No. Vincenzo comes to see me often.

ROCCO: And Ginetta?

ROSARIA *(harsh)* : Not Ginetta.

ROCCO: And you haven't gone to see her even now that the baby's been born?

ROSARIA *(resentful)* : What about the Giannellis? You think they see Vincenzo?

OCTOBER – NOVEMBER 1957.

Cecchi's gym. Inside. Evening.

Simone is in the ring working out with a heavyweight. Cecchi, the trainer and the masseur are all standing around the ring. Today's session is particularly important, since it precedes an important bout. Simone is cheerful and continually jokes. Cecchi is less cheerful and observes Simone attentively.

SIMONE *(to Cecchi)* : You still haven't learned that it's best not to touch the gloves on the eve of a fight.

CECCHI: I'm the one that knows what's best for you. All right? Let's go, come on there, lead-legs. *(To the trainer)* That's the way he is: I can't make him understand that tomorrow night he's going in with a man that can give him a very rough time.

SIMONE *(joking)* : But you always say that.

CECCHI: But this time it's true. And he's a lefty too. Look, as far as I can see you can make it only if you're fast. But here you are; you're heavier than an ox. Move! Come on! Move!

The trainer senses reproof for himself in these observations and incitements, and he answers impatiently.

TRAINER: I've worn myself out with this guy. But he doesn't listen and he doesn't understand a thing. He's counting on his roundhouse punch, he says! Roundhouse punch! But instead of hitting the other guy he may be punching the air! And then what?

SIMONE *(irritated in turn)* : I suppose it's my fault I'm not trained right! There isn't even a lefty in sight here! *(Half-joking and half-ironical, Simone points to his brother Rocco, who is exercising at the punching bag.)* I'll find one for myself. He fights lefty too if he wants to. Rocco, come here a minute. Come on!

Cecchi and the trainer gesture as if to say, "You know what you can do with this one." Rocco obediently climbs into the ring. The heavyweight who has been sparring with Simone looks to Cecchi for instructions.

CECCHI *(turning his back in irritation)* : Now you want to fool around, eh? Go on, go on, do whatever you want. I'll tell you what I think the day after tomorrow.

Rocco, urged on by Simone, puts up his guard.

SIMONE: Fight lefty! Let's see what you learned in the army.

The heavyweight has left the ring and takes off his padded helmet and belt. The trainer starts to join Cecchi, who has ostentatiously left the ringside. Suddenly the trainer stops in surprise. Then, walking more slowly, and with his eyes still fixed on the ring, he catches up with the gym manager.

CECCHI: What is it?

In response to the trainer's glance, Cecchi too looks toward the ring. Simone is unable to land a single blow as Rocco fends him off with exceptional skill and intelligence.

SIMONE *(stopping and laughing)* : Oh! You really have made progress! Who was your corporal?

Simone tries two more punches and misses both. He turns to look toward Cecchi and catches the two men looking with great interest at Rocco. Simone lands a punch. Then he immediately goes over to the ropes and slips off his gloves.

SIMONE: Will you let me do what I want to? *(In a singsong)* The day before a fight you have to let me alone. I'm nervous, understand?

Simone jumps down from the ring. Rocco is distressed by his brother's nervousness and evidently realizes too just how mediocre Simone's state of preparation is. He, too, starts to leave the ring. Cecchi signals to the heavyweight to go back into the ring.

CECCHI *(to Rocco)* : Let's have a look. *(Rocco starts to protest; Cecchi speaks in a authoritarian tone.)* Let's see you a minute.

The sparring partner begins to fight. Rocco defends himself without enthusiasm, still trying to get out of it. But his instinct immediately takes command and Rocco begins to put his heart into it.

CECCHI *(calling)*: Simone, come here. Listen to what I'm telling you. If you don't watch out this guy will run you right out of here!

Simone has come to the locker-room door and barely glances at Rocco.

SIMONE *(to Cecchi, irritated)*: Wait till tomorrow before you talk.

CECCHI *(irritated too)*: Agreed. I'll wait till tomorrow. But if things go as I think they will...

Rocco realizes that he has involuntarily provoked the quarrel between Simone and Cecchi and stops boxing. Cecchi comes up to the ring and leans casually on the ropes, preventing Rocco from leaving the ring.

CECCHI: You've made progress.

ROCCO: We did some boxing in the barracks and since they said I was doing all right, they put me in a couple of army fights. Small-time stuff, of course.

CECCHI: And how did you do?

ROCCO *(simply)*: Well, I tied twice. I won one on points.

CECCHI: Oh?

ROCCO: But I certainly don't mean to go on, you know.

CECCHI: Why not? You don't like it?

ROCCO *(emphatically, shaking his head)*: No.

He smiles timidly and again starts to climb out of the ring. Simone passes from the shower to the locker room.

SIMONE: I'm going because I'm in a hurry.

CECCHI *(to Simone)*: The massage.

SIMONE *(with exaggerated patience)*: All right, all right! Massage.

Cecchi sighs. Then he turns back to Rocco and tries to detain him.

CECCHI: You were saying…

ROCCO *(astonished)*: Nothing.

Locker room, Cecchi's gym. Evening.

Simone is lying down being massaged. He is in a bad mood because of the quarrel with Cecchi and complains and grumbles as he urges the masseur to hurry.

Now Rocco goes past them on his way to the shower. Simone watches him under the shower.

SIMONE *(raising his voice so that Rocco can hear him)*: Hey, Rocco, listen to me. Don't let that Cecchi seduce you. He gave me the same line, like he does to everybody….

Rocco leaves the shower and again goes past Simone's cot as he dries himself.

ROCCO *(distracted)*: Come on, he likes you….

SIMONE *(turning over on his stomach)* : He's a bastard, that's what he is.

Rocco, engrossed in dressing and in combing his wet hair with great care, seems not to have heard. Then he suddenly turns, aware that Simone has been watching him.

SIMONE *(laughing)* : Going wenching?

Rocco smiles at him as he puts on his jacket.

ROCCO: Why? Anything wrong with that?

SIMONE *(after a brief, perplexed pause)*: Nooo... I should say not! *(Mockingly)* But do you know how?

Rocco laughs and starts to whistle a popular tune. He is about to go out when Simone calls him back.

SIMONE: Come here. Tell me.

Still whistling, Rocco shakes his head.

SIMONE *(commenting ironically to the masseur)* : How cheery he is. *(Calling to his brother)* Rocco, be careful! Women are dangerous.

But Rocco does not even turn. Simone jumps off the cot and catches him by the shoulders. Rocco turns and his eyes betray some slight apprehension, which disappears immediately at Simone's question.

SIMONE: Have you got a cigarette?

ROCCO: You know I don't smoke.

SIMONE: You might have changed. Everything about you's changed.

ROCCO: And don't you smoke either.

SIMONE: I do what I want to. With your permission... *(Simone goes back to lie down on the cot again; to the masseur.)* Hurry up.

Rocco has left. Simone remains absorbed in his own thoughts for a moment, until the masseur's voice recalls him.

MASSEUR: He's in love, eh?

SIMONE *(a little worried)*: No. He's got a girl back home....

JANUARY 1958.

Outside Cecchi's gym. Evening.

Rocco leaves the gym and immediately starts to run across the street, skill-fully dodging the cars and buses. He reaches the next bus stop, where Nadia is awaiting him. She has changed completely: now she is all sim-plicity, smiling, even a little apprehensive toward Rocco.

ROCCO *(panting)*: I'm sorry... I'm a little late.

Nadia offers him her cheek to kiss. Rocco squeezes his arm around her waist. The bus pulls up and the couple gets on.

Back platform of the bus. Night.

Nadia and Rocco are standing on the back platform as the bus heads toward the outskirts of town. Their words are inaudible but they are plainly in love. They smile. The wind whips through the girl's hair....

Café. Night.

Several young men are sitting around a card table in the back room of the café with which we are already familiar. Three or four are playing cards; others are seated at the corners of the table or standing behind the chairs. One of the players is Simone. Ivo stands behind the player facing Simone.

A vulgar-looking girl stands at the arch dividing the two rooms. She seems impatient.

GIRL *(whining)*: Ruggero! Let's go.

One of the men sitting beside the players answers with a patient sigh.

RUGGERO: I'm coming. *(To the men)* Well?

SIMONE: Well, I can't. I have to fight tomorrow.

RUGGERO: I told you.

One of the players lays down his cards angrily.

PLAYER *(violently)* : When the time comes everybody here has some excuse. But when it's time to divide up the take, everybody's there....

RUGGERO: In my case, if you don't mind... even if I don't come I'm the one that's lined up the deal.

PLAYER *(still angry, to the girl)* : Listen, Marcella! Can't you go wait outside? *(To Ruggero)* Sorry, but here we really have to change our way of doing things. *(Calming down somewhat and indicating Simone)* I mean him most of all. If he's there when we divide up he has to be there first, too.

Simone looks at Ivo, vainly seeking solidarity. Ivo lowers his eyes.

SIMONE *(instantly getting angry)* : When have I ever skipped out?

RUGGERO: Well, Simone! Let's not go into that.

SIMONE *(defensively)* : We need ten of us to go take a tiny little car. Not even if we had to pick it up and carry it...!

PLAYER: Don't worry about that! You coming or not?

Simone is defeated. He pours another glass of brandy.

SIMONE: No. Not tonight.

IVO: Pray God you win, because you'll be in pretty bad shape if you don't.

FEBRUARY 1958.

Principe arena. Inside. Night.

His opponent's insistent attack has clearly overcome Simone. He tries to cover himself from the shower of blows, but he is breathing hard and is obviously on his last legs. Nor can he summon up his willpower: there is a certain passivity in his behavior.

The overflow audience is in a state of extreme excitement: all are shouting, urging, protesting.

SHOUTS: Come on, Simone! Give it to him! Come on, Simone, hang on!

Cecchi, Rocco, and Vincenzo, huddled together at the corner, just outside the ring, seem dumbstruck by what they are witnessing.

VINCENZO: What's happening to him?

CECCHI *(enraged)*: He's a damned son of a whore....

Ciro and Luca, in the first row, are suffering the torments of hell.

LUCA *(softly, imploring)*: Come on, Simone, come on... Oh, dear Jesus, help him.

Beside him, two members of the audience comment loudly.

FIRST MAN: He looked like he was headed for the top. He's got the body, he's got the fist.... He's bad....

SECOND MAN: Come off it. I always said he didn't have the stuff.

Simone, forced against the ropes in one corner, takes another flurry of punches. His head is fearfully battered. He pulls himself up with an effort. He begins to wave his arms around wildly, but his opponent parries the attack and is ready to pass to the offensive again. Simone slowly sinks to his knees. The referee immediately goes to him and begins the count.

REFEREE: One... two... and three... four...

Simone gets up with an effort and goes toward his corner.

SIMONE *(whispering)*: I can't go on.... I give up.

TRAINER *(lying)*: Don't lose your nerve, stupid. He's tireder than you are. Tire him, tire him out with your right. Keep to the center and...

Another bell signals the beginning of the next round. But Simone does not want to go out.

SIMONE *(desperate)* : Throw in the sponge. I can't go on....

TRAINER *(in a last attempt to persuade him)* : Are you crazy? I tell you he's... Grit your teeth....

Cecchi, Vincenzo, and Rocco are all close to Simone's corner. The trainer questions them with a glance. Simone turns toward them with the exasperated fury of a wounded and terrified beast.

SIMONE *(with a violently furious shout)* : Throw in the sponge, I tell you....

A stream of blood flows from his lips. Cecchi shrugs.

TRAINER *(at the acme of scorn)* : All right.

He throws the towel into the center of the ring, as the arena explodes with screams of protest, boos, and insults directed at Simone.

VOICES : Clown! Yellow! Fake!

Luca and Ciro try to catch his eye but Simone ignores them. Luca's eyes are filled with tears. He murmurs to himself, imploringly.

LUCA : Simone!

Locker room, Principe arena. Night.

Confusion reigns in the locker room. The admirers of the victors come to congratulate them; the medical aides administer to the wounded. A terrified Luca cringes in one corner. Ciro comes up to him and puts his hand on his shoulder.

CIRO : Come on home; Rocco and Vincenzo are staying.

Luca follows Ciro somewhat unwillingly, and turns to look back toward the room where Simone is lying on a cot. A medical aide is making him rinse out his mouth. Ivo affectionately attends his friend. Vincenzo goes back and forth between Simone's cot and a group gathered around Cecchi, who is overcome by rage.

CECCHI *(softly but furiously)*: And since he hasn't got a thing inside him, he'll always be a failure. He's got no heart, he's got no dignity, no passion. You need to be serious in this business.

FRIEND OF CECCHI: Calm down. He's been taught a lesson and you'll see, it'll do him good.

ROCCO: Simone's not the same as he used to be. I realized it as soon as I came back.

CECCHI: Don't you defend him; you know what the story is better than I do.

Rocco stops in embarrassment. Looking at him, Cecchi seems to calm down a bit. He puts his hand on the boy's shoulder.

CECCHI: Now you see you can't tell me no any more. You have a debt of conscience, after all the disappointment your brother's given us.

Vincenzo looks questioningly at his brother. Ivo is at the door of the room where Simone is lying; he turns now to go back to his friend.

Simone has pulled himself up to a sitting position and is looking in a hand mirror at his smashed eye and swollen cheek.

SIMONE *(to Ivo, hoarsely)* : What are they saying?

IVO: Nothing. *(Simone gets slowly off the cot and begins to take off his robe.)* Cecchi blew up, but he's calmed down now. He was saying he wants your brother. Is it true he's so good?

SIMONE: Rocco? *(Ivo takes Simone's clothes from the hook and hands them to him; Simone speaks gloomily.)* How should I know?

Simone puts on his shirt. Ivo is now sitting on the cot.

IVO: He'll have to calm down now too. With women, I mean.

SIMONE *(laughing heartily)*: Rocco'll be world champ at that.

IVO: Eh? With that bloodsucker that once almost ruined you? *(Simone turns to look uncomprehendingly at Ivo.)* Don't tell me you don't know. Everybody knows the great love story. They go around everywhere together. *(Simone still does not understand.)* With Nadia. Oh, come on, Simone... What d'you mean, you didn't know?

SIMONE *(frowning)*: No.

IVO: Well, that's that. She's supposed to be really in love with him. You know who told me? Remember Alberto? Well! He always used to go with Nadia. Well, he says she didn't want to see him any more. Not him or anybody else. She goes to secretarial school. A little saint she's turned out to be.

Rocco is entering the little room with Vincenzo, and Simone motions Ivo to silence. He stares at his brother as if seeing him for the first time.

FEBRUARY 1958.

Café. Inside. Evening.

The customary bar of Simone and his friends. Simone, Ivo, and two other young men are standing at the bar. The card player slaps Simone on the shoulder.

PLAYER: If you'd come with us instead of getting your head bashed in, you'd have been better off.

IVO *(warningly)*: Let him alone!

PLAYER *(snickering, vulgar)*: Why?! Didn't he get licked? They say the noise sounded like a bunch of firecrackers going off.

ANOTHER YOUNG MAN *(indicating Simone)*: Forget it.

The card player whispers to Ivo with a malign air that tries to pass for innocence.

PLAYER *(softly)*: Why? He really did so badly by us?

IVO: What d'you think? He enjoyed it? And then Cecchi threw him off the team, too. And he took his brother on as an added insult.

PLAYER: Whose brother?

Until now Simone has feigned not hearing. But now he turns darkly and angrily.

SIMONE: Idiots.

The player is sincerely astonished this time. But he immediately gets red with anger and is about to throw himself on Simone.

PLAYER: Oh! What d'you mean by that?

ANOTHER: We told you. Forget it!

The charged atmosphere is now interrupted by the entrance of a seventeen-year-old boy, who approaches the group shivering with the cold and clutching his leather jacket tightly around him.

BOY: Who pays for this bet?

IVO: Stupid. Whoever loses.

BOY: Well, they'll pay for a coffee for me too, with some brandy for the cold.

YOUNG MAN: Well?

BOY *(watching Simone)*: Well, I followed him. And when I left him he was walking around the fields with a little brunette. Toward the underpass.

SIMONE: So what? Maybe it isn't her.

IVO *(laughing)*: You're sure stubborn!

SIMONE *(to Ivo, after a very short pause)* : Then let's go. *(He turns to the boy, who is now drinking his coffee.)* Where're Camisasca and Rigutini?

BOY: They're still tailing him... near Figone. On the Roserio road.

Simone strides out of the café, followed by Ivo.

Outside the café. Night.

As soon as they are outside the bar, Ivo pulls his coat tight about him.

IVO: It's as cold as hell. Must not be much fun wandering around the fields in this fog.

A small car pulls up with its headlights dimmed and stops a few feet from Simone. Camisasca gets out; Rigutini remains at the wheel.

SIMONE: Well?

CAMISASCA: They're there. We have to hurry. Get in. We'll take you.

SIMONE: All right. I'm coming. But if it turns out not to be them you're in for it.

CAMISASCA: Get in... come on.

Simone, Ivo, and Camisasca get into the car, which starts off immediately and is lost in the fog.

Open land with buildings under construction, on the outskirts of Milan. Night.

After only a few hundred yards, the car slows down and stops. The doors open and Simone and the other three men get out and head for a low escarpment overlooking the fields and gardens. The massive shape of the overpass looms up out of the dark; a very few cars pass over it, their headlights boring through the fog. Rigutini, who has been leading the way, stops suddenly on the edge of the escarpment.

RIGUTINI: Down there in the field, near the hedge... They just got here.

SIMONE *(to the others)*: You go around that way... behind the underpass. I'm going down here. Wait for my signal.

IVO: You're going alone?

SIMONE: Yes.

Camisasca and Rigutini crouch down and start to circle from the right. Simone lets himself slip down the escarpment in the dark. The night is alternately lit by the moon and obscured by passing clouds.

Simone is followed by Ivo. He suddenly seems to hear a rustling sound. He falls to the ground and motions to Ivo to do the same. He lies still a moment, waiting for the sound to be repeated. Then, reassured by the absolute silence (except for the distant roar of the vehicles crossing the bridge), Simone gets up again and goes on, stepping over one of the low hedges separating the vegetable gardens.

He reaches the darker mass of a fairly high hedge. Still crouching, Simone tries to separate the branches silently in order to see beyond the hedge. As he does so, he hears a low, indistinct sound of voices and at the same time the rustle of leaves and bushes. Simone stops to listen intently. Though he leans forward, Simone cannot hear Rocco's and Nadia's words. But their behavior hits him like a whip. He shifts position slightly and can now get his head through a small opening in the hedge. He sees Nadia and Rocco sitting on the ground on her raincoat; Rocco is caressing her hair, her forehead, and her eyes with his lips. Simone's eyes are feverish. As he moves to get a better look, the branches rustle. Rocco lifts his head to listen.

ROCCO: What's that?

NADIA: Nothing. Must be a cat... What else?

Simone leaps out of the hedge and finds himself almost on top of them.

Rocco has turned completely and gotten halfway to his feet. But Simone stops him and shouts peremptorily (though not very loudly).

SIMONE: Don't move!

Still lying on the ground, Nadia gazes at him in terror. Rocco again starts to get up but Simone orders him again.

SIMONE: I said don't move!

ROCCO: What is it? What's the matter with you?

Simone's expression does not escape them. He comes a step closer.

ROCCO: I can certainly go with whoever I want to....

Nadia, too, gets up. She stares at the two brothers, not yet comprehending what is happening or what she herself should do. Simone looks at Rocco and answers him.

SIMONE: With whoever you want to, yes, but not with her that was my girl. I don't like being cuckolded by you. Understand?

Rocco looks at Simone in amazement and tries to smile.

ROCCO: But if it's almost... two years since you were seeing her...

Simone's answer is to put two fingers in his mouth and emit an ear-splitting whistle. The forms of Camisasca, Rigutini, and Ivo emerge from the darkness at a run. Rocco is ever more stupefied. Nadia watches the three new arrivals suspiciously.

SIMONE: To start with, ask me to forgive you.

ROCCO: Why?

Simone does not even let him continue but slaps his face. Taken by surprise, Rocco staggers back. He is unable either to hit back or to defend himself. Nadia is immediately at his side and catches him.

SIMONE: Thataboy! Let women hold you up!

NADIA: Simone, what do you want? *(Looking at the others, who are awaiting orders)* What do you all want?

SIMONE *(to Rocco)*: Come on, ask me to forgive you. *(Rocco is paralyzed; he continues to stare at Simone, who insists, exasperated.)* I said ask me to forgive you.

But Nadia intervenes.

NADIA *(shouting)* : Stop it! *(She takes Rocco by the arm and tries to drag him away.)* Let's get out of here, don't you see he's drunk?

But Rocco remains anchored to the ground.

NADIA: What are you doing, Simone?

SIMONE: What I want to... Me! Me cuckolded by him?... Look here, you want to see what your Nadia's like? *(His voice is bitter; he grabs the girl and pulls her to him.)* You want to see how to screw your woman?

Nadia struggles but Simone does not loosen his grip.

NADIA *(screaming)*: Simone!

Rocco follows the scene with horror-stricken eyes, incapable of stirring or intervening. Simone continues wildly.

SIMONE: Why? Didn't I screw her before you? So? Look at him, Nadia, your lover. Don't you see he doesn't give a damn for you or anybody else? He might come over here and give you a hand. He might jump on me, try to strangle me. What did our mother make you out of?

Simone forces Nadia to the ground, then falls on her and immobilizes her legs with his own, searching for her underpants with his hands. He turns to glare at his brother as he overcomes her last resistance and pulls them off. Then he flings them in Rocco's face.

SIMONE: Here, take them and kiss them if you have the guts to. You only know how to make love to these things anyway.

Rocco hurls himself on Simone, grabs his shoulders, tears him from Nadia, and pulls him to his feet. Simone is caught unprepared; he hesitates a moment. Rocco stares at him. But Camisasca, Ivo, and Rigutini fall upon Rocco from behind and immobilize him.

SIMONE *(shouting to the three men)*: Hold 'im tight, let 'im get a good look... so he'll remember.

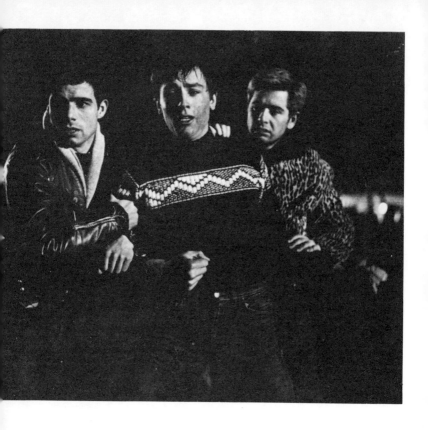

He turns to look for Nadia, who has managed to get a few steps away. She is about to cross the hedge when Simone reaches her and clutches her about her waist.

SIMONE *(to Nadia)*: Where're you going? Here, you have to stay right here, right in front of him so he'll see who you are and what you are.

He forces her to the ground again and immediately falls on her. Two of the men hold back Rocco. He hears Nadia's lament and Simone's panting. His face is transfigured with horror and almost surrealistic pain.

Then there is total, dense, dramatic silence. The two men loosen their grip, leaving Rocco inert. Nadia is lying with her face hidden in the grass, her clothing disheveled. Simone has gotten to his feet; he brushes the dirt and grass from his clothes. He looks at Rocco, whose face is flooded with tears.

SIMONE: And the rest at home, just you and me.

But Rocco's silence alarms him. Ivo and the other two men step a few paces away, commently softly among themselves. Simone lifts up his brother's chin to force him to look him in the eyes.

SIMONE: Learned your lesson now?

ROCCO *(whispering)* : You make me puke.

SIMONE: Say that again.

ROCCO *(slowly)* : You make me puke.

Simone punches him in the face. Rocco takes it but falls to his knees.

ROCCO *(softly)* : You're my brother.

SIMONE: Couldn't think of that before, could you? Now you're scared, you remember I'm your brother?

ROCCO: I'm not scared.

SIMONE: Then come on, show me you're not yellow.

He kicks him to the ground. Then he leaps on Rocco and hammers him with his fists. Rocco reacts; he succeeds in getting to his feet. They glare at each other, holding their breaths. Then they hurl themselves on each other. It is a savage, beastly battle.

A stream of blood flows from Rocco's eyebrow as he takes his bloodied hand from his face. Ivo now prudently tries to intervene and separate the brothers.

IVO: That's enough!... Simone...

But Simone is now uncontrollable and does not even hear his friend. Nadia is heard shouting. She has managed to get away unseen and is calling for help in the distance. Ivo and the other two are terror-stricken.

IVO: Somebody might come. Are you crazy?

RIGUTINI: I'm cutting out. If he's trying to get into trouble, why do I have to be involved too?

Rigutini, Camisasca, and Ivo slip away into the fog. Rocco and Simone continue to battle in the now deserted field. Mighty and impassioned, they begin to tire but continue to fight proudly on to the bitter end. Now and then they slow down momentarily, glaring at each other like beasts. Rigutini's car passes nearby. Simone knocks Rocco to the ground, then runs toward the car, which races away after he gets in.

Vincenzo and Ginetta's apartment. Night.

The doorbell rings desperately in Vincenzo's apartment. Ginetta is the first to hear it. She sits up in bed and looks over at the still-sleeping Vincenzo, wondering who it can be at this hour. Little Antonio, sleeping between his parents, begins to whimper and Ginetta picks him up as she runs to the door.

She opens the door without unhooking the safety chain. Through the crack she sees Rocco leaning against the wall, his clothes muddied, his hair disheveled, and his face bloodied. Ginetta is horrified. She flings open the door.

GINETTA: Holy God in heaven! Rocco?

ROCCO: Let me in.

Ginetta immediately releases the chain and lets him in. Vincenzo appears, even more stupefied and horror-struck than his wife, and hurries to prevent his brother from falling.

VINCENZO: What's happened?

Rocco speaks with effort.

ROCCO: Vincè, let me stay here tonight. I'll explain later. If you can, tell them at home so they don't worry about me.

He is barely able to get out the last few words before falling forward in a dead faint.

GINETTA *(shrieking)* : Holy Mother of God!

She is trembling violently. Vincenzo tries to pick Rocco up but cannot manage it alone.

GINETTA *(weeping in horror)* : Holy Virgin...

VINCENZO : Keep calm. Get me some cold water.

But Ginetta is too distraught to move. Vincenzo gets up and goes to the kitchen sink himself. He returns and bends over his brother again. He gazes at Rocco's lips anxiously as they begin to move.

VINCENZO *(softly)* : Rocco, Rocco...

Rocco opens his eyes but only to stare straight ahead: a vitreous stare which seems not to see. Vincenzo awkwardly passes his hand before his brother's eyes. Then he turns to Ginetta, who is still trembling as she leans against the wall with the baby in her arms.

VINCENZO : Put the baby down and help me get him on the bed.

FEBRUARY 1958.

Piazza behind the cathedral. Day.

The air is cold but clear; the skies are serene. It is noontime and the streets and sidewalks are crowded with people leaving the offices and stores of downtown Milan. Just behind the apse of the cathedral, Rocco and Nadia have met and are now gazing at each other in some embarrassment, searching for the right words.

NADIA *(very timidly)* : Did I... make you wait?

ROCCO *(very timidly)* : No. I just got here a couple of minutes ago.

An embarrassed silence. Nadia lowers her eyes. She twists her hands together.

NADIA: Thank you for coming.

Rocco avoids looking at Nadia.

ROCCO: Why did you want us to see each other again?

NADIA *(whispering)*: Because. Because I... we...

ROCCO *(still not looking at her)* : We can't see each other any more, Nadia.

NADIA : What... are you saying?

Rocco gets up his courage and looks at Nadia. She has begun to cry without even attempting to control herself. Passers-by turn to stare curiously.

ROCCO *(almost soundlessly)* : Don't, Nadia....

Nadia attempts to control herself.

NADIA : It'll pass now....

She turns to look around. She walks back until she reaches the entrance to the stairway and elevator to the top of the cathedral.

NADIA *(still weeping)* : It'll pass now....

She stamps her foot in rage at her own impotence before these suffocating tears. A number of people turn to stare. Nadia takes Rocco's arm.

NADIA : Let's go up. There won't be anybody up there to stare at me.

Cathedral roof. Day.

Nadia leans against the balustrade with her face buried in her hands, bent over as if battling to overcome a physical pain; she is still weeping. Rocco stands near her and watches her in silence. She suddenly raises her devastated face and almost assails Rocco.

NADIA : Why shouldn't we still see each other? Instead of killing your brother, you want to kill me? What have I done to you? *(Rocco looks at Nadia without answering.)* I waited all this time for you to show up. I looked everywhere for you.... *(She is about to weep again.)* And now... you tell me we can't see each other any more. *(Raising her voice)* Say something, by God, are you out of your mind? What's happened?

*Some students draw near, joking and elbowing each other as if to say,
"Let's let them alone." They go off. Then Rocco squeezes Nadia's hands
in his own and begins to speak, still without looking at her.*

ROCCO *(with sad irony)* : Why didn't you tell me what there had
been between you and my brother?

NADIA *(astonished and defensive)* : What should I have told you?
You know everything perfectly well. With Simone there
was what there was with everybody else. I haven't hidden
anything from you. *(Suspicious)* You knew everything.
Don't lie. I told you everything.

Rocco shakes his head.

ROCCO *(his voice weary)* : I didn't know Simone was so in love with
you. I knew something had happened to change him. But
I didn't know that something was you.

NADIA *(sincere)* : It's not true.

ROCCO *(not listening)*: Just a person who's been driven to desperation could do what Simone did the other night.

NADIA *(aggressive)* : Just a cowardly vulgar bully like him.

Rocco looks into Nadia's eyes for the first time.

ROCCO: I'm... still a simple person, born and raised in the South.
For me a person who betrays his own brother, takes away
his woman...

NADIA *(with cold determination)*: If you keep on that way I'll throw
myself over the edge. *(Almost hysterical)* I'll kill myself,
understand? *(She does not raise her voice, but her words are intense in the extreme; softly.)* You came to look for me. You
persuaded me my life was all wrong. You taught me to love
you. And now, all of a sudden, on account of the stupid
crime of a poor bastard who wanted to mortify you because
he's scum, because he's jealous of you, of everybody...
on account of the brave deeds of this devil, all of a sudden

none of it's true any more. What used to be holy, and just, is guilty now.

A group of tourists looks out over the balustrade. The guide points out the landmarks. Nadia tries to control herself. She breathes with difficulty.

NADIA: I don't feel guilty.

ROCCO: We are guilty, Nadia. Me more than you. *(He passes his hand over his eyes; he stops and turns slowly toward Nadia, and speaks with a lifeless voice.)* You have to go back to Simone.

NADIA *(almost jumping in her astonishment)*: What?

ROCCO *(his voice still lifeless)*: Simone has only you. He needs you or he'll be lost. You're his woman.

The tourists have gone off. Nadia tries to control herself. She even makes an effort to smile, and some of her former vulgarity reappears.

NADIA: Listen, my pretty boy. Let's say your brother needs me. But doesn't it occur to you that I count for something too? So then what? How do we solve that one?

Rocco pulls his raincoat closer around him, as if to ward off the cold.

ROCCO: I believe you love Simone too.

NADIA *(stupefied)*: But you're crazy; you're out of your mind!

ROCCO: You wanted to start another life with me. We didn't think that we were hurting other people.

NADIA *(indignant)*: If I wanted to hear a sermon I'd go to church. *(Breathless)* Rocco, listen Rocco... *(Pulling him by the sleeve)* Listen to me, Rocco. I love you. *(Beginning to weep)* What can I do? Rocco... why do you torture me this way?

ROCCO: I can't make you go back to Simone. But I ask you, I beg you to go back to him....

*The three students are crossing the roof again. Nadia starts to say some-
thing, then breaks abruptly away from him.*

NADIA *(shouting)* : You'll regret it, you know. Oh, how you'll
regret it. And it'll be too late. I hate you, I hate you, oh
God how I hate you....

*She races away as the three students stare after her, moved for a moment
by her violence and emotion. Then, as if making an effort to show off their
cleverness and irony to each other, they elbow one another. Nadia pushes one
of the young tourists aside as she makes her way into the elevator which
some of the group have already entered.*

Nadia's bedroom. Evening.

*Nadia is seated before the dressing table, studying her face in the mirror
and trying to read her own eyes. But she evidently cannot see anything but
the external signs of exhaustion and of precocious aging. Slowly, almost
in boredom, she takes a cosmetic pencil from the top of the table and begins
to outline the corner of one eye. Then she angrily turns on the dressing-
table light and begins to make up her face with energetic determination.*

Clandestine gambling joint. Inside. Night.

*Cigarette smoke has rendered the air turbid and suffocating in the small
room where a "chemin de fer" table is operating. The virtually complete
silence is broken only by the monotonous hoarse voice of the croupier.*

*Simone is among the players, all of whom wear a tense, strained expression.
Simone's eyes are exhausted and feverish as he watches the cards being
drawn from the shoe. He plays his last thousand lire and loses. He swears
softly and looks around. After a moment's hesitation he makes up his
mind, unbuckles his wristwatch, and hands it to a man sitting not far off,
apparently following the game with only slight interest. Without a word,
the man weighs the watch in his hand and estimates it.*

PAWNBROKER *(softly)*: Twenty and four...

SIMONE: And three...

The pawnbroker gestures to indicate his acceptance of 3 per cent interest and hands Simone two ten-thousand-lire bills, which Simone immediately transforms into chips.

A feminine laugh is heard from the adjoining room, which is separated off by a heavy velvet curtain. Simone barely turns his head; another man at the table calls for quiet. The pawnbroker (who is presumably also the owner of the apartment) gets up to silence the offender. As he passes into the adjoining room, we see Nadia seated on a couch between two men. She is dressed flashily; there is a bottle of brandy at her feet. She is laughing convulsively and does not seem to notice the pawnbroker.

NADIA *(continuing her story)*: And I just stood there like a fool... up there with all the saints and the madonnas, weeping and wailing... I was so hung up on that guy, let me tell you...

Her laughter becomes almost hysterically shrill. One of the two men slaps her on the thigh.

MAN: Poor Nadia. You'll get over it. Everything has an end....

Simone has appeared in the doorway, exhausted and distraught. Nadia looks as if a wasp has just stung her. She straightens up and turns toward Simone.

NADIA: You can ask him; he should know. Hey you, isn't it true?

SIMONE *(gloomy)*: True what?

NADIA *(with a forced laugh)*: That you have a brother who's... *(Gestures)* not all there?

SIMONE *(nervous)*: What are you talking about? That night again?

Nadia has suddenly stood up. She faces Simone.

NADIA: No. I'm talking about afterwards. What your little brother did. You know what he did?

SIMONE: No. And I'm not interested.

Nadia seems not to have heard his answer. She is again overcome by the convulsive laughter, which greatly resembles a sob. Evidently she is also drunk. Simone squeezes her arm to attract her attention.

SIMONE: Hey! What's the matter with you? You want me to take you away from here?

NADIA: Sure… away! And you and me together! That's just what he wants…. You didn't know that?

SIMONE: I don't know what you're talking about. *(With a slightly sinister smile)* But if that's what you want I'm ready….

NADIA: Ah! You're ready? I'm sure you are… clever guy! *(She looks suspiciously at him.)* You two aren't in cahoots, by any chance? *(Talking somewhat haphazardly now)* Right! Because we've hurt you so much, poor boy! We've ruined you… ruined you!

Simone does not understand. He approaches the girl again, but she interprets his gesture in her own way and breaks violently away from him.

NADIA: Get out of here! Over my dead body! If you come any closer I'll spit in your face.

The pawnbroker intervenes once again.

PAWNBROKER *(to Simone)*: Get her out of here. I don't want any trouble here, understand? And I don't want any drunks either. Go on, out.

Nadia has thrown herself down on the couch again. One of the young men beckons Simone over.

Nadia is weeping. Simone approaches her. He tries to look into her face and involuntarily presses her to himself. Nadia rebels a little but without much conviction.

NADIA: Leave me alone... I told you!

SIMONE: Come on... don't be so nasty... If you want to, I'm still willing ... you know?

Nadia stares at him with a terrible ironical and bitter expression.

NADIA: With your little brother's permission? *(Simone does not understand and shrugs his shoulders; Nadia stares into his eyes.)* We'll be together now or always.... *(Laughs)*

SIMONE: Always, if you want...

Nadia begins to laugh again softly. She sits up on the couch, examining herself in her compact mirror, then powdering her face.

NADIA: All right! It's all the same to me. I told you that once... you or somebody else...what difference does it make? *(Her eyes suddenly fill with tears; she closes the compact abruptly to avoid seeing them.)* Get me a drink.

Someone is playing a record at the other end of the room. Taking another glass of brandy, Nadia rises unsteadily and moves in time to the soft music.

Simone gazes at Nadia with feverish eyes, as she dances slowly in the middle of the room. The voice of the croupier and the clatter of chips are heard from the next room.

NOVEMBER 1958.

Service station owned by Franca's father. Inside. Day.

A small truck, sleek and robust, is parked before the garage entrance. Vincenzo and Ciro are gazing admiringly at it through the office window, visually caressing the truck as if it were a blooded racehorse. Franca's father comes up behind them. Ciro turns to him with an almost guilty expression.

CIRO *(as if asking forgiveness)*: I was just having another look at it....

FRANCA'S FATHER *(with typical Milanese cordiality)*: Go right ahead. *(Proudly)* It can stand being looked at!

VINCENZO *(diffident)*: And the terms are...what you said... *(Somewhat ashamed)* Forgive me for asking again, but the money for the down payment isn't mine, it's my wife's....

Vincenzo clears his throat.

CIRO *(correcting)*: The installments though...we're splitting....

FRANCA'S FATHER: Yes. I'll go broke. It's just something hare-brained I want to do for you... because of Ciro here whom I've known for so long....

Ciro turns to his brother and gives him a little shove.

CIRO: You see? What're you scared of? *(Raising his voice)* Come on, run and get the forms for the promissory notes, and we'll settle everything right now!

FRANCA'S FATHER *(to Vincenzo)*: Wait, I'll come with you, and I'll tell you what due dates to buy them for.

The two men go out. Alone, Ciro goes back to the window to admire the truck with shining eyes: it is the acme of his dreams. But he is startled by the sound of a door opening and hears a voice calling.

FRANCA: Papa!

Ciro turns and sees Franca, who looks particularly lovely today. She is dressed as a young lady now and seems much older than the last time we saw her with Ciro.

CIRO: Hi. *(Corrects himself)* Good morning.

FRANCA: Hi. Look who's here.

CIRO: Your father's just gone out for a minute.

FRANCA: Are you coming back to work here?

CIRO *(laughing)*: No, no. This time I'm just a customer.

Franca gazes at him with infinite good will.

FRANCA *(a little coy)*: Can I help you? *(She moves toward the display window, pointing out the various articles.)* We've got everything here, oil, grease, shammies....

CIRO *(laughs again)*: No, no: I'm buying something else.

He points outside. Franca is astonished.

FRANCA *(amazed)*: The truck? Hey, did you win the lottery, by any chance?

CIRO: Almost. I found out that your father can give it to us on installments. *(Changes his tone)* So we'll be meeting again.

I'll be coming here to pay once a month. *(Sighs)* On the eighth.

FRANCA: I don't come here very often. Today I just happened to stop in.

Ciro reflects, as if remembering the past.

CIRO: When you were younger, I remember, you used to spend more time here.

FRANCA: It was fun. *(As Franca talks, Ciro cannot help hanging on her words.)* But girls change a little when they get older... maybe they think about other things.

CIRO *(comically suspicious)*: About what?

FRANCA: I can't tell you what...just other things...

FEBRUARY 1959.

Principe arena. Inside. Night.

Some of the spectators are conversing as they lean against the wall. Shouts of the crowd. The bell rings.

FIRST SPECTATOR: These are things that happen every once in a while. Remember Tunney?

SECOND SPECTATOR: Come on. That was just a lot of talk too. He'd been through the ranks, and how.

FIRST SPECTATOR: Cecchi's no gambler. If he has a fault it's keeping a man back.

SECOND SPECTATOR: And I say you're wrong. If he feels he can take a chance, he takes a chance. He has a whole career to defend.

FIRST SPECTATOR: He hasn't brought out a single new man lately. A real man. He needs to take a chance.

THIRD SPECTATOR: Damn it. You think a serious manager could take a crazy risk like this if he didn't know he had an ace up his sleeve? He's kept him under wraps because he had the ace. Here he is, just look at that stuff. *(Bell)* He's as fresh as if he just got out of bed.

In the corner of the ring, Rocco is getting up from his stool to enter the last round of a match against an opponent apparently a good deal more vigorous than he. Cecchi is near the ropes and whispers a last warning to Rocco, who nods.

FIRST SPECTATOR: You'll see, he's going to make him knock him out.

SECOND SPECTATOR: Sure. Because he's the one that decides.

The two contenders are in the middle of the ring, and silence has fallen on the arena. Rocco's opponent starts a furious attack with the intention of sending the young boxer to the ropes. Rocco's footwork is skillful as he parries all the blows. Then he begins his own precision attack, and the steady rain of blows forces his opponent back. Shouts of the crowd.

FIRST SPECTATOR *(extremely excited)*: Bravo! He looks like a kid... and... *(Shouting)* Baby Face! Come on, Baby Face!

Rocco turns slightly as if seeking Cecchi's advice. Then, with a short sharp uppercut, he sends his opponent to the canvas as the crowd roars. The referee begins to count.

REFEREE: One...two...three...four...*(Rocco stands with legs wide apart, alert lest the other man should get up before the end of the count.)* ...five... six... seven...

The crowd is spasmodically tense and mute.

At the count of ten the crowd roars joyfully. The referee raises Rocco's arm to signal his victory. Vincenzo and Ciro push their way through the crowd toward ringside. The shouts and applause continue.

Cecchi runs toward Rocco's corner screaming like a madam.

CECCHI: Thanks! Bravo! Bravo!

Rocco goes slowly toward his corner and like an automaton lets them slip on his robe and take off his gloves. The fanatics shout and continue to applaud. A boy is hoisted up to the ring with a bouquet of flowers. Rocco lets them put the flowers in his arms. Vincenzo and Ciro exchange glances.

VINCENZO: It's the emotion. Look how overcome he is.

Rocco now climbs slowly out of the ring. Everyone crowds about him. Cecchi slaps him on the shoulders, then exuberantly embraces Vincenzo.

CECCHI: Now we're talking, now!

Ciro embraces Rocco, who submits without participating.

CIRO *(worried, whispering to Rocco)* : What's wrong, Rocco? You feel bad?

Rocco shakes his head slightly. He tries to smile. He turns to Ciro with the astonished expression of a child who has just discovered the existence of evil. With the same expression, he turns and watches his defeated opponent going toward the locker room. Now Rocco is almost overcome by an impulse to weep. In Ciro's arms, he murmurs brokenly.

ROCCO: No. He was easy to beat because I couldn't see him in front of me any more. It was like seeing someone to take out my hate on, all the hate that's built up inside me! It's horrible, Ciro! If this is the way it is…it's horrible! It's horrible!

Ciro has not in the least understood his brother's drama. He has understood only that Rocco feels all right, and he therefore laughs contentedly and starts off with him and the others toward the locker room.

CIRO: You're just the one to talk about hatred; you wouldn't hurt a fly. Come on, come on, Rocco, cheer up. You're going to be a champ.

Superimposed on the scene appears the word : CIRO.

NEW YEAR'S DAY 1960.

Outside a dance hall on the outskirts of Milan.

Some very modest festive decorations at the entrance to the dance hall (the Alfa Romeo recreation center) welcome in a "Happy 1960."

The cold wind whips through the paper decorations. The sound of the orchestra is heard from within. Some young men and girls (almost all of modest circumstances) are leaving the dance hall, mostly in small groups which rapidly break up outside under the stimulus of the bitter wind. The young people shout out their farewells and holiday good wishes as they start up their motorcycles or run toward the bus stop.

A tall, thin young man with a cheerful face (the typical "life of the party") comes outside still singing along with the orchestra and dancing around. He is a fellow-worker of Ciro's at the factory, and he parodies a serenade to Franca, who smiles with pleasure and a little embarrassment as she comes out on Ciro's arm.

Ciro is dressed in his holiday best and seems very proud. Franca points out a little truck parked in the street.

FRANCA *(to Ciro)* : Look, Papa's already here and waiting for us.

She quickly says goodbye to the assembled friends, many of whom she has evidently met only this evening.

FRANCA: Goodbye and best wishes to everybody. Goodbye...

CIRO'S FELLOW-WORKER: Best wishes to you too. *(To Ciro)* Nothing to him. He's already been too lucky, the dog. *(Still joking)* But I'll steal her away from you yet, you know.

Franca laughs, holding Ciro's hand. He reacts energetically to the jest.

CIRO: That's what you think. I have nothing to worry about. Franca doesn't like beanpoles like you.

Franca has run toward her father, who has gotten out of the truck. Ciro's friend continues to joke with him, calling him a southern hick, dwarf, etc., until Ciro motions him to keep quiet.

ANOTHER FELLOW-WORKER *(to the first)* : Shut up, here's his future
father-in-law.

*Both the young men wave courteously to Franca's father. Ciro, very stiff
and formal, has now come up to the father.*

FRANCA *(to her father)* : We had such a wonderful time. Ciro's
friends are such fun.

FRANCA'S FATHER *(to Franca)* : Did you tell him to come tomorrow
night?

FRANCA *(laughing)* : No. How silly of me. Ciro, Papa wants you
to come to our house tomorrow night because he wants to
talk to you. *(Still laughing gaily)* He wants to know if we
have serious intentions.

CIRO *(with great emotion)* : I can tell him right away.

FRANCA'S FATHER *(cordially)* : Tomorrow night, tomorrow night. *(To Franca, joking)* Let's at least give him a last chance to escape. *(Ciro, extremely serious, starts to protest; the father turns to the girl.)* Get in, it's cold. *(Franca runs toward the truck, followed by her father. She turns back to give Ciro a gay little kiss on his cheek, then runs toward the truck again.)*

FRANCA *(turning to shout)* : Don't go back in there, you hear? Go right home. You mustn't ever dance without me.

CIRO: It wouldn't even enter my mind.

But Ciro's words are carried off by the wind and almost entirely muffled by the roar of the truck motor starting. Ciro gazes in ecstasy at the truck, holding his hat with both hands so that the wind will not carry it off. His tall thin friend comes up to him.

CIRO'S FELLOW-WORKER: Well?

CIRO *(extremely serious)* : I may be getting engaged.

CIRO'S FELLOW-WORKER *(jeering)* : And you haven't been for a whole year now?

CIRO: Not officially.

He gives his friend a playful shove and the two start off, passing in front of the dance hall from which the music can still be heard.

Street in front of Rosaria's apartment building. Evening.

Ciro walks rapidly and cheerfully into the building, whistling the dance tune heard in the preceding scene.

Rosaria's apartment. Evening.

The small entrance hall is dark but the kitchen light is on. Ciro goes toward the kitchen. But he stops at the door, surprised and embarrassed. Inside the kitchen is Nadia, calmly smoking in her bathrobe in front of the stove, where a pot of water is boiling. Luca is near her and watches her preparing a hot drink.

Nadia barely turns to look at Ciro.

NADIA: Hello. You're number four, aren't you? We've met before.

LUCA *(to Ciro, conciliating)* : You remember her. She's Simone's girl. Simone's back too. He's in there. We're sleeping here in the kitchen tonight.

VOICE OF ROSARIA: Ciro! Come here a minute, Ciro!

Ciro answers Nadia's greeting and goes to Rosaria's room. Nadia shrugs her shoulders and beckons to Luca.

NADIA: Where are the knives?

Luca races toward the table in the center of the kitchen, circling around the bed which has been moved in; he opens a drawer and takes out a knife which he hands to Nadia. She cuts a slice of lemon peel and throws it into the boiling water. Then she takes a cup from the shelf over the stove and fills it with the boiling liquid.

NADIA: It's the only thing that'll cure your brother's hangover.

Voices of Rosaria shouting and Ciro answering. With an ironical half smile Nadia turns to look toward Rosaria's bedroom. Ciro is heard arguing with his mother, but the words are not distinguishable. Luca is watching Nadia with a mixture of curiosity and friendliness.

LUCA *(friendly)* : And you'll be living here always now?

NADIA *(laughs)* : I don't know. I do what he wants.

LUCA: I say that with a little effort we can get along. *(He gestures toward the door, through which Rosaria's excited voice is audible.)* You'll see, after a while… *(Hesitates)* You'll get along with Mama too.

NADIA: Well, that'll take some doing.

LUCA: She's always that way in the beginning. With Ginetta too, it was such a long time before she made up with her.

NADIA: Who's Ginetta?

LUCA: Vincenzo's wife. *(Proudly)* Did you know I'm an uncle? I have three nephews already.

NADIA *(distracted)*: Oh, really?

She is starting to go toward the room where Simone is when Ciro comes up to her.

CIRO *(coldly)*: I'd like to talk to my brother a minute.

Nadia withdraws with mock ceremony. She holds the cup out to Ciro.

NADIA: Well, give him this then. He has to drink it hot. Try to make him throw up.

Ciro does not answer and does not take the cup. He enters the room and closes the door behind him. Nadia turns to Luca, shrugging her shoulders and sighing. She sips the boiling liquid and grimaces in disgust.

NADIA *(smiling at Luca)*: Ugh! It's horrible!

Simone is sitting on the bed in the adjoining room, which is in a state of extreme disarray. An open valise lying on a chair is piled high with feminine garments. Simone is speaking to Ciro, with an air of extreme irritation.

SIMONE: Now don't you start in on me too.

Ciro leans over his brother's bed, speaking softly but violently.

CIRO: Here's the money to go to a hotel. You are absolutely irresponsible. Just out of consideration for our mother.

SIMONE: Consideration of what?

CIRO: If you can't figure it out for yourself...

Simone takes the money, looks at it, and hands it back to Ciro.

SIMONE: Here. So I pay the rent. Happy now? It's a good rate for a room like this. You're making a good bargain, as usual....

CIRO: You're drunk.

SIMONE *(raising his voice)*: You don't think for a minute I want to hear a sermon from you? This is my house. And I bring home whoever I want to. I have a bill of sixty thousand at the hotel. Will you pay it? And give me another sixty for this month? Doesn't suit you, does it? So leave me alone.

They hear the door opening. Ciro turns. Nadia has come in.

CIRO *(to Simone)*: We'll talk about it tomorrow.

SIMONE: We'll talk about it when I decide to. Good night.

NADIA: I'd like it to be clear that I am not responsible for this. I've got the worst deal of anyone, believe me.

Nadia comes over to the bed and straightens the sheets and blankets. Ciro looks at her wordlessly, then walks out, slamming the door behind him.

As Ciro enters his mother's bedroom, Rosaria immediately rushes to him and puts her hands on his shoulders.

ROSARIA *(softly and intensely)*: What is that woman doing? Did you throw her out? Throw her out, for the love of God!

Ciro closes the bedroom door and looks at his pale and disheveled mother, who stares back at him with dilated eyes.

CIRO: Calm down, Ma. Simone's not feeling well. Tonight we can't... but tomorrow we'll fix everything.

He takes her wrists with a patient but not affectionate gesture. Rosaria frees herself from his grasp with a hysterical outburst.

ROSARIA *(softly and very distinctly)*: Throw her out. You must throw her out, right away.

CIRO *(ironical)*: You think Simone would allow it?

Ciro has hit home. Humiliated, Rosaria lowers her eyes.

ROSARIA *(lamenting)* : My poor boy! That woman's put a spell on him....

Ciro sighs and nods in assent. He treats his mother with the patience usually reserved for the sick and the innocent.

CIRO *(calmly)*: Maybe you're right, Mama. *(He crosses the room and looks out the window; calmly.)* Now go to bed. You'll see, tomorrow...

ROSARIA : How will it be any different tomorrow? *(Ciro turns to look at his mother, struck by the trembling desperation in her voice; he finds her staring at him with feverishly dilated eyes.)* Swear to tell me the truth, Ciro. You have to swear by the memory of your father. *(Ciro looks questioningly at his mother, who takes his hands and squeezes them compulsively.)* Is it my fault all of this has happened? Is it my fault if I had the ambition to bring my fine strong sons to the city, so they could get rich and make a life for themselves instead of withering away on the land like their father who died a hundred times before he closed his eyes for the last time?

CIRO *(extremely upset)* : What are you saying, Ma? I don't understand you. Nothing's your fault. Nothing at all.

ROSARIA *(raising her voice)* : Your father never wanted to leave our town. But I did. I dreamed of it for the twenty-five years we lived together. I wanted it for Vincenzo, and for Simone, and for Rocco. I don't know what I wanted for them. The whole world would've seemed too little. At one point I thought I'd gotten all I'd dreamed of. The people treated me with respect, in such a big city, because of my sons. *(Again in a tone of lament)* But then what happened? Rocco has left home and he looks like a man who's seen the face of hell. Simone's in the clutches of a tramp. *(Raising her voice)* A curse on the day I brought you away from the land of your fathers. *(Weeping hysterically)* Ciro, you must

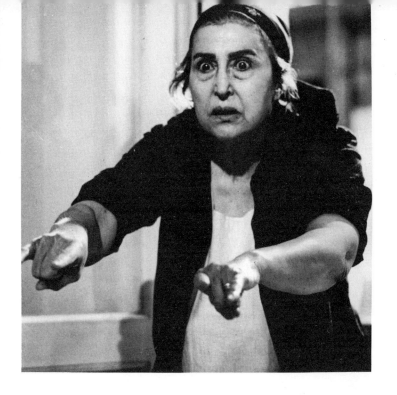

protect your mother's home! Do something! It's your duty to do something.

Ciro puts his arm around his mother's shoulders, trying to lead her to the bed.

Milan park. Foggy dawn.

An area of the Milanese park where the athletes come to work out at dawn. They move like ghosts through the light fog. Among them is Rocco, with his usual assistants.

Now Rocco interrupts his exertions, covers himself with a towel, and comes over to where Ciro is sitting on a low wall. The two brothers resume a conversation broken off only shortly before.

CIRO: Think of our mother, who has to make that woman's bed in the morning.

ROCCO: I know, and I feel shame just like you do.

CIRO *(with a burst of anger)*: Brother or no, I don't want to have anything more to do with him. We're like seeds from the same pod, seeds that have to bear healthy fruit themselves. If among us there's a sick one, a rotten one, then he's got to be separated from the rest like when Mama used to give us the lentils to clean. Think of the danger for Luca.

ROCCO: Simone hasn't changed. He's just wounded in his pride. I still have faith in him. Let me try. It's for me that I'm asking you. I know how to do it.

Rocco's eyes suddenly fill with tears. To hide them, he turns his face away. Ciro answers him a little hostilely.

CIRO: I can't do a thing. But even if I could...

At Ciro's words, Rocco smiles disconsolately. He gestures to interrupt him.

ROCCO *(slightly out of patience)*: Let me try. We should never have left the old place. But this was our destiny... yours, mine, and Simone's too.

CIRO: But think what our life would have been if we'd stayed there.

ROCCO: We'd still have all been together.

Ciro does not answer but smiles. Rocco responds with a sad smile. Then Ciro claps him on the shoulder and says goodbye.

CIRO: I'm going.

He turns rapidly and goes off as Rocco prepares to resume his exertions.

FEBRUARY 1960.

Locker room, Principe arena. Night.

The noise and shouts of the crowd in the arena are heard in the locker room. Cecchi is pacing nervously back and forth. The trainer observes him with a fairly ironical gaze.

CECCHI *(violently)* : I could kick myself! Damn me for giving in to him. Damn my good heart. He's a bastard. A good-for-nothing. Not even great God in heaven could pull him up again.

ASSISTANT : Something must have happened to him. He left home at eight with his little brother.

A boxer comes out of his cubicle, his curiosity aroused by this outburst.

BOXER: What's going on?

ASSISTANT: Simone hasn't shown up yet.

BOXER: Well, it's no great loss.

Cecchi shakes his head. He is enraged. Over the loudspeaker they hear the lengthy applause of the audience marking the end of a bout. The applause continues as the contenders in the preceding match appear in the locker room, Vincenzo and Ciro behind them.

CECCHI: Do you see? Was this my idea?

VINCENZO *(in consternation)*: And he wanted the reporters to eat their words, what they'd said about him.

CECCHI: He'd have done better to save his breath for the ring. And less chitchat.

Principe arena. Outside. Night.

The street is deserted; all the spectators have entered by now. The empty street echoes from time to time with the explosions of enthusiasm, the applause and cheers of the crowd within.

At the corner of the street, Simone stares at the building in terror. His forehead is beaded with sweat and his lips are trembling. Beside him, Luca holds his bag and watches him with heartstruck affection. He wants to comprehend his brother's suffering completely. He wants to help him. And he does not know how. He addresses him.

LUCA: Well?

SIMONE *(extremely nervous)*: Let's wait just a minute more.

He wipes the sweat away with a trembling hand as another wave of shouts billows out from the arena.

Morini's car pulls up in the parking spaces reserved for associates at the entrance to the arena. Morini gets out of the car.

SIMONE *(to Luca)* : Go over there. Call that man. You see him? That one. Tell him I'm waiting over there for him.

He points to nearby café, toward which he now walks rapidly. Luca remains there a moment, uncertain. He starts to call his brother back, then decides against it and runs toward Morini.

Café. Inside. Night.

From the café we see Luca speaking to Morini, who then comes slowly toward the café. Luca remains alone near the arena entrance. Morini sees Simone paying the cashier, going over to the bar and ordering a brandy, which the bartender serves him immediately.

Café. Outside. Night.

Morini pushes open the glass door and enters the oppressive, noisy atmosphere of the little café.

Café. Inside. Night.

Simone is drinking his brandy, his eyes lost in space.

MORINI: What's up? Scared?

SIMONE: I don't feel well.

MORINI *(with an effort)* : Then what are you doing here? *(He claps a hand on his shoulder.)* Come on, I'll take you home. And if you want we'll stop at my place and have a drink in peace and confort.

Simone looks him in the eyes for the first time, as if to understand Morini's intentions.

SIMONE *(murmurs)* : All right.

He tosses down the rest of the brandy. They leave.

Principe arena. Outside. Night.

Morini and Simone walk toward the car. A short silence. Luca sees Simone, desperate, about to get into the car.

LUCA: Simone!

SIMONE *(with extreme violence)*: Leave me alone. Get out of here. *(To Morini)* Got a cigarette? *(Morini gives him the pack and Simone feverishly takes three or four; he apologizes.)* I'll keep the other ones for later on.

He lights a cigarette, takes a long drag, and feels a little better.

MORINI *(looking straight at him)*: Feel better now?

SIMONE: When we're far away from here...

MORINI: You're scared, I know, and then too... *(He smiles with a strangely detached air as he gets into the car.)* ...you don't

like to have your profile messed up. You really don't want that. *(Passing his hand over his own face, as if caressing it).* A person does like to look good.

He laughs.

Inside Morini's car. Night.

The car drives off. Morini addresses Simone, with his usual air of ambiguous superiority.

MORINI: Well, where do we go?

Simone looks at him as if imploring his protection.

SIMONE: We said your place.

Morini smiles with an air of triumph.

MORINI *(intentionally ambiguous)*: I knew you'd be the one to ask me some day. *(Glances at Simone)* I see you're getting back your courage.

SIMONE *(with an expression of surrender)*: A person learns. *(Morini accelerates as Simone, fragile and whiny, whimpers as if in self-justification.)* I need money. A lot.

Rosaria's apartment. Day.

Ciro is washing in the bathroom before going to work when he hears voices in the entranceway. He opens the door and looks out into the hall, where he sees Rosaria, a coat thrown over her nightgown, talking to a uniformed policeman who is holding a sheet of paper in his hand. As she hears the door opening, Rosaria turns to Ciro with a look of desolation.

ROSARIA: They're looking for Simone.

Ciro comes to the front door.

ROSARIA *(weeping)*: They want him at police headquarters. He says there's a warrant for his arrest.

CIRO *(to Rosaria)*: Go on inside, Ma. *(To the policeman)* My mother
must have told you that my brother Simone wasn't here
last night. He doesn't always sleep here. Actually, he's
not here very often at all. You can see for yourself if you
want.

*The policeman enters the hall. Luca looks out of the bedroom and listens
apprehensively.*

CIRO *(softly, to the policeman)*: Can you tell me why they want
him?

POLICEMAN *(brusquely but courteously)*: I just have an order to take
him back to headquarters.

CIRO *(following the policeman through the house)*: But if I came down
to headquarters could they tell me?

POLICEMAN: I don't know.

Ciro puts on his jacket and follows the policeman out.

*Weeping desperately, Rosaria goes through the motions of her usual
routine: talking a pot off the stove, lifting a cover, drying her hands.
Then, as if coming to a decision, she goes toward one of the bedrooms and
flings open the door.*

*Nadia is lying on the bed in her slip, smoking and polishing her fingernails.
Hearing Rosaria enter, she raises her head slightly. Rosaria stares at her
with hatred.*

ROSARIA: The cops are looking for him. What's he done? Do you
know?

NADIA: Well, I don't know what he's done this time, but I can
imagine. He's a criminal. *(Nastily)* Did you know that,
that your son's a criminal?

*Trembling with wrath, Rosaria is barely able to keep from hurling herself
on the girl.*

ROSARIA *(uncontrollable)*: What are you saying? You...you...

you have the nerve to insult other people? Since you've been here I've been too ashamed to look out the window!

Nadia bursts out in an insulting laugh.

NADIA *(ironical and nasty)*: Oh, no! But you've kept me here yourself, for fear of losing your son.

ROSARIA: You're getting something out of it too.

NADIA *(laughing)*: He agreed to keep me. *(Looking around)* But do you think this is any way to keep a woman like me? He can't do anything. He works badly, he steals worse. *(Seeing Rosaria's horrified face, she insists.)* I said steals, did you hear me all right? Steals! But he's no good at it.

ROSARIA: You're the one who's a criminal, you're the one who's ruined him for me! He was my best son. And you'll see, when he gets free of your clutches, he'll be the best of all again.

Nadia begins to put a bathrobe on over her slip.

NADIA: If that's all the matter is, you can feel easy. I'm getting out.

Rosaria is taken aback. Her tone of voice is no longer as resolute and firm as before.

ROSARIA: No, not you. He's the one that has to tell you.

NADIA: Who's going to stop me? I've seen him go to the bottom. That's what I was waiting for. Now I can go away happy. *(Raising her voice)* Now you tell Rocco all this good news for me. That he should understand once and for all just who he's sacrificed me to. And tell him that I don't even want the pleasure of telling him so myself any more. *(She turns toward Rosaria with a weary, desperate air: grimacing to hold back her tears.)* I just want to get out of here and never see another one of you again.

Extremely pale, Rosaria remains immobile, looking at Nadia, who begins frenetically to gather up her things, which are scattered all over the room. At a certain point a mirror drops from her hand and shatters on the floor. The two women gaze on the fragments in horror. Rosaria desperately makes the gestures for exorcising evil.

Café frequented by Simone. Day.

The café is deserted. A waiter in shirt sleeves is cleaning up. Luca comes up to the waiter and speaks to him.

We cannot hear, but we understand that the waiter cannot answer Luca's question. The boy remains there perplexed and thinking for a moment, then starts slowly out of the café, still reflecting. Then he starts to run.

Morini's apartment. Day.

Pale and extremely wrought up, Morini paces up and down before Ciro, Rocco, and Vincenzo, who gaze at him apprehensively.

MORINI *(speaking with an effort)* : He thought I was scared. "If you take that money I'll tell the cops," I told him. He began to laugh and he broke the desk drawer open right before my eyes.

ROCCO *(his voice expressionless)* : You can still tell the cops you made a mistake: you found the money you thought had been stolen. I'm ready to sign a promissory note for you right now. Cecchi can guarantee me.

MORINI *(screaming hysterically)* : Ah, because you think I've compromised myself for seventy thousand lire? It's been two years that that bum has been blackmailing me. Yes, gentlemen. Almost two years.

Vincenzo and Ciro lower their eyes, tremendously embarrassed by Morini's confessions. Rocco rises to wind things up quickly.

ROCCO: Tell me what my brother owes you and that'll be the end of it.

MORINI: It's not just a question of money. I've jeopardized myself for him. And more than once. I've had to pull all kinds of strings to get him off when they picked him up for some petty smuggling. He's an ass.

Ciro is profoundly disgusted. He looks at the extremely pale Rocco, who speaks again with a vibrant voice.

ROCCO: I asked you: how much does my brother owe you?

MORINI: Four hundred thousand.

Ciro and Vincenzo are stunned. And even more horrified as they hear Rocco's calm answer.

ROCCO: All right. I'm prepared to sign you ninety-day notes.

CIRO *(to Rocco)*: Are you crazy?

VINCENZO *(to Rocco)*: I can't do a thing. The truck still has to be paid off.

ROCCO *(to his brothers)*: This is my business.

CIRO: But you can't. Where can you find that kind of money?

Morini watches the three attentively.

MORINI: You're sure Cecchi will guarantee you?

ROCCO: You can ask him yourself.

There is a moment of silence. Morini goes over to the telephone. Ciro and Vincenzo immediately begin to protest excitedly to Rocco.

CIRO: Even if Cecchi is so crazy as to guarantee you... tell me how you can pay him back.

ROCCO: Cecchi's offered me a lot of money if I make a ten-year contract with him. He'll present me in Brussels, and then... then what does it matter to you?

Ciro and Vincenzo look at each other. Morini is heard telephoning Cecchi.

VINCENZO *(to Rocco)*: But you always said you wanted to quit boxing. So? You want to change your whole life for that poor devil?

ROCCO *(wearily)*: Well... do you have anything better to suggest, besides abandoning Simone to his fate?

MORINI: Listen a minute, will you? *(Ciro and Vincenzo stop talking, the three brothers turn to Morini, at the telephone.)* Cecchi's on the wire. He says he'll guarantee this only in the case... that Rocco knows.

*Rocco motions Morini to wait and comes to the telephone. Vincenzo turns
excitedly to Ciro.*

VINCENZO: We have to stop him!

CIRO: If Rocco wants to pay this debt there's nothing we can do
about it. We can't help him.

*Vincenzo starts to rush to Rocco's side, but Ciro's attitude stops him.
Both brothers watch Rocco at the telephone.*

ROCCO *(to Cecchi, on the telephone)*: This is Rocco. I understand
perfectly. It was obvious. If I ask you for this guarantee
it means I accept everything.

*Rocco does not even wait for Cecchi's answer before handing the telephone
back to Morini. He takes a few steps and then stops, leaning on the back
of a chair.*

Vincenzo looks at Ciro, serious and pale. Then he goes over to Rocco.

VINCENZO: You can still take it back. Your life is more important than this... this...

ROCCO *(softly)* No. Ten years go by. But if we don't save Simone now...

Ciro, too, has now come up to Rocco. He says nothing. Vincenzo looks at Ciro, then at Rocco, then back at Ciro again.

VINCENZO *(as if clearing his conscience)*: You're the one who's deciding....

MORINI: Let it be clear that I want your assurance that he won't bother me any more in the future either.

Vincenzo and Ciro look at Morini as Rocco, extremely pale, leans against the back of the chair, his head lowered.

CIRO *(angrily, to Morini)*: You can rest assured. But let it be clear that our obligation takes effect only when we have official word that your accusation has been withdrawn.

Hotel room. Night.

A tiny, squalid room in a cheap hotel. Luca sits on a stool by the window and looks at his two older brothers. Simone is sitting on the bed, unshaven, with his coat on over his undershirt. Ciro is standing in front of him. He, too, is wearing his coat and he does not sit down, in order to emphasize the brevity of his visit.

CIRO *(indicating Luca)*: I imagine he's already told you everything.

SIMONE: He told me you've gotten yourselves cheated by Morini. Dopes. Did Rocco already sign the notes? He should have given me the money, it would have been better spent.

Ciro takes a few bills from his pocket.

CIRO: This is for you, and you'll do us all a favor if you get out of Milan for at least a little while. *(Ironical)* It's not as if you were going to lose a job. One city or another ought to be all the same to you. Anyway you're not coming back home again.

SIMONE *(ironical in turn)* : Is that the sentence of the brothers' tribunal? *(Raising his voice)* Who wants to go home anyway?

CIRO *(trying to finish)* : That makes it easier.

Ciro starts to go out, but Simone stops him, waving the money.

SIMONE: Listen. Let's make a bargain. Since you've got so much dough you can just rain it down on that bastard Morini, I imagine you have something more to give your brother. Two hundred thousand and I really will go.

Simone looks at the few bills, then laughs loudly.

CIRO: We'll give you another hundred thousand after the fight.

It's impossible right away. The second installment of the contract. Cecchi'll pay it after the fight on Sunday.

SIMONE : I'll wait.

Ciro turns to Luca.

CIRO: Let's go. *(To Simone)* And you leave him alone.

SIMONE *(jumping up in extreme irritation)* : Ooh! Ooh! Take it easy there. I'm not a leper. I'm sick of listening to your preaching. Who do you think you are? A skilled worker at Alfa Romeo! What a career! You can afford to be so high and mighty.

Simone takes Ciro by the lapels of his coat. Ciro remains impassive and pale.

CIRO: I feel sorry for you.

SIMONE: How sweet! Did you hear, Luca? He feels sorry for me.

Ciro opens the door and goes out.

CIRO *(calling)* : Luca!

Luca whispers to Simone.

LUCA: I'll be back tomorrow. Leave me a message if you change hotels.

Arena. Inside. Afternoon.

All the light in the sports arena are suddenly turned on in unison. The clock reads 8:30.

Café. Outside. Afternoon.

Simone leaves the café at the same hour and walks rapidly away, raising the collar of his coat.

Arena. Inside. Outside. Afternoon.

Employees of the arena open the entrance doors to let in the crowd which has been gathering outside for some time. A torrent of spectators rushes inside.

Arena. Boxers' entrance. Outside. Afternoon.

Some spectators have gathered outside the boxers' entrance, too. They are the fanatics of the sport, fans of one or another of the contenders who are waiting the appearance of their favorites. A car pulls up and Rocco's trainer and seconds get out, then Rocco himself with Luca. Rocco is bundled up in his overcoat, and a woolen scarf protects his mouth from the cold air. His fans greet him. Rocco rapidly enters the arena with his group. Other boxers arrive.

Locker room of arena. Afternoon.

Rocco enters the locker room. Vincenzo and Cecchi come up to him immediately, apprehensive and solicitous.

CECCHI: Were you able to sleep?

ROCCO: An hour.

VINCENZO: How do you feel?

ROCCO: A little nervous.

CECCHI *(stepping in)*: Go on! Massage, now.

The masseur comes forward and prepares the cot. Rocco begins to undress. The other boxers are also coming in with their managers and their seconds, and the locker room is soon animated with feverish activity. Several languages are being spoken. The doctor appears and begins to examine the contenders one by one.

Simone's regular café. Inside. Afternoon.

Simone is with some friends in the billiard room. They are mostly older than Simone and of a social category even lower than that of his former friends.

MAN: So? You're not giving us the tickets?

ANOTHER MAN: But you promised us.

SIMONE: Who did? I didn't promise a thing! I'm not even going to the fight myself.

WAITER *(from a distance)*: He's not going or he'd eat his heart out.

MAN: You're really not going?

ANOTHER MAN: Since he quit he doesn't even like to watch anybody else. That's understandable.

ANOTHER: But why did you quit?

SIMONE: Because I didn't want to fight any more. All right?

ANOTHER MAN *(snickering from the back of the room)*: Sour grapes. You know the story of the fox and the grapes?

SIMONE *(with an angry gesture)*: No, I don't know it.

ANOTHER MAN: Get someone to tell it to you.

Ivo has entered the bar with a slouchy expression. He goes over to Simone and stands protectively behind him.

IVO: Listen. Me and some other guys saw with our own eyes how he licked the champ one night at Bovisa. Who was there, you remember?

MAN: Water under the bridge. I'd like to see the two Parondis fight now. Then you tell me who licks who.

IVO *(laughing vulgarly)*   We can always try it again. This time we'd have to go to the lake. *(To Simone)* You know what they tell me? That Nadia's working out around Ravizza Park. She rents a room and a car from someone. *(Laughs)* A whore on wheels, get it? She picks up customers in Maino Boulevard and takes them to the lake, near the soft-drink stand.

SIMONE *(interested)*: Are you sure?

Ivo laughs heartily, pointing to Simone.

IVO: Look how he perks up his ears. If you want we can set up another evening like the one I was telling you about. *(Laughing still more heartily)* But is your brother still whoring? He's aiming higher now, isn't he?

All laugh.

Arena. Inside. Afternoon.

The seats inside the arena are almost all filled. The first bout has begun. The contenders are two lightweights, a Frenchman and an Italian. The audience follows the bout with interest. Its cries, underlining the good punches, are heard intermittently even inside the locker room, where the boxers are making their preparations.

End of bus line at the lake. Afternoon.

The bus has reached the end of the line virtually empty. Simone gets out and immediately starts along the path circling around the lake toward the soft-drink stand, whose dim lights are visible through the darkening air. The fog has settled on the still black waters of the lake. The large, still, artificial lake has something strangely sinister about it. There is not another living soul in sight; the silence is absolute. Simone continues around the edge of the lake. The sounds of the city are dimly audible in the distance.

Locker room of the arena. Afternoon.

Rocco is being dressed. His group is gathered about him. Vincenzo enters the locker room at a run, breathless.

VINCENZO: What a time I had finding Gina a seat. They're all there together now. In a good spot. Gina, Franca, her father and mother. What a crowd! My God! Did you see? Loi, Mazzola, all the big names are here tonight.

ROCCO *(to Luca)*: Give me a little water. My throat's dry.

CECCHI: Just rinse out your mouth. But stop drinking. You'll swell up like a balloon!

LUCA: Would you rather have a lemon?

ROCCO: Give me a lemon.

Luca takes half a lemon and squeezes the juice between Rocco's lips; he licks them avidly. He looks around with eyes somewhat worried and feverish and clasps his jaw. The masseur has bent down to work over his calves with liniment.

At the opposite corner of the locker room is Rocco's opponent, a typically Teutonic-looking blond, surrounded by his seconds and his trainer. He jumps around a bit to loosen up.

The doctor continues to check the boxers. He tests the German's blood pressure and heart.

DOCTOR: Fine. All right.

He translates into German. The boxer thanks him.

The doctor now comes toward Rocco; Vincenzo and Ciro watch him with somewhat tense expressions. The doctor seems to be taking quite some time in his examination of Rocco.

DOCTOR: How come your pressure's high?

Cecchi intervenes before Rocco can answer.

CECCHI: It's the nerves, Doctor.

The doctor turns back to Rocco.

DOCTOR: Have you eaten?

This time Ciro answers for Rocco.

CIRO: Yes, doctor, eight hours ago.

DOCTOR: The pressure's high. Too high. *(To Rocco)* You've been feeling all right these last few days?

ROCCO: Of course.

Vincenzo echoes his brother's assertion.

VINCENZO: He was training till yesterday.

DOCTOR: All right. Anyway I'll check it again later on. Try to stay calm. Don't see anybody; don't talk to anybody.

The doctor continues on his rounds.

CECCHI *(to Vincenzo)*: Such a fuss! All for a couple of heartbeats.

Lake. Near the soft-drink stand. Late afternoon.

The area around the soft-drink stand is deserted, too, and Simone walks cautiously through the dripping trees. He looks all around him but sees not a soul. He goes as far as the lake side and stares for a moment at the water.

A car is heard in the distance. The sound draws steadily nearer. Simone listens. He shivers and hunches his shoulders against the cold. Now the sound of the motor is closer and the headlights are visible intermittently on the far bank. The car is seen taking the road parallel to the lake and approaching the soft-drink stand. Simone crouches down in the bushes and waits with an anxiety that becomes spasmodic.

A small car slows down and halts. The headlights are switched off and then the motor. Silence again envelops the area. Simone advances cautiously toward the car, making no sound. He bends over a moment to peer through the rear window, then reaches the door and flings it open. The occupants— Nadia and a terrified middle-aged man in eyeglasses—are startled from their embrace.

SIMONE *(to the man)* : Get out of here.

MAN *(stuttering)* : But... who are you, what do you want?

Simone grabs him by the lapels of his coat and drags him brutally out of the car.

SIMONE : I said get out of here. Get out or I'll kill you. *(Shouting)* Understand?

Terrified, the man steps back, then runs away. Meanwhile Nadia has gotten out of the other door of the car. Her face, too, betrays terror. She looks at Simone across the car. Simone moves toward her but Nadia, still watching him, tries to circle around the car. Then she steps back in an attempt to flee. But Simone reaches her instantly and grabs her arm. Uncertain, disconnected words tumble from her lips.

NADIA : Help! What do you want? Why? Help!

SIMONE *(covering her mouth with his hand)* : Wait. Stop it. Don't shout.

NADIA *(her voice muffled by Simone's hand)* : Aaaah! What do you want?

SIMONE : Come here. *(Trying to drag her toward the bushes)* Calm down. I'll explain.

NADIA: Leave me alone. *(Freeing herself with a violent effort)* Let me
go.

*She looks at him in terror, her eyes dilated, her breath short, her mouth open
to scream again.*

SIMONE: Calm down. You're afraid? Look how I'm trembling,
and you're the one who's afraid?

Nadia feigns a courage she does not feel.

NADIA: I'm not afraid.

*She takes a few steps, mainly to try to gain control of herself. Simone,
trembling like a leaf, continues to watch her. Nadia takes a cigarette from
her handbag. Her hand trembles and she looks at Simone to see whether he
has noticed. With her free hand she grasps the other, holding the match.
She notices that the bag is still open, and speaks.*

NADIA: Is it money you're after?

*She shows him the inside of the bag, stretching it open with both hands.
The cigarette hangs from her lips, and she grimaces from the smoke. Simone
makes a negative gesture.*

NADIA: See? Well? What're we doing here? Let's get out of here.
(Indicating the car) I'll take you back to town.

Simone comes up to her.

SIMONE *(pleading)*: Listen, Nadia...listen...look, this is what I
came to tell you.... *(Feverishly)* The two of us... if you
want... we can go away together. That way I can start
again too....

He has made a great effort to say this much. He stops to catch his breath.

NADIA: Go away? Where? With you? Get that idea right out of
your head. Listen, Simone, leave me alone. I've told
you... I've starting working again and it's all over with
you, all over for always.

SIMONE *(pulling some bills from his pocket)*: I'll pay you, like the others do.

NADIA: No. Never again with you... not even once.

She throws the cigarette on the ground. Simone is suddenly upon her. He takes her by the shoulders and pulls her to him with savage violence. He speaks desperately to her, in her neck, on her face.

SIMONE: You know I could kill you? You know you can scream all you want to here and nobody'll hear you? You understand?

Nadia struggles desperately to free herself and finally manages to pull free, leaving her coat in his hands. She starts to run toward the lake. Simone throws her coat on the ground and follows her; he catches up with her at the edge of the water. He snatches at her sweater and rips it. Nadia screams. The handbag soars through the air, scattering its contents here and there. Simone, blinded by fury and madness, is upon her again, shouting.

SIMONE: Oh! No… not like that! You can't!

He begins to slap and punch her. She tries to ward off the blows, but Simone's fury continues unabated until Nadia slips to the ground, her head almost in the water.

Simone suddenly stops. He bends over her and calls her name; he lifts up her head. Nadia's upper lip is bleeding. Simone takes a handful of water and trickles it over the wound. Nadia is still immobile, her clothing ripped away, her face bloody, testifying to the wrath of the storm that has swept over her.

SIMONE: Oh God! Oh God! Forgive me. I've hurt you? It's nothing… it's nothing. Cover yourself… cover yourself… it's cold.

He picks up her coat and places it over her. He clutches her convulsively to him. She lies there, inanimate. A long moan escapes her half-closed lips, an infantile moan. Simone wipes away the blood still flowing from her lip with a dirty handkerchief he takes from his pocket. The pain evokes a still louder moan from the girl. Simone hugs her to his breast with sudden convulsive tenderness.

Nadia regains consciousness little by little. She passes her hand over her forehead as if to soothe her great pain. Then she pulls back her hair with the same hand.

Simone stares fixedly at her. With his right hand he takes her face, turns it gently toward him, and kisses her at length, softly and cautiously, on the mouth. She does not try to turn away. Simone draws away from her lips and lets his head fall on her shoulder without daring to move again. Nadia, too, is still. After a short while she begins to speak with enormous effort; her voice is calm and pitifully broken.

NADIA: You can't know how I hate you. You are vile, you are an animal, you're not a man. Everything you touch turns vulgar, filthy, horribly ugly. I want to spit in your face. *(Simone kisses her again; Nadia continues in the same piteous voice.)* So then I'll be free of you forever. You were the one

who filthied the only clean thing in my life. But I love him…
him… only him.

She is silent. Simone lets his head fall back on her shoulder.

Now Nadia takes Simone by the hair and pulls his head back. He is destroyed. He no longer weeps but on his ashen face are all the signs of desperation and disaster. His features are distorted: his eyes oblique, his mouth contracted.

NADIA *(whispering)* : Do you understand, jail-bait? *(Simone nods.)* Now you can do whatever you want. I don't care about anything anymore.

She takes a few steps away from him. She seems to him to be weeping: she hides her face in her hand and her shoulders heave with irregular sobs. He comes up to her and takes her hand from her face. But Nadia is actually laughing to herself: hysterical laughter, but soft and infantile rather than shrill.

Her handbag is on the ground. She takes a few steps and bends down to pick it up. She looks at it: it is empty; the few objects it contained are now in the water. Disconsolate, she hurls it far out into the lake. An indescribable melancholy pervades her face. She stares out over the water to the spot where her bag has gone under. She sniffles; she yearns for tears which do not come.

Simone has been silent for some few moments now. But Nadia, absorbed in her own thoughts, does not seem aware of this. The appearance of a car's headlights on the far bank seems to bring her back to reality again.

NADIA : Over there… a car… *(Simone does not answer.)* It's stopped, see? They've turned off the lights. They've come to make love. *(Another pause)* It must be a couple in love with each other and happy to be together, snug in the warmth inside there. And the windows steaming up little by little… and nothing can be seen outside any more… the smell of cigarettes…

Nadia sighs. Hearing no answer, she turns. She sees Simone standing stock-still only a step away from her. Only the knife blade glimmers dully.

Nadia does not even start. She stands still, waiting. She waits for Simone to come nearer. Simone takes a step. He is beside her; he virtually covers her with his own bulkier body. He pulls her to him. There is a pause, then Nadia screams like a wounded beast. Simone thrusts the knife carefully into her side; her inert body collapses on him, and since her scream has become a prolonged gurgle, like that of a leaking sink, Simone thrusts the blade into her side once again and Nadia slips down into the water, almost dead.

Arena. Inside. Sundown.

Rocco is now fighting his German opponent. It is the sixth round. The impassioned audience follows the seesaw phases of the bout. Their roars underscore each well-landed blow, whether it is the Italian's or the German's.

Rocco is hit by a heavy left which has taken him unawares. His left eyebrow begins to bleed. Stunned, he seems for a moment about to go to his knees. The audience holds its breath. The referee stops the German from taking advantage of Rocco's momentary daze. Rocco is on the ropes; he shakes his head to clear it of the blood.

Cecchi, Vincenzo, Ciro, and Luca, at the corner, are in a state of extreme tension. Cecchi lets an insult directed at Rocco escape him.

CECCHI: Christ! That idiot! Why doesn't he close?

VINCENZO: His eye! Now we're in for it.

Rocco shakes his head two or three more times. Then he springs off the ropes and charges toward his opponent with lowered head. He lands a series of extremely effective and accurate one-two's. The crowd jumps to its feet, shouting encouragement to Rocco, but the bell interrupts his hammering and the blows lose force and efficacy. Back in his corner, Rocco does not answer Cecchi's questions. He simply looks at him, his gaze almost severe, but firm and clear-eyed. Cecchi nonetheless continues to shower him with feverishly intense suggestions.

The bell brings the contenders back into the center of the ring.

AUDIENCE: Give it to 'im! Kill 'im! Down, send him down!

Urged on by the audience, Rocco attacks with firm decision. After a few accurate blows his opponent is on the canvas and the referee is counting.

REFEREE: ...Three... four... five... six... seven... eight... nine... ten.

The bell rings and pandemonium breaks loose among the crowd. Rocco feels himself hoisted up almost bodily, with many people around him: Cecchi, Vincenzo, and Ciro have brought him back to his corner.

Rocco's opponent is still lying down; now he is being carried back to his corner. Rocco's robe is thrown over him; a sponge removes the blood from his face. The verdict is announced by the referee and the crowd goes wild. Rocco is in the center of the ring; his arm is raised up high.

Rosaria's apartment. Evening.

Rosaria, Rocco, Ciro, Luca, Vincenzo, and Ginetta with their oldest son are gathered around the table. Dinner is over. Flowers are pathetically mingled with the plates and bits of bread around Rocco's place.

LUCA : I was scared when he got you with that left. Did you feel him?

ROCCO *(smiling)* : No, I didn't even see him in front of me. It seemed as if I was shadowboxing, like when I work out.

Ciro turns to Rosaria with an unusually gentle expression.

CIRO : You could have come too. You wouldn't have been frightened, I assure you. Are you happy? Do you know he'll be the champ of Italy? And maybe...

Rosaria gazes at Ciro with gratitude. She senses that Ciro's words are the answer to her outburst the night that Simone and Nadia came to the house.

ROSARIA *(softly)* : Yes. But I'll really be happy only when I see all five of you together again around this table. Five, united like the fingers of a hand.

She raises her right hand in a fist, like a symbol.

CIRO *(a little impatient)* : Oh please, Ma.

Rosaria sighs and nods as if to say, "I know, you can't have everything." Then she gets up and with ostentatious gaiety pours wine into the empty glasses.

ROSARIA : Drink. Give some to Luca too. Tonight even the littlest has to get drunk.

Ginetta passes the glass of wine to Luca. Vincenzo rises to begin the toast. All hush to listen.

VINCENZO *(in Lucanian dialect)* : Let me drink one glass of wine....

Ciro raises his glass in turn.

CIRO *(in dialect)*: This wine so, so sweet and fair... *(He stumbles, searching for the right words; no longer remembering his home-country dialect, he concludes hesitantly in Milanese.)* To everybody's health.

VINCENZO *(shouting gaily)*: Aren't you ashamed of yourself? You don't know your own language anymore. You've turned more Milanese even than Ginetta. Rocco, you finish it. Let's hear you.

ROCCO *(in dialect)* : This wine I drink...

ROSARIA *(interrupting)* : I thought I heard somebody knocking.

All are silent for a moment. Ginetta gets up and goes to the door.

GINETTA : No, there's nobody there, Mama.

CIRO : Come on, Rocco. Finish the toast. I want to hear if you're better than me.

ROCCO : No, Ciro. I'm not better than you. I just wanted to say that some day, even if it's a long time away, I want to go back to my town. *(Interrupting himself as if struck by a sudden sad thought)* And if I can't... maybe it'll be impossible for me... some one of us will want to go back. *(Looking at Luca)* Maybe you... isn't that so?

LUCA : With you, with you I want to go back.

ROCCO *(hesitantly, moved)* : Remember, Luca, that's our home; the town of olives and of moonlight madness...and of rainbows...

Spellbound, Luca listens to him with open mouth. The others listen, too,

Rosaria with ill-concealed emotion. Vincenzo and Ciro exchange glances.

ROCCO *(continuing)* : You remember, Vincè? *(He seems to have lost his train of thought and passes his hand over his forehead.)* Remember how when the master mason starts a new house, he throws a rock in the shadow of the first person that passes by?

LUCA *(eagerly)* : Why?

ROCCO *(looking each person gently in the eye)* : Because there has to be a sacrifice for the house to be built strong.

His voice breaks. His mother and his brothers look at him. There is a moment of real embarrassment and tension. In the silence the doorbell rings loudly and insistently. Everyone is startled. Rosaria gets up. All turn to watch her go toward the front door.

VINCENZO *(getting up too)* : I bet it's Cecchi. He hasn't forgiven you for coming back home.

Their expressions are transformed as they see Simone enter the front hall. He is in a pitiful state: disheveled, unshaven, his eyes wild and hallucinated. His raincoat is filthy and ripped, his trousers and shoes full of mud.

ROSARIA *(touched)*: My blessed son. Come, come inside. You've made your mother happy. *(In her joy at having her son with her, Rosaria seems not to notice the state he is in; to Ciro.)* He's come, too, to celebrate his brother's victory. You see?

Rocco has stood up, extremely pale, and gazes at Simone. Simone avoids Rocco's eyes and his mother's, goes to the table and pours himself a glass of wine.

ROSARIA: Have you eaten? No? I'll heat up something right away for you. What would you like?

Simone drinks the wine in one gulp, then puts down the glass.

SIMONE: Nothing. *(He lifts his lifeless eyes to Rocco and asks hoarsely)* Did you win today, too?

VINCENZO: It was fantastic. Why didn't you come?

Simone turns slowly to look at Vincenzo, and his gaze is such that the words are extinguished on his brother's lips. Luca comes to Simone's side and remains beside him. By now Rosaria has noticed something odd in her son's appearance, and she questions Rocco and then Vincenzo with a desolate gaze.

SIMONE: Well? What were you saying?

He pours another glass of wine, but his hand shakes so violently that some spills on the tablecloth. Everyone is still and they all exchange alarmed glances.

CIRO *(to Simone, coldly)*: What did you come here for?

Rocco whirls on Ciro.

ROCCO *(reproving)* : Ciro, no!

Simone looks first at Rocco, then at Ciro.

SIMONE *(to Ciro, with bitter irony)*: See? I've got a defender.

ROSARIA *(softly, nearly weeping)*: My son, what's the matter, I was
so happy....

SIMONE *(harshly)*: Rocco. Tell her to keep quiet, too. Tell her!

CIRO *(disgusted)*: He's drunk.

ROCCO: Come here.

He has placed his hand on Simone's shoulder and tries to push him into the kitchen. Simone frees himself violently from his brother's touch. Rocco lowers his hand. As he does so, he notices that it has been soiled by a dark substance. He tries furtively to clean off his hand on a napkin. Simone notices; his eyes grow ever more desperate and the tremor of his limbs more obvious.

ROCCO *(his voice lifeless)*: Come here. I have to talk to you.

SIMONE : I have to talk to you, too. But I can say what I have to right in front of everybody. I didn't come to congratulate you on your successes. I don't give a damn about them. I just want money. All you've got. Right now.

CIRO *(coming resolutely toward Simone)* : We had an agreement, I believe.

Simone kicks a chair to the floor to block his path. Rocco now takes Simone by both shoulders and violently pushes him forward toward the kitchen.

ROCCO : Tell me what you want. Me! But you're hurt?!

As he removes his hand from his brother's shoulder, Rocco again notices that it is covered with blood.

SIMONE *(convulsively)* : No. I have to go away. Right now.

Rocco touches his brother's shoulder firmly once again, to assure himself that Simone is not in fact wounded. A terrifying fear begins to depict itself on Rocco's face.

ROCCO : You're not hurt. But this? What's this?

SIMONE : Blood.

He hurls his brother violently against the wall. Rocco remains with his shoulders nailed to the wall, staring at his brother in anguished terror.

SIMONE *(to Rocco, ferociously)* : It's blood. She hung on to me. I couldn't get away from her. She wouldn't die.

ROCCO *(almost soundlessly)* : Simone!

The others listen in horror.

SIMONE : While you were in the ring, at the same time... I killed her.

ROCCO *(almost soundlessly)* : No!

Simone turns angrily toward the sound of Rosaria's suffocated sobs. He seems about to hurl himself on his family. Rocco moves quickly to block his path and embraces Simone.

ROCCO (*softly, speaking rapidly, almost hysterically*) : For the love of God, Simone. Talk to me. Talk to me.

SIMONE : Nobody saw me and there's no reason they should suspect me. (*Turning ferociously on Rocco*) So it's all over. You happy now, champ? You wanted her to come back to me? That's what you wanted, wasn't it?

ROCCO (*still embracing his brother*) : It's my fault, I know, I know!

Simone thrusts Rocco aside once more. Vincenzo and Ciro bring Rosaria into the adjoining room. The mother falls on a chair, moaning.

ROSARIA (*crossing herself and speaking softly*) : She was a tramp.

VINCENZO : You're sure no one can suspect you?

SIMONE : They can suspect me or him or you or anybody. Anybody who knew her, that is. I left her there near the water. She was with a man....

ROSARIA (*turning to her sons, justifying Simone*) : It was jealousy. Jealousy!

VINCENZO : The man she was with didn't see you?

SIMONE *(suddenly terrified)* : Yes. But it was dark. He didn't see my face.

Simone's face suddenly contracts in a grimace of infantile weeping. For the first time he turns imploringly to Rocco.

SIMONE *(weeping)*: I'm a poor devil. I'll go away forever if you'll help me. If I can get across the border...

ROCCO: Of course.

Now Ciro comes forward. In the silence that now prevails he speaks harshly.

CIRO: You have to go give yourself up. *(All look in embarrassed astonishment at Ciro, who continues with extreme emotion.)* Don't you all think that's what he must do?

Ciro trembles with emotion and indignation.

ROSARIA *(violently)* : He's your brother!

CIRO: I know. Unfortunately!

SIMONE *(raising his voice)*: He's just thinking about the money it'll take.

Simone comes up to Ciro.

CIRO: Just the fact that you can think such a thing shows what you are.

ROCCO *(with extreme emotion)*: Ciro, listen carefully to me. I don't believe in the justice of men. It's not for us. We must only defend him... help him.

CIRO: That's not true. That's not the way to help him. Not the way you want to.

ROSARIA *(almost shouting)*: He's avenged his honor, Ciro!

CIRO: Mama! You too! You're out of your minds!

Rosaria comes up to Ciro.

ROSARIA *(with great violence)* : Shame! Shame!!! You're your
mother's enemy!

*She slaps his face with extreme violence. Ciro remains immobile, without
reacting. Then he suddenly covers his face with his hands.*

*A horrible silence weighs on them all. Simone has fallen prone on the
bed, his face buried in the pillow. Rocco is immobile, backed against the wall
as he watches the scene. Luca has taken refuge in a corner, his eyes terrified
and swollen with tears. Only Vincenzo moves, trying to lead Ginetta
lovingly out of the room. Rosaria also remains immobile among her sons,
who dare not speak or move or look at one another.*

Rosaria lifts her arms to heaven and screams a curse.

ROSARIA: Jesus Christ must repent of all he's done to us!

Rocco starts at Rosaria's cry and turns to her.

ROCCO: No, Ma! Don't curse! *(He starts for the bed on which Simone
has collapsed.)* What good is it? Who listens to us? Everybody's an enemy. That's what we've become: an enemy
family. But why curse? We've made a mistake and we have
to pay for it. We have to pay for it.

*Ciro can no longer bear his brother's words. He suddenly turns his back
on them and rushes out of the house.*

Luca is the first to realize what's happened. He cries out.

LUCA: Ciro! Ciro's leaving!

*Rocco starts. He races after his brother. Rosaria can no longer hold back
her desperate shrieks.*

Stairway, Rosaria's apartment building. Evening.

*Followed by his mother's cries, Ciro rushes on down the stairs as Rocco
appears at the doorway of the apartment.*

ROCCO: Ciro! Where are you going? *(Rocco follows him down the*

stairs; some neighbors come to their doors to look out.) Ciro, listen
Ciro... Wait!

Rosaria appears in the doorway with Vincenzo, shrieking and wailing.

Street in front of Rosaria's apartment building. Evening.

Rocco catches up with his brother in the street and stops him. He forces Ciro to listen to him.

Luca has reached the street, too, by now. He follows the scene from the center of a small group of people who have stopped to watch.

Rosaria's cries are still audible from inside.

ROCCO: What are you doing?

CIRO *(struggling)*: Let me go. Let me go!

ROCCO: In the name of our father, don't do this, Ciro!

With a final tug Ciro frees himself from Rocco's grasp and flees. Rocco remains standing there, watching. Luca comes up to him.

ROCCO: Now it's finished!

Luca huddles against Rocco as if seeking protection. Superimposed on the scene appears the word: LUCA.

Alfa Romeo automobile factory. Outside. Day.

In a field in front of the factory gates, some of the workers are playing soccer with a rag ball as others eat their lunch in the pale sun of an early spring day. An intimidated and uncertain Luca appears at the far end of the open space separating the factory from the first buildings of the city. He looks toward the factory as he approaches, seeking his brother Ciro among the workers. When at last he sees Ciro sitting slightly apart at the edge of the field, Luca comes slowly toward him. Ciro does not notice him at first. When he does, he turns for just a moment, then looks straight ahead again.

CIRO: What did you come for?

There is short silence. Luca too avoids looking at Ciro, and when he speaks it is with an evident effort.

LUCA: They took him away this morning at seven. They found him up on the roof, in the room where the water tanks are. He'd been sleeping there for three nights. *(Another pause; Luca sits down, but his back is to Ciro.)* He was supposed to leave tonight. Rocco had gotten him a passport. He wanted to go to France. But they put the handcuffs on him and they dragged him down the stairs like a sack of potatoes. Mama was screaming so loud everybody came out to look.

Ciro covers his face with his hands. Luca turns to look at him and is stupefied and slightly hostile to find Ciro weeping.

LUCA *(hostile)*: What are you crying for? You should be happy... since you wanted to turn him in. Now you can come home and be the boss again.

CIRO *(after a pause)*: When you get older you'll understand you've been unjust to me. You've all been unjust. None of you loved Simone as much as I did. When we left home I was the age you are now. Simone was the one who explained to me what Vincenzo hadn't understood. Simone said that down home we were living like animals that had to depend on the whim or the generosity of their owner. He explained that we had to learn to stick up for our rights, after we'd learned to know our duties. Simone forgot all these things, afterwards. I've tried to learn to know my rights and my duties. *(Struggling with his tears)* That's why I can't... *(Ciro bites his hand to suffocate his tears; in an almost irritated tone.)* What have I got to gain from a misfortune like what's hit us? I'm proud; I have ambitions. I want to succeed in life. Don't think that tomorrow, when the picture of my brother the murderer hits all the papers,

it'll be very pleasant for me to keep on working in there...
side by side with my friends who like me, who respect me.
Or present myself to my girl! It would have been much
better for me if no one had ever found out. If they had
accused just any poor devil, wouldn't it? *(In the brief pause
that follows, Ciro passes a hand over his face; his voice is even
softer as he continues.)* I didn't inform on him, but it's as
if I had. Simone's a sick man who poisons everything.
He's sowed hatred and disorder in our house. He was
ruining you, who has to become the best of all of us, because you're the youngest and you can profit by all our
experience. And Rocco's goodness is as harmful as his evil.
That seems odd to you? It's the truth. Rocco's a saint.
But in the world we live in, in the society men have created,
there's no more place for saints like him. Their pity creates
disasters.

Luca's expression is upset as he watches Ciro.

LUCA: If Rocco goes back home I'll go with him.

CIRO *(sadly)*: I don't think Rocco will ever be able to go back
again. What do you think will be different down there?
Our town will become a big city too, where men will
learn to stick up for their rights and to impose duties.
I don't know if that kind of world is nice, but that's the
way it is, and if we're a part of it we have to accept its
rules.

*At sound of the factory sirens, the workmen start back toward the gates.
It is the end of the lunch hour. Ciro carefully folds up the paper in which
his lunch was wrapped and stands up.*

CIRO *(bending over his little brother and caressing his hair)*: Kiss Mama
for me.

*He starts back to the gates. Luca remains standing there, watching Ciro.
His eyes fill with tears. Suddenly he shouts out, raising his hand.*

LUCA: Ciro! *(Already in the midst of the other workers near the factory gates, Ciro turns.)* Come home tonight. We'll be waiting for you!

Ciro smiles at him and waves. Luca now starts off for home again. He is smiling slightly as he crosses the grassy open space where groups of workmen are still standing. He walks along a sidewalk with a quick step and breaks out in short spurts of running.

He suddenly stops, his attention attracted by a newspaper stand. The dealer has displayed a number of copies of a sports magazine in neat order all around the stand. The cover picture is repeated as in the infinite reflections of a set of mirrors. Luca is pleasantly struck by the display, for the cover photograph is of Rocco. A large headline announces an important world tour of the young champion: Brussels—London—Melbourne, etc. After contemplating the images of his brother, Luca continues on for home, followed by the ear-splitting shriek of the sirens.

THE END.

The Job (1962)

(An episode from *Boccaccio '70*)

Credits

Producers:	Carlo Ponti, Antonio Cervi
Director:	Luchino Visconti
Screenplay:	Suso Cecchi d'Amico, Luchino Visconti, from an idea by Cesare Zavattini based on Maupassant's short story, *Au Bord du Lit*
Director of Photography:	Giuseppe Rotunno
Editor:	Mario Serandrei
Art Director:	Mario Garbuglia
Music:	Nino Rota

Cast:

Pupe:	Romy Schneider
The Count:	Tomas Milian
The Lawyer:	Romolo Valli

Entrance hall and first drawing room of Ottavio's and Pupe's home. Inside.
Evening.

Under the titles, three or four enormous pedigreed dogs race barking across
the room and hurl themselves against the door. A servant, somewhat afraid
of the dogs and attempting to defend himself against them, makes his way
toward the same door. From the outside is heard the insistent sound of a car
horn.

FIRST SERVANT *(under his breath)*: Damn you! Get away, down,
      down! Masaccio! Down! Here!

The sound of the horn rouses the dogs to ever greater cacophony. With
some effort the servant finally manages to thrust his way through them
and open the door. In the meantime another servant hurries into the
entrance hall upon hearing the dogs and the horn. End of the titles.

The dogs race out as the door is opened, almost knocking the first servant
down and hiding from view their young master, who is coming up the last
part of the stairway. Recovering his balance, the first servant greets the
master in perfect form, rapidly readjusting his jacket which the struggle
with the dogs had disarranged.

FIRST SERVANT: Welcome home, sir.

The second servant runs toward the door, careful to keep his distance from
the dogs.

SECOND SERVANT: Good evening, sir.

The count comes forward surrounded by the ecstatically barking pack of
dogs.

COUNT *(bored)*: Evening.

The chauffeur follows him in, carrying suitcases and a briefcase. With a suddenly more relaxed expression, the count greets his dogs with affectionate slaps on their necks and sides.

COUNT *(to the dogs)* : Saint. Sympathy.

CHAUFFEUR : Your instructions, sir?

Of all the servants, the chauffeur is evidently the one most terrified of the dogs. He deposits the suitcases in the entrance hall and immediately retreats to await the orders which the count is far from thinking of imparting, totally absorbed as he is in extracting something from behind one of the dogs' ears.

COUNT *(to dog)* : What've you got here behind your ear?

The chauffeur looks at the first servant as if to ask instructions from him. The servant's answer is to shrug his shoulders. The chauffeur shrugs in turn, glances with aversion at the dogs, and gestures as if to say, "I'll be downstairs." He begins to go downstairs.

COUNT *(to first servant)* : Is the lawyer gone?

FIRST SERVANT : No, he's waiting in the drawing room.

COUNT *(bored)* : Hell. *(To the dog he is cleaning)* Dirty beast. Saint. Sympathy.

The count finishes cleaning the animal's ear and dismisses it with a last slap. Meanwhile the servant has opened the door to the drawing room and smiles at the count as if to compliment him on his cleaning operations as he starts to try to hold back the dogs.

COUNT : Let 'em go.

The servant immediately steps back in fright as the count passes into the drawing room surrounded by the dogs. Overjoyed by this unhoped-for concession, they leap forward, upsetting everything in their way.

Drawing room, Ottavio's and Pupe's home. Inside. Evening.

The dogs' entrance into the drawing room is greeted by the noise of chairs being pushed back and by a confusion of voices.

VOICE OF AN ELDERLY MAN *(shrill)* : Hey, no, by God!

Four men are standing in the room, and all but the lawyer Zacchi are rather terrified of the dogs. The oldest of them, Professor Berardelli, does not even attempt to smile.

COUNT *(to Zacchi, without a smile and with the same air of boredom)* : What's going on?

ZACCHI: Professor Berardelli's afraid of Michelangelo.

Ottavio, with a tired gesture, turns to look at Professor Berardelli, at whom the largest of the dogs is snarling and barking furiously.

COUNT *(with a smile, immediately repressed)* : They can tell right away if you don't like them. *(To the dog)* Michelangelo. *(With extreme kindness)* Take it easy, Michelangelo. Masaccio, come here. Don't you get into it too. *(The count goes to the door, opens it and calls with sudden irritation.)* Antonio! *(The first servant appears immediately.)* Why didn't you tell me Zacchi wasn't alone? *(To dogs)* Go on out. Take them away.

FIRST SERVANT *(weakly)* : I did say. But perhaps you didn't hear me, sir.

The dogs try to regain their master's confidence by lying down.

COUNT *(without raising his voice)* : I said get out.

With this final word Ottavio makes his decision irrevocable and the dogs go out behind the first servant, whining and growling one last time at Professor Berardelli.

ANOTHER LAWYER *(with forced cordiality)* : They're splendid animals. What breed are they?

The count does not answer. He is watching Zacchi with a questioning expression on his face, as if asking for an explanation of the presence of so many people.

ZACCHI *(to Ottavio)* : This is Professor Berardelli, Mr. Simoni, Mr. Alcamo. Since the situation was so serious, I felt...

The count acknowledges the introductions with a courteous but distracted nod and motions his guests into the library, whose door Antonio has opened. As they enter the library, his eyes fall on a folder in Zacchi's hand. Zacchi notices Ottavio's glance.

ZACCHI: Here're all the papers, arranged according to political stand. Have you seen them yet?

OTTAVIO *(letting himself fall into an armchair)* : On the plane. The French ones... here they are... *(Hits the table)* Eyewash.

ZACCHI: Not quite. If I thought it necessary to disturb my eminent colleagues... *(To Ottavio)* Where were you? I called you in Paris, in London. Where were you?

COUNT *(bored)*: How should I know?

Zacchi's three colleagues exchange glances.

ZACCHI: Well, anyway, luckily you called yourself this morning. But there's one thing I don't understand. You called me because you heard…

COUNT *(in the same detached tone, picking up a folder of newspapers)*: No. I called because I ran out of money. Now that I think of it, have some money sent to… *(Remembering the presence of the others)* I'll tell you later. *(Reading from a newspaper)* "We're just good friends, says the call girls' count." What kind of stuff is this?

No longer exhausted and pained, the count reveals sudden interest through his expression.

ZACCHI *(triumphant)*: Then you've only seen yesterday's papers. Today's are *all* running the news on the front page. And for once they're all on the same side, rightists and leftists. It could be good for a laugh. *(Emphasizing)* You've carried out your plan.

The count does not appreciate the lawyer's "brilliant" witticism in the least and darts an ever more disgusted look at him, almost compassionate. The lawyer hurries to conclude.

ZACCHI: We've filed suit for defamation against the lot of them. Without proof, of course.

The count tosses the papers onto the table and points to one with his foot. It is an illustrated news magazine.

COUNT *(thoughtful)*: That was a very bad move. For once it would have been right to buy off these jackals. I suppose they came around first, as usual, to ask you to pay…

ZACCHI: We were negotiating. But after the police got into it the word got out to the dailies, and then the whole thing broke loose. *(Excited)* Once the bomb went off their demands became exorbitant. I couldn't take the responsibility for so much money all by myself. Do you want to know how much?

COUNT *(indifferent)* : You could have asked my wife.

ZACCHI: Your wife, eh? *(Counting on the effect of his revelation)* And where was your wife?

COUNT: Where was she?

ZACCHI: That's what I'd like to know. She's disappeared since yesterday.

The other lawyers, poker-faced, nod approvingly and await the young count's reaction.

COUNT *(still calm)* : Disappeared. She's around somewhere. You think she should stay shut up in the house waiting for you to call? Ask Antonio, he'll tell you where my wife's disappeared to.

Ottavio reluctantly slides out of the armchair, where he has been reposing comfortably with his legs dangling over the arm, and goes to ring for the servant.

ZACCHI *(abruptly stopping him)* : You can't seem to understand how serious this is! Your wife went out yesterday morning saying she was going to the hairdresser's, and she hasn't been seen since. Her father's called several times and left word for her to meet him immediately at Burgenstock. But she still hasn't showed up at Burgenstock. I can assure you that she hasn't crossed the border in her car or by train or plane. This morning, with Professor Berardelli's help, we put the police onto it, top secret of course. *(Checks his watch)* We should be calling them now. *(To the count, who is ringing nervously)* Understand? It's quite beyond your Antonio.

COUNT: We'll have him bring us something to drink. *(Returning to his armchair)* Anyway, instead of worrying about my wife you should have taken care of these characters.

Ottavio points to the papers scattered over the low table.

ZACCHI *(interrupting the count and speaking rapidly, with exasperation)*: We've been worrying about your wife for an infinite number of reasons that I'm astonished you can't comprehend. First of all, there's a human factor involved. *(The lawyer is so upset that he stammers.)* It may be that your wife—and the facts unfortunately bear this out—your wife, a young woman and a foreigner, has been upset by this scandal. Because it is a scandal, no point in hiding it, and there's no telling what the consequences will be. Even for taxes, you'll see. *(Old Professor Berardelli nods in agreement.)* And then we needed her because if she'd stepped in, it would have had an immediate effect. Her solidarity *(Rhetorical)*, her defense. *(Citing a hypothetical headline)* "The beautiful young wife of the count, et cetera, et cetera, confidently awaits the results of the investigation of the million-lire call-girl scandal in which her husband is said to be implicated. A happy marriage, unbeclouded, et cetera, et cetera." *(Suddenly changing his tone, coldly)* But instead... You know your father-in-law's frozen the bank accounts? Yes, sir. Yesterday morning. He had the power to do it. Everything's in your wife's name, in Switzerland.

COUNT *(piqued, to the others)* : That was for tax purposes.

ZACCHI: And it was the right thing to do. But we're in your father-in-law's hands. As long as we're all one happy family it's an excellent ploy. The day you begin to talk about divorce they can screw you. Pardon me.

There is a brief silence. A discreet cough is heard: Antonio has entered the room silently and stands near the door trying to make his presence known.

COUNT *(distractedly)* : Oh. Antonio. Where's my wife? *(Catching himself)* I mean: bring something to drink. Or would you gentlemen prefer coffee?

ALCAMO *(lugubrious)* : Coffee for me, thanks.

PROFESSOR BERARDELLI *(also very grave)* : Just water. With a bit of sugar, if you don't mind.

ZACCHI *(still emphatic)* : Right. Cold water. Ice; very important: ice.

Antonio turns to his employer.

COUNT *(to Antonio)* : Fix it up. Bring the ice and an Alexander for me.

Antonio bows and, before leaving the room, says without raising his voice:

ANTONIO : Madame is in her room.

Antonio is about to go out when Zacchi reaches him and clutches his arm.

ZACCHI : In her room? Since when?

Before answering, Antonio turns to his master as if asking his permission. Ottavio gets up again from the armchair, shaking his head as if pitying his lawyer's incompetence.

COUNT *(ironically, to Zacchi)* : Call the cops.

ANTONIO : She returned shortly after you, sir. When she heard these gentlemen were here she didn't want to disturb you, so she went right to her room.

Antonio leaves the room and Ottavio is about to follow him when Zacchi clutches him in turn and speaks excitedly:

ZACCHI : Wait a minute. Where are you going?

COUNT *(calm and ironical)* : To my wife. You've been looking for her for two days and now you don't want...

The lawyer closes the door with an air of mystery and speaks softly.

ZACCHI: Fine. But get this. *(Summoning his colleagues' support with a glance)* We have to get a statement for the papers right away.

SIMONI: It would be disastrous to announce a separation.

PROFESSOR BERARDELLI: The money.

ZACCHI: We have to be able to maneuver... *(Ottavio opens the door again and starts to walk out; Zacchi approaches to whisper softly after him.)* What'll you tell her? Remember all those women gave your name to the cops. All of them. I'd advise you to deny it all the same, but...

Zacchi finds himself face to face with Antonio, who is returning with the ice. The lawyer is reluctantly forced to give up his exhortations.

ZACCHI *(louder, after the count)*: We'll be waiting here.

The lawyer returns to the library immediately, followed by Antonio, who is pushing along a tea cart. Zacchi sits down in an armchair and addresses his colleagues in the slightly false tone which Antonio's presence imposes.

ZACCHI: He's a fine boy at bottom. A fine boy.

And the lawyer begins to gather together the newspapers, in which the portrait of the fine boy, Count Ottavio, appears in various poses beside photographs of buxom, scantily clad girls whose faces are largely concealed by black strips. The headlines repeat, in all dimensions, "Count Ottavio, etc., etc., implicated in the million-lire call-girl scandal."

Pupe's apartment. Inside. Evening.

COUNT'S VOICE: Pupe, Pupe...

The lights are on in the room but no one is to be seen save some Persian cats sprawled out voluptuously on the huge sofas; they barely lift their heads at the disturbance before falling back asleep.

COUNT: Pupe...

He is answered by a sudden burst of music. Ottavio stops, turns, and walks slowly toward one corner of the room, where he finds his wife lying on the carpet beside the sofa on which are lying two of the cats.

This must be Madame's favorite corner, judging from the books piled up here and there on the floor, the magazines tossed about, the telephone and the phonograph, which the young woman turns on and adjusts with her bare foot, employing much more energy than if she had simply arisen and used her hands. Toilet articles are also scattered about on the carpet: a mirror and some cosmetics.

COUNT: Hi.

The lady's only response is to halfopen her eyes, throw a little kiss into the air, and motion slightly to the phonograph, from which a guttural voice is croaking out.

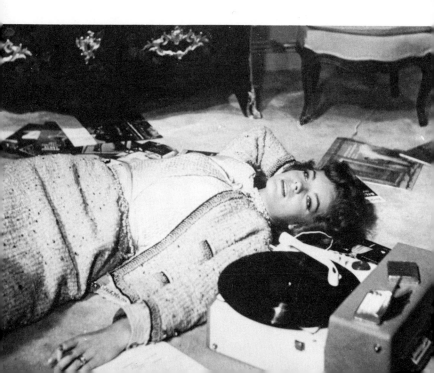

SINGER'S VOICE: "Here I am, baby. Drunk and sleepy and lonely."

Ottavio nods toward the phonograph as if acknowledging the singer's statement, then slips to the floor to sit beside his wife, pushing aside some papers and a notebook.

With a disgruntled expression Ottavio indicates the newspapers lying around on the floor.

COUNT: I see that...

The singer's voice limits itself to croaking out the title of the song. Now it is silent, submerged by the lamenting cry of a trumpet. Pupe motions her husband to be still.

PUPE: Just a minute, sweetheart.

Pupe looks about as if she is trying to find something: the papers and note-book which Ottavio swept aside in sitting down and which she now tries to pull toward herself, using a book held in her outstretched hand.

COUNT *(courteously)*: What do you want? This?

The count hands the notebook and papers to his young wife, who takes them and, raising herself slightly, reads something from them as she whistles silently, trying to follow the rhythm of the music. This continues for a brief moment. Satisfied by her efforts, Pupe puts down the notebook, lowers the volume of the music with her foot and turns to her husband.

PUPE: What?

COUNT *(again pointing to the newspapers)*: More lies than words. I'm sorry for your father, who as usual will believe anything.

PUPE *(sighing gravely)*: Mm, yes.

A brief silence. Ottavio hunches up with a peevish air.

COUNT: What makes me mad, besides the lies, is the tone of these articles. Like an operetta. What shit. *(Pupe has stopped listening; she is looking through her notebook.)* What's the matter, Pupe?

PUPE *(as if rousing herself)* : Nothing. I want you to listen to something. We'll talk afterwards.

It must be something important because Pupe curls around on the carpet until she is able to reach the arm of the phonograph and place it back at the trumpet solo.

COUNT: No! I'm too wrought up to listen to music.

PUPE: It's not the music. Now you'll hear it.

She motions Ottavio to be patient.

COUNT *(still upset)* : Where were you yesterday and today? He says they looked everywhere for you. The cops too.

PUPE *(following the music)* : I was out. I saw a lot of things. I was thinking. I've made some important decisions. I stood for ages in front of a wall. A long white wall. Actually, it was there…. Listen. *(Pupe picks up the phonograph arm and places it a few grooves back; she reads from the notebook, heavily stressing the meter.)* "I love you, cypress tree, for my melancholy is like as thee."

Pupe raises her eyes and gazes at her husband.

COUNT: What is it?

PUPE *(very proudly)* : Poetry. I wrote it myself. You like it? Say you like it. I adooooore it.

COUNT: Maybe I didn't hear well. *(Pupe immediately picks up the arm again and searches for the trumpet solo ; the count continues, bored.)* Forget the music.

PUPE: They go well together. Here it is. "I love you, cypress tree, for my melancholy is like as thee."

COUNT *(after a brief pause)* : It's a nice idea. But there's something wrong with it. You can't write poems in Italian, dear. You don't know the language well enough. I don't think you can say "like as thee."

PUPE *(offended)* : And why not?

COUNT : Because.

PUPE : But it's poetry.

COUNT : So what? Grammar has rules.

PUPE : What's the rule?

COUNT : I can't explain it. I can't remember the theory. I just know it's not right. *(Irritated)* Does this seem like the right time... *(Catching himself)* Write it in German, dear. It'll certainly sound better.

PUPE : No. I speak German well because it's my language. But I never studied it. I studied in France and England.

COUNT : So write it in French or English.

PUPE *(becoming irritated in turn)* : But now I know Italian much better. Anyway it just came to me. Poetry is inspiration.

COUNT : But if it's wrong...

PUPE *(ever more disappointed)* : You mean it's ugly, I have no talent, I should forget it? All right. I'll forget it. I'm sorry, because it was so important for me, for us...

COUNT : It sounds wrong to me. But I'm no expert.

PUPE : Right. You're an expert only about girls.

COUNT *(tired)* : Come on, Pupe. There's almost no truth in what the papers say. The lawyers will take care of denying it. The little truth there is isn't important. You're too intelligent not to know how much value to place on certain things.

PUPE : I really didn't know what value.

COUNT *(picking up some of the papers)* : Are you talking about money value? *(With a little laugh)* You really think I...

PUPE: I know it for certain. I've talked with the girls.

COUNT: You?

PUPE: I was there all yesterday afternoon. First Mirella, then Lilli, then... They're all out on bail.

Ottavio glances rapidly at his wife. He still does not know how to interpret her attitude.

PUPE *(combing her hair)*: I wanted to get it all clear. I talked with the manager, too. Imola. That's her name, isn't it?

Pupe has bent her head to one side and is combing out her beautiful blond hair.

The telephone rings. With an impatient gesture Ottavio reaches for the receiver, but Pupe gets to it first.

PUPE *(to the telephone)*: Yes, Antonio. Put him on. Wait, Antonio. I'm a little hungry. Yes. Here, please. For the count too. *(In German)* Hello, Papa. Call back in a little while if you don't mind. Take it easy. It's just that I can't tell you anything for sure yet. No, no, I haven't changed my mind. Call back later.

Pupe is still speaking as Ottavio, leaning over with unusual warmth, whispers to her.

COUNT *(softly)*: Explain that it's a political frame-up and ask why yesterday morning he ordered...

Ottavio has not yet finished his thought when Pupe hangs up.

PUPE: Oh, I'm sorry. Did you want to talk to him?

COUNT: I wanted to know why he gave orders...

The telephone rings again.

PUPE *(into the telephone)*: Antonio? Oh. *(To her husband)* Antonio wants to know what those gentlemen are supposed to do who are waiting for you.

COUNT *(impatiently)* : They should wait.

PUPE *(into the telephone)* : They should wait. Yes, thanks, Antonio.

COUNT *(bleaker)* : It's the lawyers. You should have told your father... there're a lot of complications here...

PUPE : Don't ask Papa for money. He's already so angry. He says you can't amuse yourself at my expense.

COUNT : Who's amusing themselves? *(Warming to the subject)* And listen. We've never gone into "mine" and "yours." I never said this mansion is mine, this furniture's mine, the estates are mine.

PUPE : All things that don't bring in any money.

COUNT : So let's sell them. But you want the mansion, you want the jewels, you want the hunting reserve...

PUPE : That's what we got married for. *(Dramatically)* Water under the bridge. Now I don't want anything.

COUNT : What?

PUPE : I told you I've made some important decisions. Either we get a separation, as Papa would like...

COUNT *(interrupting)* : Oh, that's what he'd like, is it?

PUPE *(calm)* : You know how it is. Papa was happy we got married, because of the prestige. But he's never had much affection for you, as a person. He doesn't even believe you're worried. He says you're just stupid.

COUNT *(profoundly offended but making an effort to smile ironically)* : Ah, yes. I'm glad to know it. While we're on the subject, let me tell you what I think of him.

PUPE *(interrupting, bored)* : I already know.'

COUNT *(impatiently)* : If he doesn't believe what I tell him he can at least read. Let him read; there are a thousand writers

who can explain whether or not our generation is amusing itself.

PUPE *(still bored)* : He's a very simple man. Is it his fault? He thinks a man like you who pays seven hundred thousand lire to sleep with a girl does it to amuse himself, not to bore himself.

COUNT *(tiredly)* : And I suppose you believe it too, even though you should know me better. *(As if deciding reluctantly to give an explanation)* You want to know how this story got started? It was because of old Imola. When I was a kid Imola was about thirty. You might say we all began there, Alberico, Stefano, myself. Then over the years Imola disappeared. One day we happened to hear she was back in action here, and we sort of wanted to look her up. You know, like going up to the attic to look at the toys you used to play with.

PUPE: And what have the girls got to do with it?

COUNT *(shrugging)* : God, Pupe. I tell you we just wanted to give the old girl a present.

PUPE: She's a pig. You gave her seven hundred and she gave four hundred to the girls. If you wanted to give Imola a present you could have given her three hundred and saved yourself the four hundred for the girls you weren't interested in. Or maybe they were able to interest you, since you went back there... *(Checking her notebook)* ...eleven times. *(Generous)* Pretty girls, too. Especially one. Lilli, I think.

COUNT *(vaguely)* : Yes, yes.

PUPE: So you admit it. You liked them.

COUNT *(with lazy surprise)* : What's going on, Pupe? Is this a jealous scene?

PUPE: For gracious' sakes. Each of us is free to do what he likes. That's our arrangement. The real marriage is between you and Papa. And as a matter of fact he's the one who's gotten mad.

Preceded by a discreet knock on the door, Antonio appears with a large silver tray laden with all conceivable delicacies.

PUPE *(to Antonio)* : Set it down here, Antonio.

She points to the floor. Antonio approaches cautiously, glancing distastefully at the cats, who have awakened and are sniffing the air hungrily.

ANTONIO *(discreetly)* : Madame didn't say what she would like, so I thought...

COUNT: All right, all right, Antonio.

Antonio sets the tray down on the floor and goes to find a low table on which to lay the plates.

ANTONIO *(to the count)* : Mr. Zacchi...

COUNT: Ah, yes. *(To his wife, somewhat embarrassed)* Please listen, dear. Zacchi's still here. The lawyers say that if you have a statement to make to the newspapers... *(To Antonio, impatiently)* That's all right, Antonio, we'll fix it up ourselves.

Antonio is about to leave when Pupe calls him back.

PUPE: No; please, Antonio. Take the cats downstairs. Give them something to eat and get their baskets ready. I may be leaving tonight, and if so I'll be taking them with me.

Antonio bows his head slightly in assent and reaches out to pick up one of the cats lying on the nearer sofa. But the cat—which evidently returns Antonio's distaste for it—escapes to the arm of a chair and from there to the floor. Sighing, Antonio prepares to pursue the cats and must pass in front of the count.

ANTONIO *(to count)* : Excuse me.

COUNT *(angrily, to Pupe)* : Does he have to get them this very minute?

PUPE: Of course. It'll only take a second. *(Ottavio bites his lip to control his impatience; he watches Antonio, who is still very close to him, and begins to eat angrily.)* Hungry?

COUNT *(eating)* : No.

PUPE: You mentioned the lawyers. They can make any kind of statement they like. It's none of my business. That's what they're paid for, to make decisions.

COUNT *(controlling himself)* : This is something that concerns you. Give it some thought. You've mentioned leaving, separation. The point is real solidarity, moral and material.

A cat meows. Pupe turns. Antonio has managed to catch one of the cats by the tail.

PUPE: Give him to me, Antonio. Quick, get Moby Dick before he gets under the sofa.

Antonio hurries to hand the first cat to Pupe, who puts it on her lap. He immediately starts after the others, followed by Ottavio's vexed glare.

PUPE: I mentioned separation because I don't know whether you're going to agree or not to my plans for the future. *(Pupe has set a plate on her lap next to the cat, which begins to nibble at its contents.)* Your girls have been as good an occasion as any to set me to thinking about a lot of things. *(After a pause)* I'm going to go to work.

The telephone rings. This time Ottavio gets to the receiver first.

COUNT *(into the telephone, agitated)*: Oh, yes. Sorry, Zacchi. I'll be right with you. My wife's agreed in principle to the statement.... Sorry, there's a long-distance call. *(To his wife)* Burgenstock. It's your father again.

Pupe elongates her neck and motions to her husband to hold the telephone next to her ear, her hands being occupied with the cat and the plate.

PUPE *(into the telephone, in German)*: Hello, Papa. I still don't know. I'll tell you a little later. But anyway I'm not changing my mind, you can be sure of that. I don't know if I'll need it. I'll tell you. What did you say? And I'm convinced I'll win.

With a look, Pupe gives her husband to understand that the conversation is over. Ottavio hangs up the receiver.

COUNT: What did he want this time?

PUPE: We made a bet. For a hundred million. Papa bets I won't be able to earn my living by myself.

Antonio approaches with all the cats in his arms. Pupe starts to hand him the one in her lap, and the plate spills all over her dress.

PUPE *(looking at her dress)*: Now I've done it. *(To Antonio)* Don't worry about it, Antonio. You take care of the cats. *(To her husband, picking up the discussion where it had been interrupted)* I have to start from scratch. As if the only thing I owned were the dress on my back. *(Beginning to unbutton it)* Or maybe a clean one. You wouldn't be amused by the idea of my working?

COUNT: Why should it amuse me? The idea that work isn't boring went out a long time ago. Ask Antonio. *(Calling)* Antonio! *(Antonio has just reached the door, with his armful of cats, and turns in alarm.)* You're bored, aren't you?

Antonio tries to control himself, but the cats squirming around in his arms put his patience to sore trial. His answering mutter is therefore in the affirmative.

ANTONIO: Eeeeh.

PUPE *(spiritedly plunging into the dialogue)*: But it's not horrible boredom. It doesn't worry you. *(Antonio gazes at her worriedly.)* Perhaps you have some material worries. Your salary or whatnot.

ANTONIO *(coming to life for a moment)*: Ah, yes. My salary. Madame had promised me...

One of the cats is about to squirm away. Antonio clutches it again, interrupting his thought.

PUPE: Some other time, Antonio. You may go. *(Antonio leaves the room; Pupe slips lazily out of her dress, remaining in her slip.)* You didn't have to ask Antonio. I can judge for myself. But you can be sure that even if he's bored he'll never get to the point of ending up in the newspapers because of this kind of thing.

Pupe lifts up one of the newspapers with her foot.

COUNT *(losing his temper for the first time)*: Because no one cares if Antonio goes and pays seven hundred lire for one of the girls out on the boulevards. *(He stammers in his great indignation.)* No... no one puts that on the front pages of the papers. But it's exactly the same thing.

PUPE *(spiritedly)*: That's what you say. If poor Antonio, after a long day's work... *(Interrupting herself and changing her tone of voice)* You don't understand a thing, and if you think you're going to change my mind you're wrong. I've made up my mind. *(She looks at the notebook in which her poem is written.)* I'd like to write, but... maybe later on. I'll do something else for a start. There are hundreds of thousands of even more remunerative kinds of work in this world.

As Pupe speaks, the telephone begins to ring. But she places her hand on the receiver and raises it only when she has completed her thought.

PUPE *(into the telephone, annoyance in her voice)*: Who is it? *(More courteously)* Oh, Mr. Zacchi. Where are you calling from? No, he's still here, poor thing. *(Listens briefly)* Professor who? How sweet. *(In a calmer tone)* You must be hungry too. *(Listens briefly)* But of course, Mr. Zacchi. I've already told Ottavio so. You can make all the statements you like. *(Listens briefly)* Deny it? No, how silly. It's perfectly true. *(To Ottavio, in a tone of protest)* That's just fine: your lawyers have the idea it's all a pack of lies.

COUNT *(snorting)*: Of course they don't. He wants to make you think that because he thinks you'd be upset.

PUPE *(into the telephone, in a tone of surprise)* : Mr. Zacchi! I don't have a petty bourgeois mind. Not even the petty bourgeois have them any more. People read, they go to the movies... *(Ever more ironically)* ...and most important, everybody does the same thing. Aristocrats, intellectuals, workers. I have to agree with Ottavio there. Let's not mention scandals, for gracious' sakes. Let's talk about banality, if you like. That's what I told my father too. What? *(Listens briefly)* Of course, of course. The accounts have been unfrozen; don't worry. Papa understands perfectly well that Ottavio's certainly not going to do anything silly at this point, so pay whatever you have to and let that be the end of it.

From his corner of the carpet Ottavio throws his wife a glance that reveals a certain interest in what the woman is saying.

PUPE *(still on the telephone, settling down more comfortably as if for a long chat)* : But get it from Ottavio. I'm not taking another penny. Me. *(In a somewhat victimized tone)* I no longer live on unearned income. I've gone to work, dear sir. *(Listens very briefly)* Don't say such a thing! Do you get bored? Are you ever worried? *(Listens briefly; then, more polemically)* You see? I've thought a lot about it, you know. Don't think it's a sudden decision. *(She listens briefly then looks toward her husband, who is pouring himself a drink; into the telephone.)* Ottavio? I don't know. Anyway I think we'll separate. *(Listens briefly)* My dear sir, I'll try to explain what I told

a boy from San Giovanni yesterday morning, to clarify my
own ideas. Yes. A soft-drink vendor I stopped to talk to
as I was wandering around. If you want you can tell my
husband too. *(Listens briefly)* Where's my husband? He's
here, dear. But I can't make him understand such things.
(Listens briefly) Yes, I'll send him to you right away. *(To
Ottavio)* Zacchi wants you in the library.

Ottavio finishes his drink, gets up slowly, and starts to leave the room.

PUPE *(into the telephone)*: Don't think, Mr. Zacchi, that when I
got married I had any illusions about breaking down the
barriers of noncommunication. I knew perfectly well I'd
be hideously alone. I married my husband because it so
happened that our fortunes wished to marry. I respect
money. The proof of that is that I've decided to make it
my *raison d'être* by earning it for myself. *(Listens very briefly)*
In order for money to amuse you, to excite you, to make
you suffer and enjoy, I mean, you have to earn it yourself, there's no way around that. *(Listens briefly)* Further
my education? But I already have one, sir, there's nothing
for it. Anyway that's all superstructure. And I'm so bored
with superstructures. I want to become an ordinary sort
of woman, with my little job, my little worries...

Ottavio has stopped in the doorway to listen. Now he leaves.

PUPE *(raising herself up to see if her husband has left, and winding up
on the telephone with a drawling voice)*: Of course. A certain
physical attraction doesn't justify a marriage, does it?
It comes, it goes... *(The drawl becomes more pronounced.)*
So long, Mr. Zacchi. You take care of everything. And keep
me informed or I won't know what's going on. From now
on I won't even have the money to buy myself a newspaper.

*Pupe hangs up the telephone, stretches her legs, and picks up her notebook.
Then she slowly gets up and starts toward the bathroom. As she passes by
the phonograph, she replaces the arm on the record and turns the machine on.*

Pupe goes back and retrieves the notebook. She goes to the bathroom, reading attentively.

PUPE *(whispering)* : "I love you, cypress tree..."

She sets the notebook down on the sink and starts to undress for her shower.

In the drawing room.

Ottavio is crossing the drawing room and heading toward the library when the door to the latter is opened and the lawyers begin to file out. Professor Berardelli looks warily around himself as if afraid of running into the dogs. Zacchi is the last to leave; he carries the folder of newspapers and a sheet of paper he shows to Ottavio.

ZACCHI: Well, we're in fair shape now. As far as the family's concerned, I mean. And that has its importance.

PROFESSOR BERARDELLI: Damnation. The family is one of Nature's masterpieces, as Santayana says.

COUNT *(ironical)* : Of course. Who's this Santayana?

ZACCHI *(to Ottavio)* : First sign this power of attorney and then I'll tell you.

Zacchi has placed the paper on top of the folder and Ottavio signs wearily as the other lawyers walk toward the entrance.

ZACCHI *(slightly worried)* : Are you quite sure the accounts have been unfrozen?

OTTAVIO: That's what Pupe said. You can count on it. *(Nastily)* If you'd been the one to say it I wouldn't be so sure. Allow me to tell you that as a lawyer you're a real... *(Rapidly)* What do I pay you for? My wife's supposed to have disappeared, and instead she's in her room. My father-in-law...

The three distinguished colleagues have stopped and turn in surprise. Zacchi gazes pleadingly at the count.

ZACCHI *(in a forced tone)* : By the way, your wife was telling me something odd. What's this business of her going to work? *(Ottavio answers with a shrug.)* Oh, not that I disapprove, of course. Quite the contrary. I may even say that at the press conference, if I get the chance. It'll make a very good impression. *(In a schoolmasterly tone)* It would be a good thing for you too.

COUNT *(distracted)* : What would?

Zacchi is about to answer but does not, partly because the other lawyers are urging him to come along with gestures aimed at making him understand that they wish to go.

Antonio has rung for the other servant. He leads the lawyers toward the door.

ZACCHI *(hurriedly)* : Well, we can discuss that later. But listen, keep an eye on your wife. She says she doesn't care a bit, but I'm sure… Not to mention the fact that the more you're seen together in public these days, the better.

With a sign of resignation Professor Berardelli heads toward the door.

Pupe's apartment.

The record is still spinning. The shower water is heard in the bathroom. Then it stops and Pupe's silhouette appears behind the filmy shower curtain.

Now Ottavio's hand lifts up the record arm and turns off the phonograph.

PUPE'S VOICE : Leave it on!

Ottavio hesitates a moment; then, with a sigh, he replaces the arm. Pupe has stepped out from behind the shower curtain, barely covered by a bath towel, her head swathed in a turban.

PUPE : Finished?

COUNT : He wanted me to sign something. *(He pours a drink.)* Now they'll be taking their cut from this business too. Devils. You talk about Imola… *(Pupe shrugs and turns to go back to the bathroom; Ottavio looks at her without interest.)* Pupe! *(Pupe turns in the doorway; he continues peevishly.)* I wanted to thank you. You were very kind, as usual. Perfect. There's just one thing…

PUPE : I have to get dried. Help me.

COUNT : No. Listen…

Pupe has disappeared into the bathroom. Ottavio is uncertain: it's a great effort for him to move. But finally he makes up his mind and follows his wife into the bathroom.

COUNT *(looking at her)*: I was saying. There's one thing I'm sorry about. You told Zacchi ours was a marriage of economic interest. Let it be said once and for all that if I hadn't liked you I wouldn't have married you. Not even if you were the daughter of the Aga Khan.

Ottavio's declaration has been delivered in a very calm voice, as he dries his wife's shoulders.

PUPE *(just as coldly)*: That's nice to hear.

Pupe goes into the bedroom. Ottavio examines himself in the bathroom mirror, checking his beard, passing his hand over his hair. Then he goes back into the sitting room. As he passes by the phonograph he stoops to turn it off, then thinks better of it.

COUNT *(toward the bedroom)*: Pupe!

No answer. Ottavio decides to go into the bedroom. Pupe is standing in front of the mirror in her slip. Her hair has been arranged differently.

COUNT: What're you doing? *(Pupe spreads out her hands as if to say, "You can see"; then she opens the wardrobe.)* Do you want to go out? Let's go to the Rock.

Pupe has taken a dress from the wardrobe and puts it on. It is a very elegant evening dress.

PUPE: I'm going out.

COUNT *(irritated)*: You mean you're going out on your own?

PUPE *(nodding affirmatively)*: Uh huh. *(Pupe finishes arranging her dress; she is in a hurry.)* I'm going to La Scala for a minute; I have an appointment with Wally. *(Brusquely)* These kinds of things don't interest you, dear. It's for my work. I'm late now, and...

COUNT *(offended)*: Excuse me, excuse me. Then I'll go to the club.

Pupe is not listening; and Ottavio, ever more offended, leaves the room. Alone, Pupe looks at herself in the mirror one last time. She completes her toilette and picks up her accessories, then leaves the apartment and crosses the drawing room.

Ottavio is alone in the drawing room, sitting in an armchair almost in the dark.

PUPE: Night.

Ottavio does not answer. Pupe continues across the drawing room. She is about to go out when she slows her steps.

PUPE *(to Ottavio, without turning to him)*: Didn't you say you were going out?

COUNT: Yes. No. I don't know. I want to read.

PUPE: Oh.

She is about to start off again, but she stops once more to look in the mirror.

Actually she is watching her husband stealthily. Then she looks again at her own image.

PUPE *(impatient)* : Damn.

Pupe turns back with resolute step. As she passes before the count he asks her lazily:

COUNT: Forget something?

PUPE: All wrong.

COUNT: All what?

Pupe stops and turns to him. She seems very edgy and impatient.

PUPE: This dress, can't you see?

COUNT: What's wrong with it?

Pupe comes over to Ottavio.

PUPE: The tone's wrong. A person looking for a job... How would you dress?

COUNT *(still half-sprawled out in the armchair)* : If you're going to La Scala...

PUPE: But I'm not going for the opera!

COUNT: Who ever goes for the opera?

PUPE *(out of patience)* : Ooooh!

She hurries out of the room.

Delighted to have found something to do, Ottavio gets up too, throws his book to the floor, and follows his wife.

COUNT: Pupe. Wait, Pupe. I'll help you choose something.

Pupe's apartment.

Before entering the bedroom, Pupe pauses to start up the phonograph again.

COUNT'S VOICE: I'll help you decide. I'm very good at it.

Pupe has opened the great wardrobes where her dresses are hung, and she contemplates them.

PUPE: Don't trust you.

Pupe has begun to pull dresses out. She looks them over one by one and tosses them aside.

COUNT· *(referring to the dresses as Pupe examines them)* : Nooo. No good, no, no.

PUPE *(turning impatiently to Ottavio)* : Leave me alone. I want to decide by myself.

COUNT *(childishly)* : I can help you, can't I?

PUPE: If you enjoy it so much, go get a job yourself. *(Sighing, as if resigning herself to sharing part of her pleasure with her husband)* Listen, what do you think I should wear?

COUNT *(coming closer to Pupe)*: Wear what you have on. It looks very good on you. You look really very pretty, word of honor. And that's what counts most, believe me. Even in looking for a job.

PUPE *(piqued)*: You see how you can't seem to understand anything? You judge with the same criterion that...

Pupe has begun to take off her dress hurriedly. But now she stops. Her movements slow down. Her voice becomes more drawling.

PUPE: I'm curious to know one thing. *(Ottavio turns toward his wife, who is still in her slip.)* If I'd been among the other girls there at your old friend Imola's, who would you have chosen? Careful. This is the game of truth.

Ottavio looks attentively at his wife, as if he were making the choice now.

COUNT: I'd have chosen you.

Pupe turns her back to him and begins to laugh, looking at the dresses but without real attention.

PUPE: That's nice to hear. *(Laughs)* Think what a scene. *(Laughs)* I...

Ottavio is still looking at her. It almost seems that the "choice" he has just been forced to make has aroused a certain interest in him.

COUNT *(distractedly indicating the dresses)*: Well?

Pupe has chosen a very simple dress.

PUPE: This one.

COUNT *(already disapproving)*: Let's see it.

But Pupe is no longer listening. She has begun to slip into the new dress while looking at herself in the mirror.

PUPE *(casually)* : How many times have we slept together since we got married?

COUNT *(sitting on the bed)* : How should I know? What kind of a question is that?

PUPE *(continuing to dress)* : It's been thirteen months. At an average of, say... wait...

Pupe fastens her dress. Then she suddenly stops. She begins to unfasten it and slips it off. Her voice is muffled for a moment as she pulls the dress over her head.

PUPE: No. Too simple. I don't want to make any wrong moves. It's better if I don't go. *(Continuing to think out loud)* Anyway nothing proves that going to work for Gianni is the right idea. *(She sits on the bed; she picks up a bathrobe distractedly.)* I won't go. I want to give it more thought. *(Turning suddenly toward her husband with a triumphant air)* A hundred and fifty times at the very least.

Ottavio watches his wife with a more aroused look in his eyes.

COUNT: A hundred and fifty what?

PUPE: Times we slept together. At the rate your little friends get, you know how much you'd owe me? Seventy million. *(Observing herself in the mirror)* Enough to buy the top floor on Via Manzoni and set up a boutique.

COUNT *(shivering)* : I say you're crazy.

PUPE: You said yourself you'd have chosen me. Notice that I've calculated the net cost. Four hundred, that is, without the tip for your Imola.

The record is finished. Pupe leaves the mirror and goes into the sitting room, passing in front of Ottavio. Ottavio follows her.

COUNT *(with comic desolation)* : Listen, Pupe. Do whatever you want, just as you always have. But I beg you on bended

knee... Go to work, get a divorce... *(Interrupting himself with
an ironical smile)* Zacchi's enthusiastic about the idea of
your going to work. He's going to tell the newspapers. He
says it'll make a very good impression. *(Resuming his former
tone)* I was saying: do whatever crazy things you want to,
but don't open a boutique. The world is just suffocating
with aristocratic ladies who open boutiques.

PUPE *(putting on a record)* : Means it's profitable. Besides it's something I could do better than the others. Or antiques...

COUNT *(with a grimace of disgust)* : Hmm.

PUPE : Public relations... hostess...

*Ottavio fingers the collar of his wife's bathrobe; it is short, a little offbeat,
and very pretty.*

COUNT : What's this?

PUPE : Chanel. Old. More than a month.

COUNT : Never saw it.

PUPE : You never look.

COUNT : Right. A kiss? Allow me? We haven't quarreled.

PUPE : Debatable.

*She offers her cheek. Ottavio puts down his glass, then embraces his wife in
a tight hug. Pupe tries to free herself.*

COUNT : Oh, come on.

With agility Pupe has been able to get away from him.

PUPE : But that's not a kiss. *(Straightening her robe and her hair)* Go
to your Imola.

COUNT *(impatient)* : Oh, come off it.

PUPE : I told you I have to work. That is, I have to get everything
ready so I can go to work.

Walking very gracefully so as to show herself off, Pupe goes toward her favorite corner and kneels down on the carpet. Turning her back to her husband, she begins to straighten up the papers and books. Now and then she surreptitiously observes her husband, who is standing still staring at her.

COUNT *(as if trying to exorcise temptation)* : Well, if that's the way it is, I'm going out. I'm going to the club.

PUPE : So long.

Ottavio starts to go toward the bedroom. Then he stops. He turns resolutely back and approaches his wife, sits down on the floor near her, and embraces her.

COUNT : Pupe.

PUPE : Cut it out. There's no point.

COUNT : Yes there is. I want you.

PUPE *(calmly)* : You feel a physical desire...

COUNT *(impatient)* : Yes. So what?

PUPE *(with the same patient tone)* : So don't go to the club, dear, go to your Imola's girls. That's what they're there for. That's their work.

COUNT *(trying again to embrace his wife)* : I want you.

Ottavio embraces his wife more tightly and pulls her down on the carpet. Pupe escapes, leaving him with the robe in his hands. She takes refuge against the sofa and from there watches her husband with an ironical smile.

PUPE *(in a childish tone)* : Really? Then pay me.

Ottavio laughs in amusement.

COUNT *(joking)* : Four hundred or seven hundred?

PUPE *(serious)* : Four hundred thousand. I'm honest. All right? It's better for you too. You save.

COUNT *(crawling toward her, his voice husky, almost drunken-sounding)* : You know you have to earn it? Lilli, for example...

PUPE *(coldly)* : I know, I know. Don't worry.

COUNT: Really? *(Piqued)* And where did you learn, if I may ask?

PUPE *(coyly)* : What do you care? *(More seriously)* I had Lilli explain it to me. I was interested. Since it was a job... It's not hard, believe me.

COUNT: You think not?

As if keeping up the joke, Ottavio throws himself on Pupe so violently that she is really a little frightened this time and escapes. This sincere feeling of fright arouses Ottavio even more. Pupe notices and is a little aroused herself. She gets up and speaks in a less controlled voice.

PUPE: Let's get out of here.

Ottavio gets up, staggering slightly, and seizes her arm.

COUNT *(in a tone of voice which tries in vain to sound joking)* : I'll pay you, don't worry.

PUPE *(who has regained her self-control)* : I don't trust you. *(After a pause)* Payment in advance?

She observes her husband as if to check the fever level. She walks slowly away from him. Little by little the game is becoming serious. Pupe is becoming cold and coy, like a professional.

She disappears into the bedroom. Ottavio pulls his wallet from his pocket. He has another drink.

In the bedroom Pupe has turned out the center light and lit only the mirror light. She sits on the bed. Ottavio comes to her, holding out the check.

COUNT: All right?

Pupe takes the check, gazes at it at length, and then throws herself back on the bed with a forced laugh. The telephone rings in the drawing room. Ottavio tries to embrace her. Still laughing, Pupe slips away from him, rolling away on the bed. Ottavio follows her, more and more aroused. For a moment Pupe lets him catch her, ready to slip away again.

PUPE *(ironically)* : Is this all right?

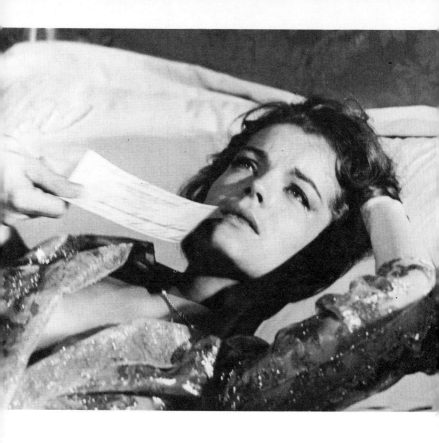

COUNT *(serious, in a hoarse voice)* : Yes.

Now telephone rings in the bedroom as well as the drawing room.
Neither Ottavio nor Pupe seems to hear it. With calculated slowness,
Pupe begins to unfasten her underwear. Ottavio too begins to undress. The
telephone rings insistently. Pupe lies back on the bed to reach the telephone.

COUNT *(more hoarsely)* : Don't answer it.

But Pupe smiles at him, takes the receiver, and immediately begins to
speak, as Ottavio lies down beside her, almost on top of her, and tries to
take it away from her.

PUPE *(into the telephone)* : Antonio? Oh. Tell Papa I can't talk to him now because I'm working. I'll call him tomorrow morning. And oh, Antonio, one more thing. Tell him: Madame wishes to say that she's found a job. Yes, Antonio. A job.

Pupe lies still a moment, staring straight ahead with an expression of mingled laughter and tears. Ottavio thrusts the receiver away; it falls to the floor but neither Pupe nor Ottavio takes the trouble to pick it up. From the receiver can be heard Antonio's voice.

VOICE OF ANTONIO ON THE TELEPHONE: Has Madame decided whether she is leaving? What should I do about the cats?

Pupe's muslin slip falls atop the receiver.

THE END.

This book was photoset in Baskerville.
It was printed and bound by
Les Presses Saint-Augustin, Bruges, Belgium.

Designed by Jacqueline Schuman.

9651